EXECUTIVE STYLES IN CANADA
Cabinet Structures and Leadership Practices in

Edited by Luc Bernier, Keith Brownsey, and Michael Howlett

Canada's political regime is centred on the existence of a federal system of government within the institutions of Westminster parliamentary democracy. This system places a great deal of political power in the hands of cabinet ministers, and while cabinet systems of government in Canada have evolved at different speeds in different federal and provincial governments, over the last two decades administrative and legislative control has become increasingly centralized.

This shift has been well demonstrated by scholars such as Donald J. Savoie regarding the federal system, but has been little examined in the context of provincial governance. *Executive Styles in Canada* looks at both levels of government, explaining how cabinet systems have conformed to or diverged from general patterns. This unique collection is the only systematic, cross-provincial study of its kind, and is essential reading for anyone interested in the structure of government in Canada.

LUC BERNIER is the director of l'École nationale d'administration publique.

KEITH BROWNSEY is a professor in the Department of Policy Studies at Mount Royal College.

MICHAEL HOWLETT is Burnaby Mountain professor in the Department of Political Science at Simon Fraser University.

IPAC **IAPC**
The Institute of
Public Administration of Canada

L'Institut d'administration
publique du Canada

The Institute of Public Administration of Canada Series
in Public Management and Governance

Editor: Patrice Dutil

This series is sponsored by the Institute of Public Administration of Canada as part of its commitment to encourage research on issues in Canadian public administration, public sector management, and public policy. It also seeks to foster wider knowledge and understanding among practitioners, academics, and the general public.

For a list of books published in the series, see page 283.

Executive Styles in Canada

Cabinet Structures and Leadership Practices in Canadian Government

Edited by Luc Bernier,
Keith Brownsey, and
Michael Howlett

UNIVERSITY OF TORONTO PRESS
Toronto Buffalo London

© University of Toronto Press 2005
Toronto Buffalo London
Printed in the U.S.A.
Reprinted 2013

ISBN 0-8020-3952-9 (cloth)
ISBN 0-8020-3785-2 (paper)

Printed on acid-free paper

Library and Archives Canada Cataloguing in Publication

Executive styles in Canada : cabinet structures and leadership
practices in Canadian government / edited by Luc Bernier, Keith
Brownsey and Michael Howlett.

(Institute of Public Administration of Canada series in public
management and governance)
ISBN 0-8020-3952-9 (bound).   ISBN 0-8020-3785-2 (pbk.)

1. Prime ministers – Canada. 2. Cabinet ministers – Canada.
3. Prime ministers – Canada – Provinces. 4. Cabinet ministers – Canada –
Provinces. 5. Political leadership – Canada. 6. Canada – Politics and
government. I. Bernier, Luc, 1959– II. Brownsey, Keith, 1955–
III. Howlett, Michael, 1955– IV. Institute of Public Administration
of Canada. V. Series.

JL97.E94 2005   352.23'0971   C2004-906387-1

University of Toronto Press acknowledges the financial assistance to its
publishing program of the Canada Council for the Arts and the Ontario
Arts Council.

University of Toronto Press acknowledges the financial support for
its publishing activities of the Government of Canada through the
Book Publishing Industry Development Program (BPIDP).

Contents

List of Figures   viii

List of Tables   ix

Preface   xi

Part I – Introduction

1 Modern Canadian Governance: Politial-Administrative Styles
  and Executive Organization in Canada   3
  MICHAEL HOWLETT, LUC BERNIER, KEITH BROWNSEY,
  AND CHRISTOPHER DUNN

Part II – The Federal Cabinet

2 The Federal Government: Revisiting Court Government in
  Canada   17
  DONALD J. SAVOIE

Part III – Provincial Cabinets

3 The Persistence of the Institutionalized Cabinet:
  The Central Executive in Newfoundland and Labrador   47
  CHRISTOPHER DUNN

4 Governing from the Centre in New Brunswick 75
STEWART HYSON

5 Premierial Governance: The System of Executive Power in
Nova Scotia 91
DAVID JOHNSON

6 The Executive Administrative Style in Prince Edward Island:
Managerial and Spoils Politics 111
PETER E. BUKER

7 Who Governs in Quebec? Revolving Premiers and Reforms 131
LUC BERNIER

8 Politics, Personality, and History in Ontario's Administrative
Style 155
TED GLENN

9 Cabinet Structure and Executive Style in Manitoba 171
JOAN GRACE

10 Saskatchewan's Executive Decision-Making Style:
The Centrality of Planning 184
KEN RASMUSSEN AND GREGORY P. MARCHILDON

11 The Post-Institutionalized Cabinet: The Administrative Style
of Alberta 208
KEITH BROWNSEY

12 The West Annex: Executive Structure and Administrative
Style in British Columbia 225
NORMAN J. RUFF

Part IV – Conclusion

13 Conclusion: Executive Institutional Development in
   Canada's Provinces   245
   LUC BERNIER, KEITH BROWNSEY, AND MICHAEL HOWLETT

Notes   251

Contributors   281

Figures

7.1   Ministère du Conseil exécutif   140

7.2   Secrétariat du Conseil du trésor Québec   141

10.1 Saskatchewan's Unaided Cabinet, 1944   188

10.2 Douglas/Lloyd Governments, 1948–1964   189

10.3 Blakeney Government, 1971–77   194

10.4 Blakeney Government, 1978–82   196

10.5 Romanow Government, 1991–97   199

10.6 Romanow Government, 1998–2001   202

10.7 Calvert Government, 2001–4   204

11.1 Ministerial Report Decision Model   220

12.1 Staffing the Centre – Office of Premier, 2002   230

Tables

1.1 Unaided, Institutionalized, and Prime Minister-Centred
    Cabinets   12

7.1 Reforms of the Public Sector in Quebec   135

12.1 British Columbia Legislative and Cabinet Committee
     Systems, 2004   237

Preface

In the 1990s a new type of cabinet organization began to emerge in several Canadian provinces. This new structure was in some ways an attempt to return to an earlier pre-institutionalized model of decision-making. But it can best be described as a reaction against what was perceived to be the increasingly cumbersome executive decision-making style of many provincial governments. This reaction to the institutionalized cabinet is the subject of *Executive Styles*.

Beginning in the 1960s and 1970s, cabinet government in the provinces underwent a process of institutionalization or bureaucratization. Complex issues were broken down into manageable units and sent to newly established committees of cabinet for study. Decisions from these new cabinet committees were then sent to an 'agenda' committee, usually chaired by the premier, for vetting. Only if the cabinet committee recommendation passed the scrutiny of the agenda committee would it be sent to the full cabinet. Powerful secretariats emerged to aid ministers in their deliberations. By the early 1990s several provincial governments believed that the institutionalized decision-making process had become too complex and a proces of reordering cabinet government began.

While there are similarities, each of the chapters in this volume reveal a different executive style. Populist right-wing governments in Alberta and British Columbia have dismantled the formal institutionalized cabinet and transformed their executive decision-making structures into what is described as a post-institutionalized model. The Harris government in Ontario, on the other hand, shared the neo-liberal ideology of Alberta and British Columbia but avoided the formal changes in executive decision-making found in the two westernmost provinces. It remains to be seen if the Charest government in Quebec with its neo-liberal inclinations will pursue any substantive reforms in its executive. As well, there is little evidence that Saskatchewan and Manitoba have altered their patterns of cabinet decision-making in any significant way. Although several authors in this collection argue that Conservative governments in the Atlantic provinces have simplified their cabinet structure, it is not clear whether this was a minor adjustment or the first step toward a new post-institutionalized model. Clearly, the pattern of executive style in Canada's provinces is still evolving.

The idea of examining the recent changes to executive government in the provinces came from several places. First, the influential work of Donald Savoie in *Governing from the Centre* pointed in the direction of change in executive government at the national level. If there was a centralization of power in the Prime Minister's Office, what was going on in the provinces with their history of premier dominated cabinets? Second, there was a lack of material on provincial cabinets. While several studies on executive decision-making were available, they were written before the recent changes. Third, the Institute of Public Administration (IPAC), through its Research and Professional Practices Committee, provided funding for a study team to assemble material for publication. Most importantly, the IPAC Research Committee provided a forum for discussion of the changes then only vaguely perceived in the executive councils across the country.

Once the study team had been approved by IPAC the task of recruiting authors began. Although it was a challenge to find scholars with an interest in provincial government, a group was brought together in a joint session of the Canadian Political Science Association and the Institute of Public Administration of Canada in June 2002 at the meetings of the Congress of Learned Societies in Toronto. Most of the chapters appearing in *Executive Styles* were presented at the all-day session. The presentation of papers and the resulting discussions made the all-day roundtable a success.

The Study Team Grant from the Institute of Public Administration of Canada was essential for the initiation and completion of the volume. Many people at IPAC need to be thanked. First in line are the staff at the Institute of Public Administration of Canada, especially Joseph Galimberti, the institute's executive director, and Patrice Dutil, the director of research. Without their assistance and support this project would never have been completed. As chair of the IPAC Research Committee, Wynne Young was instrumental in guiding the research proposal through the committee. The contributors to the volume must also be acknowledged. Their efforts in scholarship are the measure of the worth of this book.

It was the work of Donald Savoie that initiated the original conversations from which this volume emerged. Many thanks are owed to his insights and encouragement. Mark Sproule-Jones and Graham White, both fellow travellers in the study of government, made a considerable effort to attend the June 2002 roundtable on executive styles and have provided encouragement and comments since then on the project as it has developed. Virgil Duff of the University of Toronto Press has been a patient and thoughtful guide through the publication process.

Our families must also be thanked. Numerous evenings and weekends writing, travelling and editing were spent putting this project together; this is time that is owed to our children and partners.

The physical distance between us was not a barrier to collaboration. The communication and other resources supplied by L'École nationale d'administration publique, Simon Fraser University, and Mount Royal College are gratefully acknowledged. With their help, the project established a community of knowledge that will endure over considerable time.

Finally, with three editors, responsibility can be generously shared among us for any mistakes, omissions, and other faults.

Luc Bernier
Keith Brownsey
Michael Howlett
December 2004

Part I

INTRODUCTION

Chapter 1

Modern Canadian Governance: Political-Administrative Styles and Executive Organization in Canada

MICHAEL HOWLETT, LUC BERNIER,
KEITH BROWNSEY, AND CHRISTOPHER DUNN

Governments around the world change all the time. However, some aspects of government behaviour have proven more resistant to change than others. In western liberal democracies, for example, key aspects of the political regime, and especially the relationship between senior politicians and senior administrators, tend to change very slowly.[1] Even these quasi-permanent features of political-administrative relationships, however, do change from time to time, often with momentous consequences for the way the business of government is conducted.[2]

Recently, just such a claim has been made by Donald Savoie and Christopher Dunn, two leading experts on executive government in Canada at the federal and provincial levels, respectively. Canadian federal governance in the twenty-first century, Savoie contends, now operates quite differently from how it did in the past.[3] Now, say scholars such as Savoie and Bakvis, the government of Canada operates very much from the centre – that is, with an executive system of government replacing the legislature as the key features of the exercise of political power and authority.[4]

While evidence of such a development at the federal level is clear, Canada is a very decentralized federation and a major question concerns whether this phenomenon has been replicated at the provincial level.[5] In his work comparing the provinces, Dunn has argued that a more complex picture emerges than that put forward by Savoie. Identifying several different phases through which provincial executive structures have evolved, Dunn has found different provinces arriving and leaving different phases at different times, resulting in a mottled pattern of institutional adaptations and executive governments in the eleven major jurisdictions in Canada.[6]

In the chapters that follow, recent developments in Canadian executive government are examined at both the federal and provincial levels. This examination sets out the basic structures of cabinet organization and executive government for each major Canadian jurisdiction and chronicles the phases through which they have passed in the late twentieth century. The chapters examine recent development in the context of transitions in organization and process which have occurred in each jurisdiction in recent years, and historically. On the basis of these descriptions, an assessment is made concerning the nature of the current executive style found in each jurisdiction and of the dynamics that undergird change in this critical area of Canadian political and administrative life.

The Concept of a Political-Administrative Style

This book draws on several insights from comparative public administration in undertaking the evaluations of federal and provincial executive structures and assessing the implications of its findings. Over the past decade, developments in the field of comparative public administration have generated a set of concepts which are of use in analysing developments such as a shift in the nature of executive, or legislative, decision-making.

An important step in this direction was the development of the notion of a 'political-administrative style': that is, a more or less consistent and long-term set of institutionalized patterns of relationships, norms, and procedures existing between the different arms or branches of government.[7] The concept of such a style is useful for analysing political and administrative change for several reasons. First, it sets out the background against which reforms occur, providing a useful aggregate unit for describing the characteristics of a political-administrative system. And second, in so doing it simultaneously provides a standard or benchmark against which the degree of change in such systems can be assessed, as reforms alter aspects of previously existing styles.[8]

The general idea of such styles is not new, of course, with clear links not only to the foundational studies of bureaucracy and bureaucratization developed by Max Weber and others in the late nineteenth and early twentieth centuries,[9] but also to the first wave of comparative administrative studies carried out after the Second World War, which focused on the identification and elaboration of national administrative cultures.[10] Recently, however, this idea has re-emerged in the works of Christoph Knill[11] and Hans A.G.M. Bekke[12] and their colleagues, and has proven to be of use in helping to understand the difficulties encountered by the European Union in adopting EU-wide administrative initiatives.

The concept of a political-administrative style needs to be unpacked in order to be of use in the study of executive management systems and their reform. This is because the term refers to two separate but intertwined units of analysis, one structural and the other behavioural. With respect to the first issue, while the concept of a style refers to the behaviour of political and administrative agents, it has a heavily structural or institutional component, as it is assumed that these agents are not free-floating and unencumbered, but rather operate within an institutional context that at least in part determines their behaviour.[13]

In this sense, the notion of a political-administrative style can be situated within the confines of a neo-institutional approach to the study of social and political life. While the exact contours of neo-institutionalism raise some disagreement across disciplines, with different variations existing within political science, economics, and (historical) sociology,[14] these approaches share the common idea that rules, norms, and symbols affect political behaviour. In other words, the organization of governmental institutions affect what the state does; and that unique patterns of historical development constrain future choices.[15] Institutions, hence, are defined to include not only formal organizations such as bureaucratic hierarchies and marketlike exchange networks but also legal and cultural codes and rules which affect the calculations by individuals and groups of their optimal strategies and courses of action.[16]

In the political realm, institutions are significant because they 'constitute and legitimize individual and collective political actors and provide them with consistent behavioural rules, conceptions of reality, standards of assessment, affective ties, and endowments, and thereby with a capacity for purposeful action.'[17]

In an administrative context, as Morten Egeberg has noted, 'formal organization provides a ... milieu that focuses a decision-maker's attention on certain problems and solutions, while others are excluded from consideration. The structure thus constrains choices, but at the same time creates and increases capacity in certain directions. The organizational context surrounding individuals thus serves to simplify decisions that might otherwise have been complex and incomprehensible.'[18]

Thus, as many observers have noted, the structure of political and administrative organizations affects decision-making by facilitating the interpretation and reconstruction of diverse situations into existing 'frames,' making them amenable to standardized decision-making processes such as the establishment of standard operating procedures, bureaucratic routines, or operational codes.[19] And the existence of institutionalized rules of behaviour affect calculations of actors' interests and self-interests by defining the nature of the 'win-sets' which exist in given decisional circumstances, as well as the action channels these decisions will follow.[20] Together, these have an impact on the ideas that actors hold, as well as their assessments of what is feasible in a given situation.[21] As John Zysman has argued, the institutional structure of an administration creates a distinct pattern of constraints and incentives for state and societal actors. These define and structure actor's interests and channel their behaviour, while the interaction of these actors generates a particular policy logic and process.[22] Since institutional structures are different, however, it is to be expected that there are many different kinds of politico-administrative styles, each style being defined by the set of institutions, rules, traditions, and cultures of which it is comprised.

Political-Administrative Styles in Federal Systems

Zysman's point is an important insight in the Canadian case, since it implies that despite sharing a common heritage in British parliamentary institutions and 'Westminster'-style political-administrative relationships, different jurisdictions may exhibit very different executive styles, based in part on the autonomous organizations and institutions which exist at the different levels of organization found in a federal state.[23]

As Bekke et al. noted in their path-breaking 1996 work on aspects of the behaviour of civil service systems, 'although our definition refers to the state and the focus of this book is on national systems, it is not our intention to exclude other levels of government. We believe the logic and the analytic approaches can be extended to other government levels ... One basic assumption of this approach is that civil service systems, whether national, subnational, or local, vary across political jurisdictions and that this variation merits study in its own right and for its implications for the management and development of these systems.'[24]

The chapters in this book move beyond a static depiction of existing styles and instead adopt an evolutionary perspective, allowing each author to assess how changes have had an effect on the overall nature of political and administrative life in each jurisdiction.

Executive Styles in Canada

Existing work on cabinet decision-making processes in Canada has been piecemeal and has only examined specific jurisdictions at specific periods of time or in specific historical epochs. Nevertheless, Stefan Dupré and Christopher Dunn have set out the elements for an evolutionary model of Canadian executive styles. Drawing on observations from case studies of provincial executives, they have argued that a process of evolutionary institutionalization has occurred in which cabinets have moved from an early 'unaided' state to a much more heavily institutionalized form in which cabinets are decentralized into complex committee systems with central agencies created to coordinate committee activities.[25]

Dupré has given broad descriptions of the historical modes of cabinet operation in Canada. He called these the traditional cabinet, the departmentalized cabinet, and the institutionalized cabinet. The traditional cabinet, before the rise of the administrative state, had as its main business to aggregate and articulate regional and local concerns, and to dispense patronage. This was the typical type of cabinet found in the early years of Confederation and was gradually replaced as the twentieth century progressed.

The next stage was that of the departmentalized cabinet. In this type, government departments and ministers are the engines of public sector expansion. Ministers are accorded a significant degree of decision-making autonomy, demonstrate 'portfolio loyalty,' and rely on departmental experts for policy formulation and implementation.

Some scholars have termed the departmentalized cabinet the unaided cabinet, while adding some additional characteristics. The unaided cabinet is simple in structure, with few standing committees, and features restricted collegiality. The main job of the prime minister or premier is to choose cabinets and not to be the architect of the machinery of government; generally, although not always, the first minister is the dominant politician. There are central departments – that is, coordinating departments headed by a minister other than the premier. There are few cabinet-level staff, budgeting has narrow aims – usually fiscal control – and employs narrow means, and planning is optional. Cabinet decision-making sees few sources of alternative advice to cabinet other than deputy ministers.

Beginning around the 1960s (in the case of Saskatchewan, the 1940s), the institutionalized cabinet came to replace the unaided or departmentalized cabinet. This cabinet Dupré said had 'various combinations of formal committee structures, established central agencies and budgeting and management techniques [combined] ... to emphasize shared knowledge, collegial decision making, and the formulation of government-wide priorities and objectives.' There were now central agency ministers who reflected the collective concerns of cabinet, and special interest ministers who continued the older pattern of special interest politics.

The institutionalized cabinet structure is complex; there are many standing committees and expanded collegiality. The prime minister or premier's role is now enlarged to that of organizational architect – that is, designer of the machinery of government. There are now both central departments and central agencies (the latter being service-wide coordinative bodies which report to the first minister). One or more central agencies deliver both partisan (PMO-type) and policy/technocratic (PCO-type) input to cabinet. Cabinet-level staff are numerous, budgeting has wider aims and wider means, and planning is still considered optional by cabinet, but is more common than in the unaided cabinet. A 'planning-budgeting nexus,' or explicit link, is also common. Alternative sources of information to cabinet, other than the responsible minister and his or her deputy, are in place. Decision-making is more centralized, meaning that cabinet overrides departmental autonomy more, and central officials monitor departments to a greater extent. Accordingly, tension between the centre and the departments is pervasive.

One of the purposes of this book was to examine whether the provincial executives are becoming more like the federal central executive described in Donald Savoie's book *Governing from the Centre: The Concentration of Power in Canadian Politics*, which appeared in 1999. Discussions of this issue have usually centred around the relative power of the first minister, but they should instead focus around cabinet models. Savoie has implicitly posited a new model for cabinet government in

Canada, moving beyond the Dupré-Dunn framework to add a fourth model of the post-institutional or premier-centred cabinet. This model needs to be assessed to see if it exists in various provinces.

Governing from the Centre does not set out to be a critique of the institutionalized model, but it is in fact the most extensive one yet mounted. Savoie's argument is that the decision-making processes of the institutionalized cabinet, originally designed to be collective, the integrity of which central agencies protected, now belongs to the prime minister and is therefore emphatically not collegial. It is not even a case of a *retour en arrière*: 'the days of the departmental Cabinet, when individual ministers 'were very much in charge of government decision making as it applied to their own departments are clearly over, and have been since the 1970s.'[26]

Elsewhere Dunn has described the pattern he found:

> In the new phase of cabinet history, Savoie says, power has shifted away from ministers and their departments towards the centre, and at the centre, away from Cabinet and Cabinet committees toward the Prime Minister and his senior advisors. Cabinet committee decisions are rarely challenged in the plenary cabinet, but this does not imply cabinet minister power, since the chairs of these committees are hand-picked process-oriented choices of the Prime Minister. Central agencies, rather than being neutral facilitators of collective decision making, are now engaged as actors in the process itself, as extensions of the prime minister. Comprehensive policy agendas are ignored as prime ministers govern by 'bolts of electricity' – a handful of key objectives that they pursue and push through the system. In pursuing these priorities, the first minister, finance minister and central agencies have essentially made the decision making system a bifurcated one: there is one set of rules for the (nominal) 'guardians' like the Prime Minister, Finance Minister and president of the Treasury Board (whose major job traditionally was to protect the public purse) and the 'spenders' (who traditionally tried to evade them). The priority programs of the guardians sail through with little difficulty, whereas those of regular line ministers are subject to the regular cabinet committee decision-making process, where they are subject to the contending wishes of other ministers and the control of the central agencies (that is, the prime minister) and seldom emerge as their drafters originally intended. What is involved, Savoie says, is widespread institutional failure. The relevance of Parliament is even further cast in doubt; the power and influence of Cabinet is threatened; the media have become actors, not

narrators; and the public service has become an instrument for protecting the interests of the prime minister.[27]

The three types of twentieth-century cabinets developed in the Dupré-Dunn-Savoie model are sumarized in Table 1.1 below.

The factors influencing each of these stages of cabinet evolution are diverse, but observers have identified some outstanding ones. Dupré gives the impression that interest group influence (ministers' portfolio loyalty or primary commitment to their departments, derived from the fact that they were judged primarily by departmentally oriented client groups); economic imperatives (in a Keynesian era, government departments and ministers are seen as the most appropriate engines of public sector expansion); and bureaucratic power (federal-provincial officials, bound together in trust networks and supported by powerful finance departments) are influential in policy-making.

The institutionalized cabinet had factors relating to both its initiation and its persistence. It was initiated due to jurisdiction-specific mixes of factors such as ideology, pragmatism, and historical precedent. It persisted because of endogenous factors (the premier's quest for influence, emulation of predecessors, cabinet's quest for political control, cabinet's quest for financial control, decongestion or reducing overload, ideology, and momentum), and exogenous factors (the wish for policy coherence vis-à-vis other governments, the signalling of political messages to the public, social science rationalism, and facilitation of interest-group input). Savoie gives a complex list of factors influencing the new centre-focused governance, which can be boiled down into more manageable endogenous and exogenous categories. Exogenous factors are very important: the fear of media criticism, the competitive party system and its tendency to politicize most issues, globalization, and the national unity imperative are particularly central concerns. There are endogenous factors as well, including the first minister's quest for control and the wish to reduce overload by reducing the number of effective decision-makers.

In the chapters that follow, twelve of Canada's leading students of federal and provincial cabinets and executives look at recent developments in each jurisdiction. They examine a common set of concerns, including:

1 The dominant role of the first minister
2 The first minister's relations with cabinet ministers
3 The role of cabinet committees

4 The evidence of an informal group of inside ministers
5 The central agencies supporting the first minister, the role of the cabinet secretary, and the evidence of other close advisers to the first minister
6 The first minister's relations with departmental deputy ministers
7 The cabinet secretary's relations with departmental deputy ministers
8 The first minister's relations with the Finance Department and the degree of centralization over finance
9 The degree of centralization over public relations
10 The first minister's role in federal-provincial relations

Each author provides an overview of the current structure and behaviour of executive organizations in each jurisdiction in Canada, as well as historical background on the evolution of these systems to their present state. In so doing they help develop significant insights into this most important component of Canadian governmental and governance styles.

The authors writing in this book find evidence of transitions following the Dupré-Dunn pattern in most jurisdictions they examine. However, following upon the insights of Savoie and others looking at the federal level, some, like Keith Brownsey in his study of Alberta cabinets, have uncovered evidence of the emergence of a provincial post-institutional or premier-centred cabinet along the lines identified by Savoie in the federal case. In this model, cabinets are often bypassed by premiers' offices, which centralize communications functions and policy development. Central agencies come to serve the premier's office rather than cabinet per se, altering both the fundamental behaviour of government as well as its institutional order. However, not all the authors in this volume find evidence of such a transition. This development appears to be much more pronounced in the largest Canadian jurisdictions, with pronounced moves in this direction over the last decade at the federal level and in Ontario, Alberta, and British Columbia. Most of the smaller Canadian provinces retain a system of institutionalized cabinets and Quebec remains very much the anomaly in also retaining such an executive style in a large and complex jurisdiction.

However, these styles remain fluid. Even at the federal level, where moves toward a prime minister-centred cabinet were most pronounced, the Martin government has abandoned many aspects of this model and moved back toward the institutional template. Understanding how, and why, these developments occur at the highest level of Canadian politics is the main purpose of this volume.

TABLE 1.1   Unaided, Institutionalized, and Prime Minister-Centred Cabinets

	Unaided or departmental cabinet	Institutionalized cabinet	Prime minister-centered cabinet
Cabinet	– personnel choice by first minister – dominant first minister, restricted collegiality – simple cabinet structure	– first minister now has two jobs in the institutionalized cabinet (IC): personnel choice plus design of the machinery of government – greater collegiality – complex cabinet structure	– same job as in the IC; but policy-making in any dossier as well – dominant first minister; cabinet more a discussion forum than decision forum – cabinet structure streamlined, less complex; cabinet committees effectively decision-makers for routine matters; PM discourages appeals of their decisions
Central agencies	– central departments – fewer cabinet staff – little cabinet-level analysis	– central agencies as well as central departments – more cabinet staff – extensive cabinet-level analysis	– same central bodies – number of cabinet-level staff same – extensive central agency analysis for PM's purposes; for other matters, the agencies pick their issues
Budgeting and planning	– budgeting centralized; major role played by first minister – budgeting aim: mostly control – budgeting means: traditional (annual budget cycle) – planning: optional, but either project-oriented or indicative – short-term coordination by first minister or finance minister	– budgeting collegial – budgeting aims: broader than control – budgeting means: both traditional and political/off-budget controls – planning: still optional, but where practised is collective, comprehensive – planning-budgeting nexus (balance, complementarity of the two functions)	– budgeting centralized under the PM and finance minister – budgeting aims still broad, but a new element added: performance measurement – budgeting means originally off-budget (the '94 Program Review); but old (secretive) budget process now used – planning: bolts of electricity

TABLE 1.1 (concluded)

Unaided or departmental cabinet	Institutionalized cabinet	Prime minister-centered cabinet
		– nexus problematical: two sets of rules – one for 'guardians' and one for 'spenders'; no collective constraints for the former; budget measures include broad policy measures, most presented as a fait accompli; however, nominal attention to the planning-budgeting nexus in the EMS cycle
Decision-making modes – hierarchical channels of policy advice, from senior officials to the cabinet with no competing sources – decentralized decision-making: departmental autonomy favoured over power of the central executive	– alternative channels of policy advice for cabinet and committees – centralized decision making: power of the central executive favoured over departmental autonomy	– policy advice and and briefing are primarily for the PM and his delegates, the committee chairs he trusts; media play an inordinate role in driving government's agenda – centralized decision making, meaning the PM's power: favoured over full cabinet, line ministers, and the federal bureaucracy

Source: Christopher Dunn, ed., *The Handbook of Canadian Public Administration* (Don Mills: Oxford University Press, 2002).

Part II

THE FEDERAL CABINET

Chapter 2

The Federal Government: Revisiting Court Government in Canada

DONALD J. SAVOIE

In 1999 I published a paper, 'The Rise of Court Government in Canada,' and made the case that political power within the government of Canada was increasingly being centralized in the hands of the prime minister and a small group of carefully selected courtiers. These included key advisers in his office, two or three senior cabinet ministers, carefully selected lobbyists, pollsters, and other friends in court, and a handful of senior career officials. Not much has actually changed in the machinery of government since 1999. Like tigers that do not easily part with their stripes, those who hold effective political power see little reason to part with it or even attenuate its scope. Still, there has been a great deal of talk on the part of opposition parties and Paul Martin about the need to overhaul our national political institutions to deal with what has been labelled as the 'democratic deficit.'[1]

In light of the above, it is important to revisit the notion of court government. This paper identifies the central forces that have driven the development of court government and discusses its operation. It outlines new instruments of government and policy tools now in the prime minister's hand which facilitate governing from the centre. It also challenges long-established conventions about how our government works. Gordon Robertson, former secretary to the cabinet, explained more than thirty years ago that in our system 'ministers are responsible. It is their government.'[2] The Privy Council Office (PCO) in its 1993 publication on the machinery of government argued that 'we operate under the theory of a confederal nature of decision making where power flows from ministers.'[3] I maintain, to the contrary, that power no longer flows from ministers, but from the prime minister, and unevenly at that.

The above speaks to the evolution of how policies are struck and decisions are made in Ottawa. Stefan Dupré argued that institutionalized cabinet replaced the departmentalized cabinet in the late 1960s and early 1970s. Individual ministers and their departments lost a great deal of autonomy to full cabinet, or to shared knowledge and collegial decision-making.[4] But, I argue, this era did not last very long before court government started to take root. To be sure, information was gathered at the centre. However, it was gathered for the benefit of the prime minister and a handful of senior advisers operating in the Privy Council Office and the Prime Minister's Office (PMO), not for collegial decision-making. Court government established itself in Ottawa under Trudeau and, if anything, it grew stronger under both Mulroney and Chrétien.

The Actors

It is ironic that one development giving rise to court government in Ottawa was the election in 1976 of the Parti Québécois (PQ), a provincial party committed to taking Quebec out of Canada. The impact was felt in every government building in Ottawa, and nowhere more strongly than in the Langevin Building, home to both the Prime Minister's Office and the Privy Council Office.

Their place in history matters a great deal to prime ministers. No Canadian prime minister wants the country to break up under his or her watch. No other politician in Canada feels so directly responsible for Canadian unity as does the prime minister. Indeed, briefing material prepared by the PCO for new ministers makes it clear that 'the Prime Minister has direct responsibility for the conduct of federal-provincial relations.'[5] Prime ministers invariably believe that provincial governments are much better at understanding this and applying it in their decision-making process than is the federal government. They believe that there is rarely a spontaneous or isolated initiative coming forward from a provincial government, particularly in the case of Quebec, when sovereignists hold power. The thinking is that provincial governments have a game plan in their relations with the federal government and that everything fits into it.

In interviews with current and former PCO officials and federal deputy ministers, many claimed that provincial governments are much better at coordinating their relations with the federal government than vice-versa. To be sure, provincial governments are smaller, but that does not tell the whole story. One senior PCO official, for example, reported that 'all letters coming from the Quebec Government to all federal departments and agencies are written by two people. Imagine if we tried to do that.'[6] The federal government does not try to do that, but it does from time to time ask one, several or, in some instances, all departments to check with the centre of government before launching an initiative, however limited in scope, which could have implications for federal-provincial relations, particularly in Quebec.

The preoccupation with national unity tends to recast substantive policy issues into the question of their impact on Quebec and the likelihood of securing federal-provincial agreements. There are plenty of examples. Andrew Cooper, for example, in his comparative study of Canadian and Australian foreign affairs, writes, 'a tell-tale sign of how Canada's economic and diplomatic strategy was subordinated to political tactics in agricultural trade was the routing of all important decisions in this area ... through the central agencies of the Prime Minister's Office and the Privy Council Office. The decisive impact of the constitutional issue in this matter inevitably stymied the government's ability to perform effectively in the concluding phase of the Uruguay Round.'[7] The participants directly involved in recasting or rerouting the issues are for the most part political strategists or generalists operating at the centre and are not usually specialists in health care, social or economic development policy, and so on.[8] They are also often directly tied to the prime minister and his office in one fashion or another.

In 1975 Pierre Trudeau established a central agency to deal with federal-provincial relations and federal-provincial relations have enjoyed a strong presence in Ottawa's decision-making process ever since. The responsibility has always been a part of the PCO or has enjoyed its own separate status. It has never, however, shrunk to pre-1975 days when it had only about eight officials dedicated to it.

What kind of federal-provincial issue can involve the centre of government and even the prime minister? The short answer is anything, everything, and it depends. There are no set rules. All major federal-provincial issues qualify, of course, but some minor ones can too, and on a moment's notice. The level of funding for a specific program or whether a federal program applies in one region, but not in Quebec (or vice-versa) can appear on the prime minister's radar screen, particularly if it gains media visibility.

The prime minister, it will also be recalled, was firmly in charge of the failed Meech Lake and Charlottetown constitutional accords. Neither initiative was born out of cabinet's collective decision-making. Similarly, Chrétien's speech on national unity at the time of the Charlottetown Accord, where firm commitments were made to Quebeckers, was drafted by his advisers and others at the centre. Cabinet was not consulted on its contents, let alone asked to make a contribution.

Provincial premiers have direct access to the prime minister and do not hesitate to pursue an issue with him. If the prime minister decides to support the premier, then the issue is brought to the centre of government in Ottawa for resolution. Commitments are made between two first ministers for whatever reasons, and the prime minister cannot take the risk of seeing the system or the process not producing the right decision. As a result, someone at the centre will monitor the decision until it is fully implemented. When that happens, ministers and their departments inevitably lose some of their power to the prime minister and his advisers.

The program review exercise of the mid-1990s brought home the point that cabinet is not able to make spending decisions and that the decision-making power had to be concentrated in the hands of a few individuals, notably the prime minister and the minister of finance. It became accepted wisdom in Ottawa that the reason the federal government lost control of its expenditures was that ministers in cabinet were unwilling to say no to the proposed spending plans of colleagues, knowing full well that their time would come when they too would come forward with their own spending proposals.[9] One can hardly overstate the importance of the budget to public policy and government operations. It steals the stage. When the prime minister and his or her courtiers decide to bring both fiscal policy and key spending decisions to the centre of government, they are in fact bringing the key policy-making levers.

The Media

All important files have the potential of bringing the centre of government into play, but what makes a file important is not at all clear: it depends on the circumstances. Media attention can, at very short notice, turn an issue, however trivial, into an important file. When this happens, there is no distinction made between policy and administration. A file that receives media attention becomes political and at that point the prime minister and his advisers will want to oversee its development. Without putting too fine a point on it, the front page of the *Globe and Mail*, or a CBC or CTV news report, can make a file important, no matter its scope or nature. The role of the media has changed substantially in recent decades, and they are now important political actors in their own right. They are also more aggressive. Television and its tendency to turn to a thirty-second clip to sum up major policy issues or, much more often, to report on something gone wrong in government, has had a profound impact on government operations. Former cabinet ministers in both Liberal and Progressive Conservative governments have commented, in some cases in the strongest of terms, on the changing role of the media.[10] Today, the media, much like society itself, are far less deferential to political leaders and political institutions. Nothing is off limits anymore and political leaders and government officials must continually be cautious of letting their guard down when meeting the press.

The media also home in on party leaders at election time rather than on selected party candidates, even those enjoying a high profile. Journalists buy seats on the chartered aircraft of party leaders and follow them everywhere. How well the leaders do in the debates on national television, in both English and French, can have an important impact, or at least be perceived to have an important impact, on the election campaign, if not the election itself.[11]

In the past, Canada had powerful cabinet ministers with deep roots in the party or strong regional identification and support. One can think of Jimmy Gardiner, Chubby Power, Jack Pickersgill, Ernest Lapointe, Louis St Laurent, Don Jamieson, and Allan MacEachen. We no longer seem to have powerful regional or party figures who can carry candidates to victory on their coat-tails or speak to the prime minister from an independent power base in the party. Now winning candidates on the government side are aware that their party leader's performance in the election campaign explains in large measure why they themselves were successful. The objective of national political parties at election time is more to sell their leaders to the Canadian electorate than it is to sell their ideas or their policies. Canadian elections invariably turn on the question of who will form the government. It should come as no surprise then that if the leader is able to secure a majority mandate, the party is in his debt, and not the other way around.

National political parties, at least the Canadian variety, are not much more than election-day organizations, providing the fundraising and poll workers needed to fight an election campaign. They are hardly effective vehicles for generating public policy debates, for staking out policy positions, or for providing a capacity to ensure their own party's competence once in office. Robert Young argues that 'the Pulp and Paper Association has more capacity to do strategic analytical work than the Liberal and [Progressive] Conservative parties combined.'[12] Sharon Sutherland points to the omnipresent regional factor in Canadian politics as an important reason why national political parties are not good vehicles to debate and formulate policy positions. She writes, 'We do not have party government in the national institutions because of the lack of capacity of parties to reconcile inside themselves regional interests from across the whole country.'[13] National public policy agenda, and national political parties shy away from attacking regional issues head-on for fear they will split the party along regional lines and hurt its chances at election time. The thinking goes, again at least in the parties that have held power in Ottawa, that the issue is so sensitive and so politically explosive that it is better left in the hands of party leaders and a handful of advisers.

Since Trudeau, Canadian prime ministers have made themselves into television personalities. The same cannot be said for cabinet ministers. A Gallup poll conducted in 1988 is very revealing on this point. It reported that only 31 per cent of respondents could name a *single* cabinet minister four years after the Mulroney government had come to power. In addition, only 5 per cent of the respondents could identify Don Mazankowski, deputy prime minister and one of the most powerful members of Mulroney's cabinet.[14]

The age of twenty-four-hour television and the intense competition between the electronic and the written media have placed a relentless pressure on journalists to produce something new or provocative. The electronic media can hardly follow a government decision-making process and, in any case, they have little interest in describing how it works. Their focus is on political actors and the one who matters the most to their audiences and the one who is turned to for an answer to any question in any policy field is the prime minister. In addition, today's media have a greater capacity than ever before to ferret out errors or miscues in government. Access to information legislation is one factor in this development. Giles Gherson, a leading media figure in Ottawa and a former policy adviser in the Human Resources Department, explains, 'To address the access to information issue ... I saw it myself that officials are extremely leery of putting things on paper that they wouldn't like to see made public or find its way to the media, several months later, that could be embarrassing to the minister.'[15] Conrad Winn, a pollster, argues that access to information has seriously inhibited the ability of government departments to ask the right question when commissioning a survey. He explains, 'The bottom line for the average public servant is don't embarrass the minister, that is the surest way to have your career stopped or slowed down. If you have polls that ask all kinds of questions that would reveal the truthful complexity of what people think ... then [the polls] will inevitably show the public doesn't like something the government does.'

The above explains, at least in part, why prime ministers and senior public servants are concerned to promote 'error-free' government. It has been reported that when Chrétien chaired his first cabinet meeting he had a stern warning for his ministers: 'The first person who makes a mistake will be out.'[16] Paul Tellier, secretary to the cabinet under Mulroney, announced at one of his weekly breakfast meetings with deputy ministers that he wanted 'error-free administration.'[17] There can be a thin line between error-free and controversy-free government. There is, of course, a limit to how many controversies the government can manage and the centre of government will want the 'government' to focus on the issues that matter the most to the prime minister and manage any controversies that may flow from them. Tom Axworthy, former principal secretary to Trudeau, writes that the political leadership wishes to 'master events' and argues that 'mistakes avoided are just as important as bills passed.' The best way to avoid mistakes is 'to avoid surprises.'[18] Al Johnson, a former senior deputy minister, in an 'autobiographical' perspective on public management in Canada, stressed the importance political leadership attaches to error-free administration.[19]

To avoid surprises requires a strong capacity at the centre of government to monitor developments in government departments. The Prime Minister's Office and the Privy Council Office, in particular, keep a watchful eye on ministers and departments. The centre of government, after all, now belongs to the prime minister, not to ministers.

The Centre of Government

The centre of government has remained largely intact, despite a management delayering exercise in the early 1990s, a massive government restructuring introduced in 1993, and the program review exercise launched in 1994. It has remained intact even though the workload of central agencies should have decreased substantially, given that PCO has far fewer cabinet committees to service than was the case in the 1970s and 1980s. The overall size of the government is also smaller than it was in the late 1960s: numerous crown corporations have been sold and over fifty thousand permanent positions have been eliminated from the public service. Yet in 2002 the PCO employed 441 people, compared with 209 in 1969.[20] In 2002 the PMO employed eighty-six people, compared with forty in 1968.[21]

One might well ask, then, what do officials at the centre do? When Trudeau decided to enlarge the size and scope of the PMO in the late 1960s, his first principal secretary sought to reassure critics and cabinet ministers that the office would remain essentially a service-oriented organization. He explained that it existed to 'serve the prime minister personally, that its purpose is not primarily advisory but functional and the PMO is not a mini-Cabinet; it is not directly or indirectly a decision-making body and it is not, in fact, a body at all.'[22] It is, of course, not possible to distinguish between a service function and a policy advisory function in this context. Drafting a letter or preparing a speech for the prime minister can constitute policy-making, and many times it does. There is also no doubt that several senior officials in the PMO do provide policy advice to the prime minister.

PMO staffers have the prime minister's ear on all issues they wish to raise, be it political, policy, administrative, or the appointment of a minister or deputy minister. They can also work hand-in-hand with a minister to initiate a proposal, and the minister will feel more secure, knowing that someone close to the prime minister is supportive of the proposal. They can also, however, undercut a proposal when briefing the prime minister. In short, senior PMO staff members do not consider themselves simply a court of second opinion. They are in the thick of it and do not hesitate to offer policy advice or to challenge a cabinet minister.

The role of the PCO has also changed in recent years. Arnold Heeney, the architect of the modern cabinet office in Ottawa, wrote after his retirement that he had successfully resisted Mackenzie King's desire to make the secretary to the cabinet 'a kind of deputy minister to the Prime Minister' or 'the personal staff officer to the Prime Minister.'[23] It is interesting to note, however, that no secretaries to the cabinet since Gordon Robertson have described their main job in this way. In 1997 the PCO produced a document on its role and structure, and its first page made it clear that the secretary's first responsibility was to the prime minister. It stated that the 'Clerk of the Privy Council and Secretary to the Cabinet' had three primary responsibilities:

1 As the prime minister's deputy minister to provide advice and support to the prime minister on a full range of responsibilities as head of government, including management of the federation
2 As the secretary to the cabinet to provide support and advice to the ministry as a whole and oversee the provision of policy and secretariat support to cabinet and cabinet committee
3 As head of the public service, to be responsible for the quality of expert, professional, and non-partisan advice and service provided by the Public Service to the prime minister, the ministry, and to all Canadians.

The direct link between the prime minister and the secretary to the cabinet and the PCO was made clearer in the office's mission and values statement. Its mission is 'to serve Canada and Canadians by providing the best non-partisan advice and support to the Prime Minister and Cabinet.' Its values statement made no mention of cabinet. It read: 'We recognize the special need of the Prime Minister for timely advice and support. We dedicate ourselves to our work and to the effective functioning of government.'[24]

When asked to sum up the office's work from the perspective of a line department, a former senior line deputy minister observed, 'If PCO, or for that matter other central agencies, were ever asked to ice a hockey team, they would put six goaltenders on the ice.'[25] To be sure, the PCO has a well-honed capacity to stop the great majority of proposals from line departments dead in their tracks, but it can also make things happen and take the lead in certain areas if the prime minister so wishes. In any event, in one area – the machinery of government – only the PCO has the mandate to initiate change. Still, goaltenders can be extremely useful to prime ministers in their efforts to avoid or manage errors the media might pick up and to keep things on an even keel so that the centre can concentrate on carefully selected policy objectives.

It is also important to recognize that the prime minister no longer needs to rely on regional ministers for an understanding of how government policies are being received. Public opinion surveys are more reliable, more objective, less regionally biased, more to the point, and easier to cope with than are ministers. They can also be used to deal with any public policy issue. All prime ministers since Trudeau have had their own pollsters in court interpreting events and providing advice. Surveys can enable prime ministers and their advisers to challenge the views of ministers. After all, how can even the most senior ministers dispute what the polls say?

Pollsters, again better than ministers, can assist prime ministers in deciding what is important to Canadians and what is not, what is politically sensible and what is not. A pollster in court always at the ready with data can be particularly helpful in dealing with the problem of political overload. 'Political overload' refers to a pervasive sense of urgency and an accompanying feeling of being overwhelmed both by events and the number of matters needing attention. A pollster can also advise the prime minister on hot button issues. Trudeau had Martin Goldfarb, Mulroney had Allan Gregg, and Chrétien had Michael Marzolini.

Prime ministers have decided that the best way to deal with the overload problem is to focus on a handful of policy issues and to rely on central agencies to manage the rest. All of the major policy initiatives in Trudeau's last mandate, including the national energy program, the constitution, and the 'six and five' wage-restraint initiative, were organized outside of the government's formal decision-making process. Similarly, Mulroney sidestepped cabinet in pursuing constitutional reform, the Canada–US free trade agreement, and the establishment of regional agencies. At a considerable cost to the Treasury, Chrétien paid no attention to the formal decision-making process when he decided to introduce the millennium scholarship fund for low-to-moderate income students. The cabinet was not consulted before the fund was unveiled, even though Chrétien called it the government's most significant millennium project. Chrétien, like Mulroney and Trudeau, also did not consult cabinet before striking a number of bilateral deals with provincial premiers.

So, what actually goes on in cabinet meetings? The first item is 'general discussion,' which the prime minister opens. He can raise any matter he chooses, ranging from a letter he may have received from a premier, to a purely partisan matter, to diplomacy. Although the PCO prepares a briefing note of possible talking points the prime minister can completely ignore it. However, the general discussion can be particularly useful to prime ministers as a cover to make it appear that cabinet has indeed considered an important issue which could be, for example, life-threatening or require military intervention. Mulroney, for instance, agreed to participate in the first Gulf War in a discussion with President Bush Sr, but raised the matter in cabinet, if only to be able to report that cabinet had indeed reviewed the situation.

The second item on the cabinet agenda is called 'presentations.' Ministers, accompanied by their deputies, are invited to give briefing sessions on various issues. The minister of finance and his deputy minister might present a status report on the government's fiscal position. Or the minister of industry and his deputy might make a presentation on Canada's productivity in relation to the United States. At the end of the presentation, ministers are free to raise any question or to ask for further clarification or explanation. But actual decisions rarely, if ever, flow out of these discussions. The purpose is to brief cabinet, not to secure decisions.

The third item is 'nominations.' Government appointments, ranging from a Supreme Court judge, to a senator, to a deputy minister, to a member of the board of a crown corporation, all require an order-in-council. There is always a list of appointments to be confirmed at every cabinet meeting. However, the nominations have all been sorted out well in advance of the meeting. The PMO and the PCO manage the appointment process and they consult with others only to the extent they want to. Prime ministers do not seek cabinet consensus when appointing Supreme Court judges or even senators. Suffice to note that the *Ottawa Citizen* had it right when it wrote that 'Mulroney's Supreme Court may soon become Jean Chrétien's court' because of 'an unusual confluence of expected retirements.'[26] Nor do prime ministers seek cabinet consensus when appointing deputy ministers or the administrative heads of government departments. Frequently, they do not even consult the relevant minister when appointing his or her deputy. I asked a former senior PCO official why it was that Jean Chrétien as minister of, say, justice or energy could not be trusted to appoint his own deputy minister, but that the moment he became prime minister he could be trusted to appoint all the deputy ministers? His response was simply, 'Because he became king.'[27]

The fourth item is cabinet committee decisions, presented as appendices on the agenda. In overhauling the cabinet decision-making process, at first Trudeau made it clear that all decisions taken in cabinet committee could be reopened for discussion in cabinet. In time, however, he became annoyed with the practice, and did not hesitate to show his displeasure whenever a minister sought to review an appendix item. By the late 1970s and the early 1980s, he automatically sent a cabinet committee decision back to the committee for review whenever a minister raised questions about it in full cabinet. Mulroney did much the same or relied on the operations committee of cabinet, chaired by Don Mazankowski, to sort out problems with cabinet committee decisions. Chrétien did not react well when a cabinet committee decision was challenged and, like Trudeau in his later years, he automatically referred it back to the cabinet committee without any discussion in full cabinet. The result is that cabinet committee decisions are now rarely challenged in full cabinet.

Mulroney, we now know, had little patience for the cabinet process and at one point said that he 'favoured any decision-making system that minimized the time he spent in cabinet.' He preferred to deal with the big issues outside of cabinet. The telephone and face-to-face conversation were his 'stock in trade.' Indeed, we are now informed that 'under Mulroney, important matters such as energy mega-projects were often decided without benefit of any cabinet documents at all.' The point is that Mulroney, like Chrétien and Trudeau, preferred to deal with major issues outside of the constraints imposed by the system. Those decisions that matter less to prime ministers are taken in cabinet committees, not in full cabinet, and since prime ministers do not easily tolerate ministers querying cabinet committee decisions, it was and is increasingly rarely done.

There is another problem with the cabinet committee process: ministers do not sit on all cabinet committees. In the case of the early Chrétien cabinet, for example, about half of the cabinet sat on the economic union committee and the other half on the social union committee. Accordingly, about half of the cabinet has to accept what has been decided by a committee of which they are not members and based on discussions in which they did not take part. It is also important to bear in mind that prime ministers can also direct the work of cabinet committees in various ways, even when they are not members. For one thing, prime ministers appoint all cabinet committee chairs, a task they do not take lightly.

Chrétien also established a number of ad hoc ministerial committees, often referred to as reference committees. There is no set order to establishing such committees and the prime minister, not cabinet, will decide if one is needed. We have seen, for example, ad hoc cabinet committees to review drug patent laws and support for official language minority committees. Typically, five or six ministers are invited to serve on such committees and often the chair reports directly to the prime minister, not full cabinet.

The PCO prepares briefing notes to the prime minister on virtually all proposals well before they are submitted to cabinet committees. The role of the office is to sort out issues that are potentially difficult to manage, to settle conflicts, and to seek compromise. PCO officials will make sure that the prime minister is always fully informed of potential conflicts and may well seek guidance from him on what to do. The prime minister reserves the right to keep an issue off a cabinet committee agenda for as long as he wishes or even to put a committee decision on hold by not putting it on the agenda for ratification. On occasion, he may decide to bring the issue to his own office for resolution.

Ministers have very limited means of securing advice on matters discussed in cabinet other than that relating to their own departments. It is asking a great deal for, say, the minister of Canadian heritage to request briefing on a proposal put forward by, say, the minister of health. Briefing material from the centre, whether it is produced by PCO or the Department of Finance, is off limits to ministers. Ministers are, of course, free to read cabinet documents, but we know that very few actually do.

To be sure, prime ministers do not always bypass their cabinets or only consult them after the fact. They pick and choose issues they want to direct and in some circumstances may decide to let the cabinet's collective decision-making process run its course. They may also even let the government caucus have its day from time to time and permit a government proposal or legislation to be pulled back and reworked to accommodate the views of caucus members. These are issues on which a prime minister may hold no firm view and decide that it is best to keep one's political capital in reserve for another day and another issue.

The Trudeau cabinet and central agency reforms, which have in essence lasted to this day, were designed to remove power from strong ministers and their mandarins and bring it to the centre to strengthen the hand of cabinet ministers as a collectivity. In hindsight, it is now clear that the results have fallen far short of the mark. In explaining the Trudeau reforms, Gordon Robertson wrote that 'ministers now, in many cases, have to give up some share of their authority and control to other ministers if the totality of policies is to be coordinated ... ministers have less chance to appear in roles of clear and firm decision.' There is no doubt that, beginning with Trudeau, and continuing to this day, power has not shifted to cabinet, as might have been initially hoped. Rather, it has increasingly gone to the prime minister and central agencies.

Globalization

Globalization, a word that has suffered greatly from over-use, has served to strengthen the hand of the prime minister. In hindsight, we may well have overstated the probability that globalization would spell gloom and doom for nation states.[28] Many national governments are discovering that the international environment can actually enhance their own power. In any event, Canadian prime ministers belong to a series of recently created international clubs of heads of government, from the G8 to Asia-Pacific Economic Cooperation (APEC) and la francophonie. Deals, even bilateral ones, between heads of governments are struck at these meetings.

The globalization of the world economy means that many more issues or files will arrive in the prime minister's in-basket. Everything in a government department now seems to connect to other departments and other governments, whether at the provincial level or internationally. Canadian prime ministers and premiers now sit at the centre of public policy issues and when they decide to focus on one, they can easily make it their own. National governments, precisely because of global economic forces, also need a capacity to move quickly to strike new deals when the time is right, or to change course because of emerging political and economic circumstances and opportunities.[29]

The Canadian prime minister, unlike the American president who has to deal with Congress, has a free hand to negotiate for his government and to make firm deals with foreign heads of government. The final hours of negotiations on the North American Free Trade Agreement (NAFTA) between prime minister–elect Chrétien and the United States president, through his ambassador to Canada, are telling. At one point the ambassador wondered about Chrétien's political authority to agree to a final deal, given that he had yet to appoint his cabinet. He put the question to Chrétien. 'What happens if we work all this out and then your new trade minister doesn't agree?' Chrétien replied, 'Then I will have a new trade minister the following morning.'[30] It is impossible to overemphasize the fact that the Canadian prime minister has few limits defining his political authority within the government.

To be sure, the media, opposition parties, question period, and public opinion can all serve to inhibit prime ministerial power. Similarly, what may appear at first to be a seemingly innocent incident can take on a life of its own and gain a high profile in the media and force the prime minister to reconsider a strategy or proposed initiative. But inside government, the prime minister is free to roam wherever he wishes and to deal with any file he chooses. There is ample evidence to suggest that prime ministers Trudeau, Mulroney, and Chrétien all sought to push back the frontiers of their political authority.

During the Trudeau years a new breed of advisers arrived on the scene in Ottawa and made their presence felt. Lobbyists happily took up special causes, mostly those tied to big business. They sold their expertise for handsome fees and they 'quickly amassed an impressive list of corporate clients.'[31] One would be extremely naive to assume that this development has not had a significant impact on the Ottawa decision-making process. Though it is not at all clear precisely what kind of expertise lobbyists peddle around Ottawa, we do know two things. First, their numbers have not gone down, despite the downsizing of government activities and changes in government. Second, it appears that what many peddle is political connections, and those who can claim to be connected to the prime minister do much the best. Writing about lobbyists in the Mulroney era, Jeffrey Simpson asked whether these men could have plied their trade with such success had a Liberal or NDP government been in office? The answer, he argued, could only be a resounding no. A change of government in 1993 revealed that Simpson was right. If the same question were asked today, the answer would be the same. Senior lobbyists, particularly the discreet ones, can be extremely useful to prime ministers. If a prime minister needs a second opinion on advice provided by ministers and senior public servants, he can turn to one of several lobbyists who are only too happy to oblige by reporting the views of clients or the results of public opinion surveys.

A minister in the Chrétien government has argued that cabinet is no longer a decision-making body. It is now, he claims, a 'kind of focus group for the prime minister.' This analogy is not much of an overstatement. In fact, Chrétien himself wrote before he became prime minister that a minister 'may have great authority within his department, but within Cabinet he is merely part of a collectivity, just another advisor to the prime minister. He can be told what to do and on important matters his only choice is to do or resign.'[32]

Chrétien announced to his caucus in the summer of 2003 that he would leave office in February of 2004. He subsequently revised his departure date to December of that year. The consensus among political observers was that he had no choice but to resign since he was virtually certain of losing a leadership review within his party. Chrétien's former finance minister, Paul Martin, was able to organize forces within the Liberal party to secure a vote in favour of a leadership review. He subsequently won the leadership easily and became Canada's twenty-first prime minister.

Martin has sought to offer a different vision of governing. He has made the need to tackle 'the democratic deficit' a central feature of his commitment to change how the federal government operates and decides. He declared that his purpose was 'to restore the virtues of the Westminster model' and one of the ways he would accomplish this would be attenuating the power of the prime minister and his office. Furthermore, he stated, 'We have permitted a culture to arise that has been some thirty years in the making. One that can be best summarized by the one question that everyone in Ottawa believes has become the key to getting things done: Who do you know in the PMO? This is unacceptable. We must change that reality.'

Martin's pledge to deal with the democratic deficit resonated with his colleagues in the House of Commons far more than his stand on any policy issue. It is revealing to note that in Canada a machinery of government issues, notably the power of the prime minister, would matter more than policy. The issue became more important given the Liberal party's dominance in federal policies. The opposition parties have not been able to mount a serious challenge since the collapse of the Progressive Conservative party in 1993. Opposition to the prime minister had to come from within the governing party to have any chance of success.

Time will tell how and if Martin deals with the democratic deficit by attenuating his own power and the power of his office. He will assume office with all the instruments required to dominate his government.

The Workings of Court Government

Canadian prime ministers have in their hands all the important levers of power. They are elected leader of their party by party members, they chair cabinet meetings, establish cabinet processes and procedures, set the cabinet agenda, establish the consensus for cabinet decisions; they appoint and fire ministers and deputy ministers, establish cabinet committees, and decide on their membership; they exercise virtually all the powers of patronage and act as personnel manager for thousands of government and patronage jobs; they articulate the government's strategic direction as outlined in the speech from the throne; they dictate the pace of change, and are the main salespersons promoting the achievements of their government; they have a direct hand in establishing the government's fiscal framework; they represent Canada abroad; they establish the proper mandate of individual ministers and decide all machinery of government issues, and they are the final arbiter in interdepartmental conflicts. The prime minister is the only politician with a national constituency and, unlike members of Parliament and even cabinet ministers, he does not need to search out publicity or national media attention, since attention is invariably focused on his office and his residence at 24 Sussex Drive.

Each of these levers of power taken separately is a formidable instrument in its own right, but when you add them all up and place them in the hands of one individual, they constitute an unassailable advantage. Other than going down to defeat in a general election, prime ministers can only be stopped, or slowed, by the force of public opinion and by a cabinet or caucus revolt. Even then, public opinion may not be much of a force if the prime minister has already decided not to run again in the next general election. One only has to think back to Trudeau or Mulroney's final years in office to appreciate this. As well, caucus or cabinet revolts, or even threats of revolts, are historically extremely rare in Ottawa. They are, however, not so rare in other parliamentary systems, as some British and Australian prime ministers can attest.

Canadian prime ministers have enjoyed these avenues of power for some time; however, there have been other developments lately which have served to consolidate the position of the prime minister and his advisers even further. Indeed, this is now evident even before they and their party assume office. Transition planning, a relatively new phenomenon in Canada, has become an important event designed to prepare a new government to assume power. Transition planning also strengthens the hand of court government, given that by definition it is designed to serve the prime minister. It is the Privy Council Office, however, that leads the process and its focus is entirely on party leaders or would-be prime ministers. In any event, it would be difficult for it to be otherwise, since in the crucial days between the election victory and formally taking power, the only known member of the incoming cabinet is the prime minister elect. For other potential cabinet ministers, it is a moment of high anxiety, waiting to see if they will be invited to sit in cabinet, and if so, in what portfolio.

The central purpose of transition planning is to equip the incoming prime minister to make his mark during the government's first few weeks in office. It is now widely recognized that these early weeks can be critical in setting the tone for how the new government will govern. It is also the period when the prime minister, as recent history shows, will make important decisions on the machinery of government and decide which major policy issues his government will tackle during its mandate.

In the late 1970s the PCO began the practice of preparing mandate letters that are handed to ministers on the day of their appointments and also to all ministers when they are assigned to a new portfolio. All ministers in the Chrétien government, for example, were given a mandate letter at the time he formed the government in 1993 and again in his second mandate in 1997.

What are the contents of these mandate letters? In most cases, they are brief, only about two to three pages in length. They are also tailored to the recipient. That is, a mandate letter to a newly appointed minister will be different from one to a veteran minister. For the newcomer, it will outline basic information about becoming a cabinet minister, including conflict-of-interest guidelines, and the need to respect the collective nature of cabinet decisions. In all cases the letters will delineate issues the minister should attend to and identify priority areas, if any, to be pursued. Here again there are two basic mandate letters. One states, in effect, 'Don't call us, we'll call you.' That is, the prime minister has decided that the department in question should not come up with a new policy agenda or legislative program. In these cases, the message is essentially: keep things going, do not cause any ripples, and keep out of trouble. In other instances, the letter will refer to particular policy objectives and major challenges. In these cases they can be quite specific, singling out proposed legislation, a special concern that needs attending to, or a program that needs to be overhauled. Mandate letters are now also prepared for newly appointed deputy ministers. Here again the purpose is to outline the main challenges the deputy ministers will be confronting and the priorities they will be expected to follow.

Are mandate letters taken seriously? The answer is yes. Indeed, ministers consulted said that it is the very first thing that they read after leaving the swearing-in ceremony at Rideau Hall. They know, as one observed, that 'the prime minister can always dig out his copy and ask about the status of a particular point.' More importantly, the letters reveal what the prime minister expects from them during their stay in their departments. Both present and former PMO and PCO officials report that all prime ministers, from Trudeau to Martin, take the mandate letters seriously and that they spend the required time to ensure that each says what they wish it to say.

I asked both present and former senior PCO officials if mandate letters do not fly in the face of the collective nature of cabinet decision-making. How can priorities be established and major tasks identified even before cabinet has held its very first meeting? Where, I asked, is the collective aspect of these decisions? The answer was that mandate letters are not from the cabinet, they are from the prime minister. It is the prime minister who identifies priority issues for his government, and if a minister cannot accept them, then, as one former senior PCO official explained, 'He is free to leave or to resign on the spot. He is not, after all, forced to stay in cabinet.'

The fact is that very few ministers are prepared to put their jobs on the line because they are not happy with a government policy. Those political parties which have so far held power in Ottawa do not have a strong ideological base and, accordingly, policy principles do not count for much. Thus, ministers can find any number of reasons to justify not resigning over a policy issue. This too serves to strengthen the hand of the prime minister.

In looking at the causes of ministerial resignations from confederation to 1990, Sharon Sutherland found that solidarity problems were responsible for only 19 per cent (or twenty-eight cases) of all resignations. By solidarity problems she means ministers unable or unwilling to agree with cabinet colleagues or with the prime minister. In more recent years, resignations from the Diefenbaker government comprised the following: Douglas Harkness, Pierre Sevigny, and George Hees (1963); from the Trudeau government, Judy LaMarsh (1968), Eric Kierans (1971), Jean Marchand (1976), and James Richardson (1976); from the Mulroney government, Suzanne Blais-Grenier (1985) and Lucien Bouchard (1990). There have been no resignations for reasons of solidarity since Bouchard left. It is interesting to note that, in contrast, 41 per cent of ministers who left cabinet did so to accept a political appointment offered by the prime minister.[33] It is also interesting to note that from 1976 until Paul Martin's resignation in 2002 all ministers who resigned did so over the language issue or national unity.

The difficult fiscal situation confronting governments has also had an important impact on Ottawa's decision-making process. As in the past, the number of people directly involved in putting the budget together is very limited. The key players are the prime minister, one or two of his senior advisers, the minister of finance, the clerk of the Privy Council, the deputy minister of finance, and a handful of senior finance officials.

The budget has now become the government's major policy statement and defines in very specific terms what the government will do in the coming months and where it will be spending new money. Traditionally, the government's budget process pitted guardians (e.g., the prime minister and minister of finance) against spenders (ministers of line departments and regional ministers). Efforts were made under Trudeau and Mulroney to establish various systems to allocate the spending of 'new' money, but they all fell far short of the mark.

The prime minister, the minister of finance, and their advisers now combine the guardian and spender roles. The budget exercise is no longer strictly concerned with the country's broad economic picture, projecting economic growth, establishing the fiscal framework, and deciding which taxes ought to be introduced, increased or decreased. It now deals with revenue projections and spending decisions. In addition, when the centre decides to sponsor new initiatives, it will much more often than not secure the required funding outside of the cabinet process. Examples abound and include both large and small expenditures, ranging from the millennium scholarship fund (Chrétien), the establishment of two regional development agencies (Mulroney) to the Canada Foundation for Innovation (Martin). This also applies to less costly initiatives. Indeed, some ministers became openly critical of Paul Martin when, as minister of finance, he announced a cut in what was then called the 'UI tax cut' without discussing it in cabinet. Another minister told the media that it 'was not necessarily what Canadians are asking for.' An official replied that Paul Martin had not made the UI tax cut unilaterally, but had done so 'with the approval of Prime Minister Chrétien.'[34]

It appears that the prime minister and his courtiers have become convinced that ministers are not capable of establishing priorities, that they lack the ability to look at spending proposals from a perspective broader than their respective department or region. Accordingly, the court has also taken to deciding a number of less costly spending decisions. An example will make this clear. The 1998 budget contained a $400 million provision to enable the government to deal with the year 2000 computer problem. This decision was taken by the president of the Treasury Board, the minister of finance, and the prime minister. When asked why the proposal was not taken to a cabinet committee and then cabinet, a senior minister responded: 'Who knows what ministers might have done with it? They could well have said. "This is not our most important priority," and spent the money on something else. We had no choice. We have to provide for the Y2K problem.' The prime minister's court can understand such things but not, it appears, cabinet.

The role of the clerk of the PC and secretary to the cabinet has changed a great deal in recent years and the clerk's influence in Ottawa is readily apparent to everyone inside the system. Outsiders, however, know very little about the clerk's role and responsibilities. One of the main challenges confronting a clerk is to establish a proper balance between representing the public service as an institution to the prime minister and cabinet, and representing the prime minister to the public service. The balance appears to have shifted to the latter with Trudeau's appointment of thirty-seven-year-old Michael Pitfield as clerk-secretary in 1975. The balance may well have shifted again in favour of the prime minister when Paul Tellier decided, as clerk-secretary under Mulroney, to add the title of the prime minister's deputy minister to his job.

Tellier's decision, however, probably reflected the reality of his day-to-day work. Indeed, the clerk-secretary is accountable to the prime minister, not to cabinet, and most of his daily activities are designed to support the prime minister, not cabinet. The prime minister, not cabinet, appoints him; the prime minister, not cabinet, evaluates his performance; and the prime minister, not cabinet, will decide if he stays or goes. All this is to say that not only does the secretary wear the hat of deputy minister to the prime minister, but it is without doubt the hat that fits best and the one he wears nearly all the time. A former senior PCO official observed that 'all clerks since Pitfield have done an excellent job at being deputy minister to the prime minister. As far as secretary to the cabinet, the performance has been spotty.'

The deputy minister's hat is also the one that gives him most of his influence inside government. This begins with the prime minister's power of appointment. A minute of council first issued in 1896 and last reissued in 1935 gives the prime minister the power to appoint deputy ministers.[35] All prime ministers have made it a point to retain this power in their own hands and for good reason. It is key to controlling government operations and to ensuring that the government goes in the intended direction.

The late Mitchell Sharp, a cabinet minister under both Pearson and Trudeau and deputy minister under St Laurent, wrote that 'the fact that deputy ministers are appointed on the recommendation of the prime minister means that, with the exception of the clerk of the Privy Council, who reports to the prime minister himself, they have a degree of independence from their own ministers, which gives them freedom in offering advice and administering the departments. They are in a sense part of the structure by which the prime minister controls the operations of the federal government.' He added that the 'appointment of deputy ministers also enables the prime minister to ensure continuity in the administration of a department, notwithstanding his replacement of the minister, the political head of the department.'[36]

The clerks have a direct hand in deciding who should become a deputy minister. This alone ensures that they will enjoy a great deal of influence inside government. As anyone who has worked in government can attest, no one should underestimate the power of appointment. In government, money and appointments steal the stage. The one who wields the power of appointment decides, at the highest levels in the public service, who wins, who does not, who is in the ascendency, and who is not. But that is not the clerk's only source of influence since, by virtue of their position at the centre of government, they are the prime minister's principal policy adviser. At least from the public service perspective, the clerk represents the final brief for the prime minister on all issues.

It is interesting to note that most line ministers now only meet their deputy ministers and other senior departmental staff on average about three hours a week. The problem, they explain, lies in an overcrowded ministerial agenda. However, the prime minister is able to find the time to meet with his deputy minister, the clerk-secretary, for at least thirty to forty-five minutes nearly every morning when he is in Ottawa. The minister of finance, meanwhile, can spend up to three or four hours a day, nearly every day, in briefing sessions with his senior departmental officials, particularly in the months before he tables his budget. They too have overcrowded agendas. Indeed, interviews with senior PMO and finance officials reveal that the prime minister and the minister of finance are always in constant battle to manage their agenda and to accommodate the many demands on their time. The difference may be that the prime minister and the minister of finance consider that time spent with their deputy ministers is time well spent. Decisions are made, things get done, major initiatives are planned and launched, and policy is established. Both are prepared to sacrifice other meetings to invest the time where it truly matters. The same imperatives cannot be said to be true for line ministers.

There have also been some significant changes to line departments that have served to weaken them in relation to the centre. These are most visible at the deputy minister level. A detailed study, 'Changing Profile of Federal Deputy Ministers, 1867 to 1988,' is revealing. It reports that the time deputy ministers spend in a particular department has declined to three years from the average of twelve years in the early period of Confederation. Unlike their predecessors, therefore, deputy ministers no longer stay with and retire in their department. As the profile study points out, 'They can no longer head the same department for many years.' Moreover, in Ottawa, recruitment of deputy ministers now easily crosses the boundaries between departments, while countries such as France and Germany have remained loyal to the tradition that the permanent head of the department is chosen from its senior ranks.[37] Another study reveals that 'experience in a central agency, most notably in the Privy Council Office, is now a virtual prerequisite for deputy minister appointment.'[38]

The above is not without implications for the government and the public service. The 'have-central-agency-experience will-travel' types have a different perspective from those who have come up through the ranks of a department to become its deputy minister. For one thing, the former will be preoccupied with 'managing up' – that is, looking up to their ministers but mostly to the centre of government rather than down at the organization to establish priorities and a sense of direction. A federal task force has argued that 'many senior public servants have made their careers because of their skills in managing up. They have been valued and promoted because they were adept at providing superiors with what they needed ... But if they [i.e., skills of managing up] are nourished in excess, to the exclusion of other important values, they can obscure the importance of managing down.'[39]

A well-honed capacity to manage up is much valued at the centre of government, particularly in the Privy Council Office. The office has several roles that it plays on behalf of the prime minister, and an important one, is to operate an early warning system to alert the prime minister and his staff of any political danger ahead. The system is designed to highlight departmental issues which are or may become politically 'sensitive or controversial because of their political ramifications.'[40] Deputy ministers known for their ability to manage up will know not only when to alert the centre, but also how to work with it to bring any potentially controversial issue back on track. If only because of the changing role of the media, deputy ministers now have to be particularly adroit at managing a political crisis or diffusing a difficult situation. It also explains why the links between the clerk and the community of deputy ministers have come to occupy a dominant position in Ottawa. Mitchell Sharp explained how the role of the centre had changed. He pointed out that 'back then [in the St Laurent and the Pearson governments], deputy ministers were clearly responsible for policy and for working with the minister to define policy in your area of responsibility. Your minister would of course challenge your ideas, but then he would agree on a position with you and take the ideas to Cabinet and have it out with his colleagues. Things did not work quite like that under Trudeau. It was different.' He added that 'you have to understand that the art of governing was different then [i.e., in pre-Trudeau days]. Ministers had a strong base and had strong personalities. They would go to Cabinet and take on even the prime minister. Some ministers would threaten to resign over policy, and some actually did. So it was different then for a deputy minister working with a minister. I am not sure that we bothered too much with PCO. Putting aside Pickersgill, secretaries to the Cabinet were rather low-profile people and they didn't much bother you.'[41]

A retired deputy minister discussed with me the changes at the centre of government from the time he became a public servant in 1958 to when he retired in the early 1990s. Much like Mitchell Sharp, he reported that during the 1960s the clerk of the Privy Council and secretary of cabinet did not dominate in Ottawa. Things changed with Michael Pitfield's appointment. When my respondent became deputy minister in the early 1970s, he claims that he 'would not have recognized one-third of my colleagues had I come across them on the street.' He adds, 'It was very rare that you had dealings with the clerk, perhaps a couple of times a year. You had a job to do with your minister and you went and did it. There was no such thing, for example, as a mandate letter from the clerk. But things began to change in the 1970s, particularly when the clerk started to chair monthly luncheon meetings with deputy ministers. Things changed again in 1985, when the clerk added weekly breakfast meetings and again later when deputy ministers' retreats were organized.'[42] A detailed study of the workload of federal deputy ministers reveals that on average they spend one hour out of every three on interdepartmental issues. It is interesting to note that typically deputy ministers allocate nearly twice as much time to meetings with their peers than on matters involving their own ministers.[43] With respect to issues, deputy ministers on average allocate more of their time to crisis management (16 per cent) than to human resources management (15 per cent).

Deputy ministers are now as much a part of the centre of government as they are the administrative heads of their departments. Sergio Marchi, a minister in the Chrétien government, claimed that he had more influence in Ottawa than his deputy minister because of his own connections to the centre of government. He observed, 'My deputy minister is all right, but he knows that in any showdown, I can get to the prime minister a lot faster than he can.'[44] One can scarcely imagine a minister making such a claim forty or fifty years ago, when line ministers met with their deputies most mornings, when the centre of government was less visible and involved in the decision-making process, and when cabinet actually made decisions. If there was a showdown to be had in those days, it was more likely to involve the minister and his deputy working as a team.

Court government has also had an impact on the public service as an institution. Individual public servants have become highly valued at the expense of the public service as an institution. Politicians from all political parties since the late 1970s have engaged in one form or another in bureaucratic bashing. They have accused the public service of favouring the status quo, of being unresponsive and uncreative. Yet at the same time they have sung the praises of individual public servants. This is because under court government individuals matter more than institutions and it is individuals that are to be empowered, not institutions. When the Mulroney government was plagued by one crisis after another and when his own office was in disarray, he reached out to Derek Burney, a career public servant, to be his chief of staff. When Trudeau wanted someone to help him in his desire to patriate the constitution, he bypassed the public service to appoint Michel Kirby as secretary to the cabinet for federal-provincial relations. But when Mulroney appointed Dalton Camp, a high-profile partisan, with no experience in the public service and already past retirement age to a senior public service position in the Privy Council Office, he sent a clear message to senior public servants that he had little regard for the public service as an institution.

Still, prime ministers and their advisers attach a great deal of importance to being able to deal with a political crisis. They also think short term. They have their own projects to promote and priorities to pursue and have little patience for due process. They will turn to individuals at the centre to give them a helping hand and to keep other matters under control. But this requires special skills, political skills. These, rather than an intimate knowledge of a sector or a policy field, have become of prime importance.

The way to govern in Ottawa is for prime ministers to focus on three or four priority issues, while also always keeping an eye on Quebec and national unity concerns. Tom Axworthy, former principal secretary to Pierre Trudeau, in his appropriately titled article 'Of Secretaries to Princes,' wrote that 'only with maximum prime ministerial involvement could the host of obstacles that stand in the way of reform be overcome ... [the prime minister] must choose relatively few central themes, not only because of the time demands on the prime minister, but also because it takes a herculean effort to coordinate the government machine.' To perform a herculean effort, a prime minister needs carefully selected individuals in key positions to push his agenda. Cabinet, the public service as an institution, or even government departments, are not always helpful. For example, Trudeau established an ad hoc group of officials at the centre to pursue his 1983 peace initiative 'largely because of the skepticism of the Department of External Affairs.'[45]

The result is that important decisions are no longer made in cabinet. They are now made in federal-provincial meetings of first ministers, where first ministers can hold informal meetings, in the Prime Minister's Office, in the Privy Council Office, in the Department of Finance, in international organizations and at international summits. There is no indication that the one person who holds all the cards, the prime minister, and the central agencies which enable him to bring effective political authority to the centre, are about to change things. The Canadian prime minister has little in the way of internal institutional checks to inhibit his ability to have his way. Prime Ministers Margaret Thatcher of Britain and Bob Hawkes of Australia were tossed out of their offices before their mandates were finished. Their own caucuses showed them the door. This would be unthinkable in Canada. Even at the depths of Mulroney's unpopularity, there was no indication that his caucus was about to boot him out of office. In any event, in Canada the caucus holds no such power. In Britain prime ministers must still deal with powerful ministers who have deep roots in their party and well-established party policies and positions on many issues. In Australia, the prime minister must contend with an elected and independent Senate.

In Canada, national unity concerns, the nature of federal-provincial relations and the role of the media tend, in a perverse fashion, to favour the centre of government in Ottawa. The prime minister's court dominates the policy agenda and permeates government decision-making to such an extent that it is only willing to trust itself to overseeing the management of important issues. In a sense, the centre of government has come to fear ministerial and line department independence more than it deplores line department paralysis. As a result, court government is probably better suited to managing the political agenda than is Cabinet government. The prime minister, like the European monarchs of yesterday, decides, at least within the federal government, who has standing at court. Prime Minister Chrétien left little doubt that Canada had made the transition to court government recently when he observed that 'The Prime Minister is the Prime Minister and he has the cabinet to advise him. At the end of the day, it is the Prime Minister who says "yes" or "no."'[46] Advisers, much like courtiers of old, have influence, not power.

Part III

PROVINCIAL CABINETS

Chapter 3

The Persistence of the Institutionalized Cabinet: The Central Executive in Newfoundland and Labrador

CHRISTOPHER DUNN

Much recent discussion of cabinet design in Canada has focused around the patterns identified as the unaided cabinet on the one hand, and institutionalized cabinet on the other. The literature is now starting to maintain that a new model has been apparent, called the 'prime minister-centred cabinet.' The prime minister-centred cabinet does not exist in Newfoundland and Labrador, where the institutionalized cabinet has persisted for over thirty years. Three decades of the same model in Newfoundland, when other provinces have experimented with a variety of designs, certainly deserves explanation.

There have been three public services in Newfoundland. The first public service under responsible government (1855–1934) was anything but unified and merit-based. Professionalism flourished in the second public service, but it was in the context of an artificial, paternalistic Commission of Government (1934–49) grafted on to the Newfoundland reality. The third public service began under Confederation (more precisely, the joining of the province to Canada's federal system) in 1949.[1] The Newfoundland had a traditional cabinet (the patronage-based predecessor to the unaided cabinet) until 1934; then under the Commission of Government it had no cabinet at all, but an unelected body which functioned as a combination legislature and executive; then it had an unaided cabinet under Smallwood until 1972 finally switching to an institutionalized model from which it has never really deviated.

The Unaided Cabinet

Smallwood: Unaided Premier in an Unaided Cabinet

The cabinet of Joseph R. Smallwood was unmistakeably in the unaided mould. Smallwood was a dominant premier, and did not encourage collegiality. The degree to which he was dominant, however, has been a matter of debate. Ross Johnson noted that his was not a 'one-man government,' as common wisdom had it. The premier treated cabinet as a sounding board and ratification source for his own ideas, choose all party candidates and, with the exception of the late 1960s (with strong ministers such as John Crosbie, Alex Hickman, and Clyde Wells in the cabinet), defined what constituted a of cabinet 'consensus.'[2]

Most observers have supported the one-man government thesis. John Crosbie, a member of his cabinet from 1966 to 1968, said of him that 'it was a remarkable characteristic of the Smallwood cabinet that there was no sense of collective responsibility for the actions of the government ... the members seemed to feel that Smallwood was responsible for everything.'[3] Furthermore, Crosbie says, 'The important issues of government [intergovernmental, resource development, economic development] were not subject to discussion; he didn't invite debate about his own designs for government.'[4] Ed Roberts, Smallwood's executive assistant from 1964 to 1966 and later Liberal leader, says Smallwood's domination was due to a number of factors, including articulateness and knowledge of the files. Add to that, 'he had also been around a long time; with antiquity comes authority. As well, until 1968, he was very popular. In the 1966 election he got 60% of the popular vote.'[5] The premier who could move the public could move government.

Yet Smallwood was not alone in government. He had a kitchen cabinet, a group of trusted ministers and officials so named because it met often for lunch in the premier's dining room on the first floor of the Confederation Building, and would informally vet government business.

There was a simple cabinet structure. There were no standing committees of cabinet other than Treasury Board, and no practice of regular meetings of cabinet. There was sporadic and short-term use of cabinet committees relating to specific problems. In the early 1960s, there was a cabinet committee struck to examine the estimates of expenditure of the House of Assembly. In 1967 and 1968 there was a cabinet committee struck to negotiate the detailed legal arrangements surrounding possible deals the promoters John C. Doyle and John Shaheen had been discussing with Smallwood regarding a linerboard mill in Stephenville and a paper mill and an oil refinery at Come by Chance, respectively. This committee only came about after Crosbie suggested it and, since it was largely composed of ministers suspicious of Small-wood's motives, was not effective.[6]

Reliance on central departments meant that few cabinet staff and little cabinet-level analysis were needed. There was, in short, an unaided cabinet. The major central department, the Department of Finance, had changed little from the days of responsible government. Roberts says he was the first real staff that Smallwood had, and he started only in 1964. The cabinet decision-making process was aided by only one person, clerk of the Executive Council Jim Channing, who would go on to serve in this post from 1956 to 1979. There was a Treasury Board, but no real Treasury Board Secretariat until near the end of the Smallwood years.

Centralization should not be equated with a lack of renewal of the cadre of senior ministers and officials. Just as Pearson was bringing Trudeau, Marchand, and Pelletier into the federal cabinet in 1965, Smallwood was doing the same with what came to be nicknamed the 'Kiddies' Corner' – John Crosbie, Ed Roberts, Clyde Wells, Aidan Maloney, and T. Alex Hickman – in 1966. Smallwood also allowed a wave of younger officials – people in their thirties like Vic Young, Rolly Martin, David Mercer, and Sandy Roach – to be hired by the modernizing deputy in finance, Dennis Groom, who has been credited by some insiders as starting a Newfoundland brains trust that affected the provincial public service for decades.

Budgeting practice was largely in the unaided cabinet mode as well. The revenue budget, including the annual budget speech delivered by the minister of finance, was centralized in Smallwood's hands, aided by Finance Minister Val Earle, Treasury Board officer Vic Young, and selected others. The expenditure budget was similarly centralized. Ministers had control over their expenditures only if they did not involve significant increases, changes in policy direction, or new legislation. The financial control enjoyed by the premier was not due to a desire for expenditure control – he squandered a substantial surplus left to him by the Commission of Government – but to a desire for personal power. Smallwood had a profound distrust of others and was constantly on the alert for those who would usurp his prerogatives. The annual budget cycle was used, but Smallwood's many economic development schemes made for sudden spikes in off-budget public spending.

Planning took place in the style of the unaided cabinet as well, focusing on project planning. It was very similar to the type of planning that another dominant and province-building premier at the other end of the country, W.A.C. Bennett, was undertaking. For B.C.'s Columbia River project, there was Newfoundland's Upper Churchill project. For Bennett's development of the interior there was Smallwood's rural relocation program. B.C.'s fight for recognition as a region of Canada was analagous to Newfoundland's Term 29 dispute. The projects were seemingly endless.

Decision-making was also in the unaided mode. Departmental autonomy was honoured if ministerial policies were not in direct conflict with those of the premier, or did not involve major policy or expenditure implications. The cabinet by and large did not face alternative sources of information and advice. Crosbie says that 'Departmental proposals would be dealt with in the normal way. Ministers would advise cabinet in cabinet submissions that had Background, Details and Recommendations sections. However, if Smallwood proposed it, you weren't supposed to discuss it. There was no discussion of costs and benefits; he hated cost-benefit studies, and those who suggested them didn't last too long.'[7] The reason, as Smallwood noted in the House of Assembly, was simple: 'If the young people leave, we're dead. How do you make Newfoundland an exciting province? With caution? With prudence? With conservatism? That's death, that washes us down the drain.'[8]

Symbols transmitted the message of Smallwood's power. The premier's office had a one-way intercom system which allowed Smallwood to connect with ministers and senior officials, and woe betide those who were not available to harken to his call. He had a estate, Russwood Ranch, which was intended to be a provincial version of the White House. He asserted his will over ministers for all to see in the legislature. He humiliated or otherwise silenced those who interrupted him in cabinet. In the end, such excesses left him with few supporters.

The Institutionalized Cabinet

The Moores Administration, 1972–1979

Under Frank Moores, the next premier, Newfoundland entered the institutionalized cabinet era, and there, for many reasons, it has stayed. In a way, Moores was a surprising source for institutional change. He had the reputation of being not much interested in organizational matters, or for that matter public administration in general. However, at the beginning of his time in office his advisors had convinced him that substantive change to the machinery of government was necessary; he agreed, and sold it as an exercise in democratization.

The year 1972 saw the first signs of institutionalization.[9] Following the general election of 24 March 1972, the government's speech from the throne of 19 April announced that there would be a Committee on Government Administration and Productivity (COGAP) headed by the clerk, Jim Channing, which would examine the restructuring of the civil service. Parallel to COGAP was a planning inititative. On 1 June the premier announced that a three-member Cabinet Planning Committee had been struck, headed by the premier, with a task force of twenty civil servants, operating through a system of specialized study committees. The task force was headed by his chief executive assistant, Stu Peters, who had had organizational and resource policy experience in the Ontario and federal governments as well as in the Smallwood government. On 29 June Moores announced that there would in fact be a reorganization, based on the work of the committee and the planning task force. Details of this reorganization were however not announced until four months later. The circumstances surrounding the introduction of the new cabinet model revealed factors behind its introduction.

The factors promoting the birth of institutionalization and those explaining its persistence overlapped to some extent. The December 1972 *Report of the Committee on Government Administration and Productivity* explicitly identified several of what it called 'deficiencies of the traditional cabinet system' (that is, what chapter 1 has called the unaided cabinet). These were the potential to overburden ministers, the low level of policy analysis and policy integration arising from the high volume of issues that the cabinet must approve, and the tendency for governments to be overtaken by events.[10] The necessity for decongestion of the process – that is, the need to shunt some of the business of cabinet to ministers or a system of cabinet committees – was demonstrated by the fact that for seven departments identified, there were 239 acts in force, and 653 sections or subsections requiring action by cabinet.[11] So concerned were the drafters of the report for collegial or committee-based decision-making that they stressed 'the importance of individual Ministers, except in cases of extreme urgency, not raising matters orally in Cabinet. If this is done ... there is a grave risk that the effectiveness of the whole interlocking Cabinet system could be seriously impaired.'[12] They had to go through committees instead.

The committee gave particular attention to two other jurisdictions, Ontario and the federal government. It opted for the federal 'policy groups' approach as opposed to the Ontario model, with its two-tier structure and policy ministers with no departmental responsibilities. The effects of social science rationalism – calls for coordination and policy coherence by Memorial University political scientists – also pervaded the original design exercise for the Newfoundland cabinet. The desire for intergovernmental coherence was another factor driving the new design. It explained the care taken by the designers to place the intergovernmental affairs secretariat close to the seat of government, the Premier's Office, along with negotiation responsibilities.

Newfoundland by now had an administrative tradition of hierarchy and subordination deriving from the Commission era, which Smallwood had maintained. The rationalist recommendations of the COGAP coalesced with this familiar principle of hierarchy.[13] The institutionalization of the service began soon after the tabling of the report of the committee. The cabinet became more complex, structured in a hierarchical committee system. The Treasury Board evolved into a more collectivist decision-making body but retained the control orientation that it had been developing, apparently for some time.[14] The Public Service Commission obtained a powerful mandate to enforce the merit approach in the public service.

The committee had recommended that the government establish one new coordinating committee (while continuing the existing one, the Treasury Board), as well as three policy committees of cabinet. The apex was to be the new Planning and Priorities Committee (PPC), designed to set the broad policies and priorities of government and to undertake policy and program reviews. PPC included the chairs of the associated policy committees as well as the minister of finance and the president of Treasury Board. The three policy committees were Resource Policy, Social Policy, and Government Services, and the premier was to select the chair of each of the committees. The minister of finance acted as president of Treasury Board and there would be a rotating ministerial membership of the board, at least one of which would come from PPC. It was, as Joyce commented, 'ostensibly not a two-tier cabinet with ordinary and super-minsters but in fact operating in much the same way.'[15] The Treasury Board continued its budget preparation and fiscal monitoring roles, but the guidelines for the annual budget would now be established by PPC. There was added a Routine Committee for non-policy-oriented decisions.

Despite the apparent hierarchy, there was an element of collegiality that had not been there in Smallwood's day. There was a core of powerful ministers – John Crosbie, Leo Barry, Gerry Ottenheimer, Bill Doody – and ministers felt free to speak their minds in the cabinet. If a minister did not agree with the recommendation taken by a cabinet committee, he could appeal it in full cabinet. The premier still had influence, however, especially on issues of finance and economic development, and would achieve his way by employing his personality, or bypassing ministers on occasion.

Signs of institutionalization, as evidenced by central agencies, grew. A Cabinet Secretariat established to facilitate the cabinet decision-making process, served the PPC as well as each of the policy committees. The Treasury Board was retained and served by its existing secretariat, which was moved from the Department of Finance to the Executive Council Office (ECO). Dedicated legislation created a Public Service Commission in 1973, and firmly ensconced the merit principle as an important feature of the management of the public service.[16] In 1975 an Intergovernmental Affairs Secretariat was established, one of its main functions being to coordinate with the activities of the Department of Regional Economic Expansion (DREE).

In 1978 Moores combined the Planning and Priorities Secretariat and the Cabinet Secretariat. The Cabinet Secretariat reported to the premier, the Treasury Board Secretariat to the president of the Treasury Board, the Intergovernmental Affairs Secretariat to the minister responsible for intergovernmental affairs. The Cabinet Secretariat recorded cabinet decisions as well as the recommendations of cabinet policy committees, prepared long and short-term economic forecasts, and coordinated a decentralized departmental process of social and economic planning. The Intergovernmental Affairs Secretariat operated under the Intergovernmental Affairs Act, which stipulated that all intergovernmental agreements be signed by the responsible minister. The Treasury Board Secretariat continued to operate as before.

Planning and budgeting became more common, but the connection between them that some institutionalized cabinets displayed in some jurisdictions never happened in Newfoundland. One senior cabinet official of the time said that 'In my naïveté, I thought that there should be multi-year planning and budgeting, and that [consideration of] aims should precede budgeting, but the opposite was the case. Margins for planning were slim. Major planning exercises, if they were undertaken, were determined by the federal government. These were exercises of the federal government's "spending power." They took place in transportation, regional development, even school construction.'

The paper role of the PPC notwithstanding, the powerhouse in budgeting matters became the Treasury Board, which set the envelopes that departments had to live with. The Moores government introduced a Financial Administration Act in 1973. It created a new Treasury Board, now seven members strong, to advise cabinet on matters of financial management, administrative policy, personnel management, collective bargaining, and other matters. The retention of Jim Channing, Smallwood's clerk of the Executive Council, in his position, demonstrated the move by the premier to more of a British-style professional service.[17]

The Peckford Years (1979–1989): Conflicting Signals

The Peckford government tended to reform policy, not administration. Nevertheless, it began to review its organizational design, concentrating on streamlining government and a clearer economic development focus, which would later affect the Wells government. At the same time, the government signalled its intention to become more activist.

In keeping with the importance Brian Peckford placed on relations with the federal government, coherence in intergovernmental relations was a consistent theme. In 1979 the secretariat was busy preparing submissions to DREE for subsidiary resource agreements, drawing up training plans in the Federal-Provincial Manpower Needs Committee, reviewing the federal-provincial social security system, and coordinating the implementation of the Canada/Newfoundland Subsidiary Agreement for Planning.

Some of the social science influence can be attributed to the work of economist David Vardy, who became clerk in September of 1978 and was to remain in that position until 1985, through much of the Peckford years.[18] Struck by the fact that Channing had been the only person to keep records in the previous cabinet system, he was intimately involved in the operationalization of the White paper of 1972, and in improving cabinet documentation. While he was clerk he brought in planning and public adminstration reforms, which included establishing a development program for the senior public service, initiating 'Management by Objectives' in the service, generating the five-year development plan, and participating in the negotiation of the Atlantic Accord of 11 February 1985. Vardy's replacement, from 1985 to 1988, was Herbert M. (Herb) Clarke. Clarke's experience as senior executive spanned both the public and private sectors.

Peckford's quest for influence was another factor in the design. A senior official summarized the difference between Moores and Peckford, noting 'Moores did not spend a lot of time in the office. Peckford on the other hand had a broader range of interests. He was more of a mission-driven person.' Missions were in fact a Peckford theme. They were championed in a government planning document, *Managing All Our Resources*, in 1980, which dealt with the theme of getting a fair return for the province's resources.

These various influences would result in a continuation of the institutionalized and centralized cabinet format. There were three standing policy committees of cabinet, as before: Planning and Priorities, Resource, and Social committees, as well as a Routine Committee of Cabinet. Peckford added one ad hoc committee, on Fisheries Restructuring, and one standing committee, on Memorial University Financial Affairs, both of which were also served by the cabinet secretariat.

Yet the premier increasingly had to share power. An senior official of the day says 'In full cabinet, powerful ministers would rule the roost. They would protect their own departments, in terms of budgets and decision-making ... In cabinet, Peckford was close to Bill Marshall, John Collins, Gerald Ottenheimer and Neil Windsor; they would exercise a lot of influence on Peckford.' PPC was the powerhouse cabinet committee, especially in spending and major resource development decisions. For example, it decided the fate of the Come by Chance Refinery, which had gone bankrupt under John Shaheen, and it managed the Bowater divestiture.

The Routine Committee was analogous to the Special Committee of Cabinet federally, and was the only only cabinet committee that could issue orders-in-council. It decided appointments to school boards and the disposition of crown lands and was in general used for decisions that were routine and had little policy import.

The structured approach to aiding cabinet committees continued. Each of the policy committees had a secretary who was responsible for preparing analysis and recommendations to help the ministers in the decision-making process. The intergovernmental secretariat continued in the ECO, answerable as before to the minister, and now with a permanent head called the deputy minister of intergovernmental affairs.

The Treasury Board Secretariat continued as well in the ECO. During Peckford's time the premier's office, that is, the political advice side of the ECO, also grew in importance.

There was a significant, and novel, planning effort towards the end of the end of the Peckford era, one critical of both the administrative and planning efforts to the earlier years. In 1985 the government established the Royal Commission on Employment and Unemployment (the House Commission). The author of its report, J.D. (Doug) House, would come to be a critic of cabinet operations in both the Peckford and Wells eras. The report criticized the centralized, pyramidal, over-regulated and non-communicative nature of the public service.[19] The centralist Moores paradigm had apparently discouraged a development orientation in the public service. Among other things, the commission recommended an external task force to examine the organization of the public service, and a more regionally-sensitive program and planning approach.[20]

Senior officials did not accept House's analysis. According to House, they 'believed in the Peckford Government's emphasis on resource industries and the need for the province to gain greater control over these industries ... They were not primed for a radically different report six years later [House's] with its vision of a postindustrial society and its emphases on information technology, small-scale enterprise, decentralized decision-making, and a new role for government itself in economic development.'[21] A study team composed of senior officials resisted efforts to decentralize decision-making and to review, whole scale, the organizational structure of the provincial government.

Officials were not successful in getting a 'planning-budgeting nexus' – a connection – operative. *Managing All Our Resources* was the government's first multi-year budget plan, and this had taken half the Peckford years to emerge. The original idea was to have policy reserves managed at the departmental level, but this approach eventually waned because of the tendency of cabinet ministers at estimates review, as one official said, to 'question everything – to make sure that departments were not getting away with anything.' Multi-year budgeting, which has a planning element to it, declined in Peckford's years, as it had in Moores'. Old-fashioned restraint reared its head instead. The Senior Expenditure Review Committee (the Randell Committee), set up by Peckford in 1987 to examine methods of balancing the current account budget, suggested early retirement packages, privatization options, devolution of government services to the private sector, and salary costs. It also recommended a balanced budget over a four-year period, consolidation of government departments, selected privatizations, and new ways to generate revenues. By his own admission, however, Peckford had a distaste for making difficult decisions about how to reduce the size of the government, and left politics. His successor, Tom Rideout, subsequently lost the general election of 1989, further negating the chance of any immediate effect by the report.

The Peckford government therefore conveyed conflicting intentions regarding the career public service. On the one hand it indicated its concern about the size, red tape, and layering of the government establishment, as well as the reach of government enterprises. On the other hand, it showed an interest in designing a more representative and fairly compensated public service.

The Wells Government (1989–1996): Innovation amid Retrenchment

Clyde Wells had seen the unaided cabinet in operation under Smallwood, and his distaste for it led him to continue the institutionalized format. The Wells government was again relatively consistent with past governments in both the factors and effects relating to cabinet government. Social science rationalism and fiscal control drove the Wells design, as did political messaging.

The Wells government was attuned to the newest in social science reform then currently dominant in the Western world, embarking upon a modest version of what has been called the New Public Management[22] (NPM). In general NPM sought a closer alignment between private sector attitudes and public sector practices. Its emphasized market testing, the Total Quality Movement, or empowerment (called the service quality initiative in the Wells government), partnerships, downsizing, privatization, deregulation, and governments placing priority on policy direction rather on than policy implementation. Though the government never explicitly enunciated its public sector philosophy, it was implicit in its policies of the streamlining of government, service quality, regulatory reform, and privatization.

Political semaphore was also a design factor. Planning became a catchword of the Liberal party in opposition and the Wells government in office because of a felt need to assure the public – battling double-digit unemployment, rural depopulation, and out-migration – that they were not merely the pawns of economic forces. Wells admired the work done by the House Commission, which he considered had not been given adequate follow-up by the Peckford administration.

The desire for fiscal control became an additional design factor. Wells reduced the size of cabinet to fourteen and introduced a host of measures to shrink the costs of government. Cabinet chose across-the-board cuts and streamlining rather than downsizing of departments and agencies to cap government growth. Structurally, the government created regional community health boards to coordinate the delivery of community-based services; merged the administrative divisions of the Executive Council, the Public Service Commission and the Department of Finance; reorganized the Works, Services and Transportation Department; and consolidated the administrative divisions of the Departments of Environment, Employment and Labour Relations, and Tourism, Culture and Recreation.[23]

Faced with significant challenges, Wells continued and even added to the complexity of the institutionalized cabinet. Cabinet committees were continued and an appointments committee for staffing of agencies, boards, and commissions was added. The practice of designating the premier as intergovernmental minister continued; the arrangement was formalized in 1991, when the Intergovernmental Affairs Act was changed to make the premier the minister of intergovernmental affairs.[24] A notable innovation came about early in 1994 with the establishment of an ad hoc cabinet committee composed of both federal and provincial ministers. Formed in order to deal with Newfoundland's fishery crisis, it began to coordinate federal and provincial economic development policies, and called upon officials as needed.

Ed Roberts described the dynamics of the cabinet system in the Wells years:

> Wells accepted the system he had inherited. Only ministers could generate and sign a cabinet paper, that is, put it into the system. As it was, officials generated about 90% of the business of cabinet. Everything went to a committee at the discretion of the cabinet secretary. Committees were the same as with Peckford ...
>
> Chances were that if we [ministers on the PPC, like Paul Dicks, Chris Decker, Chuck Furey, Ed Roberts] recommended something, the rest of the cabinet would go along. We would deal with the significant issues of the day, matters like Voisey's Bay or the Lower Churchill [developments]. Ministers had to be invited to come to P&P.
>
> When matters came to cabinet from the cabinet committees, you likely

had had your say already in one of the cabinet committees already. All the key ministers were on Treasury Board, for instance, so the finances [had already been gone over]. You didn't get a discussion going at cabinet unless you were *really* upset about some issue.

The Executive Council Act, introduced in 1995, signalled that the premier had the job of organizational architect, an institutionalized cabinet characteristic. This act gave cabinet the power to organize departments of government by orders-in-council. Previously, by virtue of the Rearrangement and Transfer of Duties Act, 1966, the creation of government departments had to be sanctioned by the legislature.

Continuity and elaboration were evident at the central agency level. Hal Stanley, a longstanding public servant, was appointed clerk of the Executive Council and secretary to the cabinet by the Progressive Conservative government in 1988, and remained so under Wells until 1994. Another official with significant experience in the provincial system, Fred Way, then took over as cabinet secretary. One change in 1994 was to discontinue the past pattern of having a joint post of secretary of cabinet and clerk of the Executive Council, a centralized authority which Wells felt made the official too much like a 'civil service premier,' so now the post was split. The three-secretariat ECO continued: an office to record cabinet decisions and to route proposals, a cabinet secretariat to continue in the policy advice mode, and an intergovernmental affairs secretariat to coordinate intergovernmental relations. Contrary to most institutionalized provincial cabinets in Canada, the political side was under-emphasized, with only a few special and executive assistants to handle political matters.

Yet because of the political semaphore and planning imperative, there was a new wrinkle added to the central agency configuration. Within a few months of the Liberal government being elected, Wells established the Economic Recovery Commission (ERC), which Doug House was to lead. Meant to implement the development agenda of the House Commission, the ERC reported to the cabinet but had an arm's length relationship to line departments.

With the apparatus in gear, institutionalized cabinet-style planning followed. The Strategic Economic Plan involved public consultation, including a report to the public,[25] the Strategic Economic Plan document itself,[26] and several follow-up reports.[27] The government, responding both to the strategic economic plan and to a derivative report, that of the Task Force on Community Economic Development

(1995), created nineteen economic zones which were intended to coordinate the economic development activities of provincial and federal agencies at the regional level. A Strategic Social Plan process began, initially chaired by the same official who headed the economic plan, Edsel Bonnell, the premier's chief of staff. For the time being, however, this remained an internal exercise; it was never made public while Wells was premier. Departmental commitment to strategic planning was strongly encouraged by the central agencies.

Central-departmental balance is often an aim in the institutionalized context. However, in the Wells years there were several complaints about the control-oriented nature of central agencies, especially the Treasury Board Secretariat. Departments were obliged to request permission from TBS for relatively small purchases and services expenditures. Multiple analyses by central staff in the policy secretariats and other agencies accompanied most cabinet policy recommendations, and allegedly made it hard for departments to make their own arguments in the cabinet context.

One version of the decision-making and policy development in this period comes from House. He maintained that the efforts of the ERC were stymied by a handful of old guard officials in the central agencies and in the departments. They had been in government for many years by the time House arrived and were allegedly prisoners of old economic doctrines like the urbanization/industrialization approach of the Smallwood era, and the resource management approach of the Peckford years. They were said to have used a variety of techniques, ranging from non-cooperation to overt criticism in order to subvert the work of the ERC. In addition, the ambiguities surrounding the status of the ERC were never cleared up. House met regularly with the premier, but had no link to the cabinet process; he met with P&P, but for information-sharing and not decision-making; and the ERC act mentioned the commission's power to enter into agreements with the federal government, but management of the federal-provincial interface was already the role of the Intergovernmental Affairs Secretariat. Ultimately the old guard were successful in turning Wells and Tobin against the ERC, according to House.

Senior officials and ex-ministers have given several reasons for the failure of the commission. For example, the commission had more access to senior decision-makers than most other agencies of government, so access and lack of due process was not the problem. The commission did not attempt to win over the other politicians and officials;

they never 'swam in the sea,' as one minister put it. The role of the ERC changed; originally conceived of as a planning wing, through Enterprise Newfoundland and Labrador (ENL), it began to distribute loans, a function which it did not have the background for and which detracted from the job of selling a vision. The commission did not take enough notice of the perceived threat to the traditional role of politicians that the work of the ERC seemed to indicate, which was to 'get things for the district.' The commission's vision was out of sync with the political economy of the day; as one senior official put it, 'since Newfoundland was running off federal transfers, and Ottawa was engaging in fiscal entrenchment, plus there was a fishing collapse, economic planning became crisis management almost overnight.' The ERC stood for government determining what the economic structure of the province should be, but this was exactly the era of the developing thesis that 'less government was better than more government.' Lastly, the government was simply overcome by a variety of competing concerns in the early 1990s: a deteriorating fiscal system, the need for reform of the denominational system, and the coming to the boil of thirty years of constitutional renewal issues.

Brian Tobin (1996–2000): Institutionalization Redux

Brian Tobin was also resolutely in the institutionalized cabinet mode. He had five standing committees of cabinet: Planning and Priorities, Economic Policy, Social Policy, Routine Matters/Appointments, and Treasury Board.

Tobin had the PMO/PCO split at the centre as well, with an office of the premier headed by a chief of staff, and an Executive Council Office with a combined clerk/secretary, as well as intergovernmental responsibilities. The clerk in effect became the head of the public service under Tobin. Tobin also created a new post – deputy clerk and associate secretary – to assist in the ongoing administration of the cabinet process. Cabinet Secretariat, Intergovernmental Affairs, and Treasury Board Secretariat continued as parts of the ECO. It should be noted however that the TBS, although nominally part of the ECO, was an autonomous body. This had always been the case under other premiers and continued to be the case under Tobin.

There was also an Aboriginal and Labrador Secretariat in the ECO with its own deputy minister reporting directly to the premier. This was the same kind of reporting relationship as that between the premier and the deputy minister of intergovernmental affairs. In both cases there was a nominal coordinating role performed by the secretary to cabinet, Mr Rowe.

However, by the time Tobin, the consummate outsider, entered the premier's office, the institutionalized cabinet was not operating in an optimal, or even satisfactory manner. A successful institutionalized system depended on maintaining some of the traditional Westminster goals in place: a cabinet operating as a team, a clear division of responsibilities between ministers and their deputies, renewal of the senior executive cadre, and the support of the caucus.

These things were not happening. There had been centralization of power in the hands of Premier Wells and a handful of officials: absenteeism had even begun to be a problem in cabinet and cabinet committee meetings. Wells established direct links to the deputy ministers and tended to bypass ministers in the decision-making process; they were advised of decisions instead of participating in them in the first instance. The cabinet committee system, although still nominally in place, had atrophied; instead, full cabinet would make all decisions, with major items driven by the P&P Committee. Planning activity was often coordinated more by officials like Edsel Bonnell, the premier's chief of staff, than by cabinet committees. The power of the Treasury Board and its secretariat came to be significant in the financial austerity regime established by Wells; it was the major actor in the budget process, which meant that the cabinet secretariat had a diminished capacity to engage in whole-of-government coordination. Departments began to try to play one part of the system off against the other: policy approval would be sought from the cabinet, often presenting full cabinet with a policy proposal that hadn't gone through the committee process, and then using this as leverage against the financial and personnel strictures established by Treasury Board. There were no major changes in the deputy minister ranks in the Wells years, nor any initiative to involve the caucus in development of policy. In fact, the executive government was operating in a way not unlike the pattern Savoie has outlined at the federal level.

Tobin deliberately set about to change this premier-centred central executive. He moved to a system more in line with the original model of the institutionalized cabinet, as it was conceptualized both in the province and elsewhere. He made it clear to the ministers that their attendance was necessary at cabinet business. He revived the committee system, so that policy would go through them first and only then on to cabinet; cabinet was not going to decide everything. The role of P&P was de-emphasized; it was to meet rarely. In fact it did end up having a role to play in major negotiations like the proposed Upper Churchill development, Voisey's Bay, and education reform, and was the new venue for budget planning, but it ceased to be the de facto inner cabinet it had been in the early 1990s. Actively engaging ministers in generating new initiatives became the main task of the policy committees. During Tobin's time, for example, the committees recommended changes to the Human Rights Code to ban discrimination on the basis of sexual orientation, set up the province's first French-language school board, provided funding for the Morgantaler abortion clinic, and embarked upon the province's the first land claims negotiations. Coincidentally, Tobin acted to decrease gender imbalance in the executive government. He placed the new women he had recruited to politics in positions of influence in the committees, and doubled the number of women in the senior public service, from 15 per cent at the end of the Wells era to around 30 per cent.

Planning and budgeting dynamics were rearranged to reflect the new emphasis on collegiality. Planning was returned to cabinet committees and the Economic Recovery Commission was disbanded. Treasury Board would no longer spearhead the budget process, but P&P would be responsible instead, in a series of eight to ten meetings over a few weeks. The clerk of the Executive Council became more involved in the budget process (but not decisions) in the sense of achieving a synthesis between the speech from the throne and the budget address, and coordinating departmental input into a communications strategy for the budget.

The senior administrative cadre was renewed and reoriented. There was a broad-sweeping replacement of deputies and assistant deputies early on in the Tobin administration. There had been no renewal of this class in the Wells years, resulting in a blockage of career opportunities for younger, middle management. Deputies were informed that they were not to function aside from their ministers.

There was a new philosophy of management introduced in the Tobin years. Much of it was due to the work of Malcolm Rowe, the new clerk of the Executive Council and secretary to cabinet (from March 1996 to June 1999), the posts having been rejoined. Tobin had chosen one like himself, an outsider to the Newfoundland public service whose view of public administration had been shaped by experience in the federal system.[28] Rowe's philosophy of management involved a number of points.

One was to replace the current 'command and control' system with one stressing authority and accountability. Ministers and deputies were informed that the centre was not going to be looking over their shoulders all the time. By 1997 decisions were being taken to bring the provincial budget into surplus, and the role of the Treasury Board in enforcing spending freezes was ended. Departments were now to enjoy staffing delegation, with only nominal involvement by the Public Service Commission. Ministers and deputies were given authority to manage their departments, but were to be accountable. They had to live within their budgets, or face the consequences; they should not give unpleasant last-minute surprises, nor appear too hesitant in dealing with an issue that threatened the image of the government, or face micromanagement from the centre; these happened, but rarely. Another was a premium placed on information flow: the deputy secretaries for economic and social affairs in the Cabinet Secretariat tracked every major issue in the government, and deputies were expected to provide their relevant secretariat analyst, not to have them search it out, like inspectors. Another was a realization that the government had to expand horizontal management. Some inter-departmental programs existed, regarding children, human resources, and employment, but there was a felt need to catch up to other governments in this regard.

There was also a strong commitment to coordination – or a system-wide overview – of the government's agenda. One measure to facilitate this was the use of cabinet retreats which took place three times a year. The February retreat covered the speech from the throne and the first half of the government's agenda. The deputy clerk and the assistant secretaries would track all issues and would ask the deputy ministers what they saw coming in the next several months. Another measure was a disciplined approach to policy planning. Departments were obliged to bring communication and consultation plans to cabinet along with their proposals for new initiatives. The clerk established a flow chart from these plans and worked out, in concert with the premier and the cabinet, a system of announcements which balanced social, economic, and resources matters, week by week, for the year. The department concerned would be given two weeks' notice when the time came to announce its initiative. To aid this approach, a Communications and Consultation Branch was established in the Executive Council to act under the leadership of an executive director. The branch helped departments establish their communications agendas in game plans done three times a year.

Another measure involved a systematic approach to personnel and 'machinery of government' (MOG) matters. When Rowe became clerk, there were no personnel files listing the training experiences of senior officials, along with relevant comments by ministers. There were also no histories of the machinery of government of specific departments. These lacunae were rectified. There was also a formal decision-making process engaged for MOG changes. Departments who wanted changes would put together proposals which comprised MOG, policy, and financial elements, proposals which went to the premier, never to cabinet. The 1999–2000 period saw a variety of actors change places.[29]

Predictable factors therefore influenced the Tobin cabinet design. One was the premier's desire for influence; as he noted in his political biography, the sense of risk and novelty led him to the provincial scene,[30] and he did not preoccupy himself with administrative matters which may have deterred him from his policy agenda. Emulation was another. Tobin had been in the federal system for so long that it was predictable that some elements of the Ottawa model would be ingrained. He came to the provincial scene fresh from experience with a federal system that had begun to emphasize the need to establish a rigorous fiscal plan to enable the policy agenda, to de-emphasize central agency controls, and to engineer renewal of the public service.

Decongestion was another motivating factor. There were two complementary traditions that had come to dominate the provincial scene: the dominant premier tradition and the strong Treasury tradition. Together they made departments hesitant to make decisions without running them by the central agencies to see what they thought and, by implication, what the premier thought. Tobin and Rowe didn't have time for these traditions. The premier's desire for family time was instrumental in this. The centre could not control everything, and to pretend it could was unhealthy. So it was time to cut the ties that led to the Office of the Premier and to make fiscal control a corporate issue.

The Executive and Roger Grimes (2001–2003): Continuing Collegiality

The basic approach to the institutionalized cabinet that Tobin had embarked upon also became the norm for the next government, that of Roger Grimes. This approach involved continuing the concern for collegiality, a vital cabinet committee system, and a process role for the clerk in budget-making. The other patterns that had pertained before, such as a highly differentiated central agency arrangement, a premium placed on extensive analysis, and an emphasis on planning, remained.

The factors affecting the design of the central executive appear to be two: cabinet's quest for political control, and the desire for coherence in intergovernmental affairs. The Grimes government desired to control the provincial political agenda to ward of the competitive advances of the Conservatives, and had only two years to do so. They promoted an activist government: implementing fuel price regulation, establishing a Child Advocate and televising the Assembly. In energy matters, the government was promoting or managing three offshore oil developments: White Rose, the Hibernia project, and the Terra Nova project. Successful negotiations with INCO on Voisey's Bay were completed in 2002.

In the context of Grimes's fractious leadership win in February 2001, an institutionalized cabinet made perfect sense. The premier owed a great many favours to the ministers, and indeed the backbenchers, who had helped him to the leadership (he won by fourteen votes) and could not afford the luxury of dominating the cabinet (or even a small cabinet: it grew to eighteen to nineteen under Grimes). The complexity of the policy picture called out for broad participation in cabinet and caucus.

Roger Grimes therefore continued the basic, institutionalized model bequeathed to him by his predecessors. He managed the cabinet process and instituted the organization and methods of operation of cabinet and its committees. There were the familiar five standing committees of cabinet: the Planning and Priorities Committee (seven members); the Economic Policy and Rural Revitalization Committee (nine members); the Social Policy Committee (ten members); the Cabinet Committee on Routine Matters and Appointments (nine members); and the Treasury Board (nine members).

There was a relatively collegial approach to policy development, as there had been in the Tobin government. New initiatives normally entered the cabinet process through one of the policy committees, after interdepartmental discussions. A few major projects and initiatives (e.g., aboriginal land claims) were the responsibility of the Planning and Priorities Committee, with periodic reports to full cabinet. Major issues would receive extensive consideration by full cabinet.

The central agency configuration was both familiar and complex. The premier was supported by his political staff, as well as by officials in the office of the Executive Council. The Office of the Premier was headed by the chief of staff, and was comprised of political staff who aided the premier as the head of government, leader of a political party, and member of the House of Assembly. The decision-making process as a whole was supported by central agencies, including the Office of the Executive Council, the Treasury Board Secretariat and the Department of Finance. The Office of the Executive Council included the Office of the Premier, Cabinet Secretariat, Intergovernmental Affairs Secretariat, and Communications and Consultation Branch.

Grimes, like most premiers except Tobin, chose a clerk and cabinet secretary who had significant roots in the civil service culture; like Tobin, he chose someone who had worked with him, in this case as his deputy, Deborah Fry.[31]

Central officials performed complementary roles in budgetary matters. The Department of Finance tracked revenue, developed tax policy, and performed economic forecasting. Treasury Board Secretariat managed the estimates process. The clerk played a process role in budget-making and acted with the secretary to Treasury Board and the deputy minister of finance in establishing proposed budgetary strategy. Proposals for the budget were considered by the minister of finance and the premier prior to consideration by full cabinet. However, the premier also appointed a committee of ministers, chaired by the minister of finance, to consider certain budget proposals.

There were some differences in tone between Tobin and Grimes as to the style of central government. Central agencies were less called upon in the Grimes years. The standard operating procedure under Tobin was to have Cabinet Secretariat staff attend cabinet meetings as a policy resource. With Grimes, the Cabinet Secretariat attended mostly to facilitating cabinet's decision-making process. Treasury Board played a more restrictive role than it did under Tobin, allegedly because of a more constrained fiscal situation.

Planning had begun in the Tobin years to leave the realm of appointed officials and be expanded to include both cabinet and extra-parliamentary partners. In the fall of 1999, an ad hoc committee of cabinet, the Ministerial Committee on Jobs and Growth, was created to examine and economic agenda for the future. It consulted with over three hundred bodies and individuals, and in March 2000 the Grimes government released the results of the consultation, in its *Interim Report on the Renewal Strategy for Jobs and Growth*. One of the priorities cited was the need to establish new models of strategic cooperation between government, business, and labour to guide economic renewal.

Its *Final Report on a Renewal Strategy for Jobs and Growth*, released in March 2001 as a companion policy document to the provincial budget, government outlined a more specific agenda of 135 priorities.

The Grimes government moved quickly to give effect to its new vision. It created a new Department of Industry, Trade and Rural Development in 2001 to implement many of the priorities, and set out to study and to establish the strategic cooperation mechanism identified as a need in the consultation phase. After a review of several partnership models in countries like Iceland, Ireland and the Netherlands, the government announced the establishment of Strategic Partnership Forum in January 2002. The forum was to be a semi-annual meeting among business, labour, and government leaders chaired by the premier which aims to establish areas of joint concern and action. Although it is similar to other previous provincial bodies, it was notable because of its inclusive nature. It was seen as another component of a broad planning framework It was preceded by a Strategic Social Plan that was rolled out in the late 1990s and early 2000s, and the Strategic Health Plan for Newfoundland and Labrador, *Healthier Together* (2002) which established a five-year series of targets for health and community service agencies. All of this analytic and planning activity is familiar territory for institutionalized cabinets. The centre has to monitor the blooming, buzzing confusion of it all.

The Danny Williams Government (2003–)

The new Williams Progressive Conservative government in Newfoundland and Labrador has not changed much in the machinery of government for now, but it promises to change the role of the state. There are two stories to be told here. The first is the persistence of the institutionalized cabinet. The cabinet structure has remained remarkably unchanged for three decades, and Williams shows no signs of disturbing the trend. There is also a smaller cabinet, and departmental changes that were engendered by the move to a smaller cabinet. The second story concerns the political economy of the province and involves a multi-stage transition, each stage of which shows more about the administration's plans for downsizing the state and supersizing the economy.

The Williams cabinet structure follows tradition. Williams has five cabinet committees: Planning and Priorities, Economic Policy, Social Policy, Routine Matters/Appointments, and Treasury Board. As in the past three decades, Planning and Priorities is the pre-eminent committee. It is chaired by the premier, and is a committee of committee chairs, including on it the heads of Economic, Social, and Treasury Board. As a nod to the sacrifices of the long and somewhat painful period in opposition, P&P has on it the three party leaders previous to Williams: Tom Rideout, Ed Byrne, and Loyola Sullivan. Williams has reduced the size of the provincial cabinet; in November 2003 it consisted of fourteen members, including himself.

The initial structure of the Williams central bureaucracy was a three-legged stool arrangement unusual for provincial governments. There was a clerk/secretary, a chief of staff, and a deputy minister to the premier – three instead of the usual two senior executives. The appointment of Robert Thompson as the new clerk of the Executive Council and the secretary to cabinet to replace Deborah Fry demonstrated that the practice of appointing deputy ministers to senior executive positions had solidified. Both brought extensive deputy minister experience with them. On the political side, in the Premier's Office, Williams appointed Brian Crawley to serve as his chief of staff and a Mulroney-era MP and cabinet minister, Ross Reid, to serve as interim deputy minister to the premier.

The division of responsibilities at the beginning of the Williams term reflected the talents of the trio. The clerk of the Executive Council and the secretary to cabinet continued to be the senior official in the office of the Executive Council, and coordinate the operation of the secretariats. In his cabinet operations role, he assisted the premier in setting the cabinet agenda and keeping cabinet records. As head of the public service, the clerk coordinated deputy ministers, advised on the appointment of deputy ministers and assistant deputy ministers, and chaired the Senior Management Development Committee (SMDC), established in 1998, whose mandate includes training, career planning, and performance evaluation of senior officials.

The position of interim deputy minister to the premier involved overseeing the new administration's transition and restructuring team, and the preparing the inaugural Throne Speech and Budget in 2004. Reid had not given any indication about whether he was going to stay on, as of this writing, so the design may or may not change.

The Office of the Premier is headed by the chief of staff, and is comprised of political staff who aid the premier to perform his functions as the head of government, leader of a political party, and member of the House of Assembly.

The Executive Council Office maintains its somewhat quirky but efficient format, being formed of a Cabinet Secretariat, an Intergovernmental Affairs Secretariat, and a Treasury Board Secretariat. The interesting arrangement regarding Treasury Board and the Department of Finance continued as it had since 1973. The minister of finance, who at present also serves as president of Treasury Board, is served by two deputy ministers.

Like the cabinet committees, stability is the norm in the design of the central agencies; unlike them, the departments saw change in design. Nineteen departments became fourteen in February 2004, and ten were restructured. The intent of these changes was to support the major directions contained in the *Blueprint*, the Conservative election platform, part of which aimed at a 'lean administration, while also emphasizing a new integrated approach to governance.'

Cameron and White, in their comparative study of Ontario transitions in government offer this insight: 'When do transitions begin and end? It is possible to think of transitions in a temporarily restricted fashion; for example, as the period between the election and the swearing-in of the new government, or in an expansive fashion, as the period beginning with the preparation for government, which often occurs well before the election campaign begins, to the end of the incoming government's "settling-in" period, which often can extend up to the end of the first year in office.'[49]

Williams chose the expansive version of transition. It has involved extensive pre-election planning, the handing over of power, an external financial review, a departmental restructuring exercise, and a program review. All point to a reduced role for the state.

Explaining the Persistence of Institutionalization

If this essay sounds like repetitions upon a theme, this is indeed the case. The institutionalized cabinet has persisted, and remained relatively unchanged in format, even if modified in its application, for over thirty years. Although premiers are the major political actors in their governments, and can usually bring along the cabinet with them on issues of their choosing, the prime minister-centred model does not have resonance in the province. The government, with only incremental changes, has basically had the same cabinet committee structures and central agency configurations since it switched to the institutionalized mode in the early 1970s.

Cabinet committees remained virtually unchanged in name and function over a period of thirty years. They maintained an important role throughout the period, and can thus be considered another manifestation of collective decision-making- for most of the period, anyway. One senior official noted: 'There was not much difference between Peckford and Wells ... Input from cabinet committees was important. Treasury Board made decisions, relatively independently; the Social and Economic Committees rarely made final decisions in both the Peckford and Wells administrations. The usual pattern was that the recommendation would go forward from the committee to Cabinet as to what should be done. Another function of committees was that it gave departments a chance to solve differences between them before they came to cabinet. Cabinet committees were used to explore compromises.'

There has always been a tension between full cabinet and the de facto inner cabinet, the Priorities and Planning Committee, in terms of final decision-making authority. Theoretically, a strong PPC is inimical to the idea of collegial decision-making in the institutionalized cabinet. The province has in fact seen its share of strong PPCs over the years and powerful ministers in PPC could often get other ministers to go along with them. However, it is important to point out that the plenary cabinet was not merely a cipher. Aggrieved ministers throughout the last few decades could use the cabinet to register their complaints with the decisions of a cabinet committee, including that of PPC, and they have.

The central agencies that had been established early on remained stable, with specialized, analytical, and corporate orientations. Although they tended to lapse into control orientations until recent years, they plainly had cross-government orientations, rather than just the first minister's needs, as their frame of reference. Like the cabinet committees, stability rather than change in the design of the central agencies is the norm; the organizational charts of the 1973 and 2003 Executive Council Office look very similar. The corporate orientation has come about for two reasons: administrative culture, and a circulation of departmental personnel through the central agencies. One senior official noted that

The first responsibility of the ECO is the Premier and his needs. However, we work on behalf of the whole system. In the federal system, the PCO doesn't share notes with departments. But here we do things collectively.

It's mostly a function of size, but it is also a matter of collective will: we will pull on the oar together, like true Newfoundlanders. We don't play our cards close our chests [like in Ottawa central agencies].

Another senior official said that there has been a culture of not dominating the departments, but trying to achieve a systemic view across government nonetheless.

If you are too dominant as the central agency level, departments can back away; it's easier to defer. For me, the role of the central agency was to ensure that everything was taken into account, and to consider options and views that might not have been considered. The view of the central agency was not insignificant. Several ministers would take this personally; it would then be necessary to work things out DM to DM. It is necessary to consider the big picture. ... The system has got to say why the decision should be taken.

Another way of encouraging a corporate outlook for in the machinery of government is personnel rotation. Several officials noted that the pattern of moving departmental staff through the cabinet secretariat system, a pattern in place for many years, tended to resolve much potential conflict between the centre and departments. Staff tend to be rotated out of the centre after a one-to-three-year stint.

Reviewing decades of experience at the centre, one senior official said 'premiers have had two things in common: strong central agencies and a strong Intergovernmental Affairs Secretariat (IGA), because of the strong role that federal government transfers play in our provincial system.' Federal-provincial relations are indeed important for the province: needing to cultivate a close relationship with federal authorities, governments of Newfoundland and Labrador have to establish a structured central executive to study it intensively. COGAP took special care to place the IGA in the Office of the Premier. The Peckford government gave the impression of engaging in pitched battles with the federal government on the matter of resources, but its IGA liaised in more prosaic areas such as tourism, agriculture, forestry, fisheries, urban infrastructure, manpower, and planning. Wells's years saw emphasis on constitutional matters, and Tobin used the IGA group, in part, to follow up on his Ottawa contacts. The persistence of institutionalization has much to do with the need for coherence in the intergovernmental sphere.

Social science rationalism was another exogenous factor at work in the design of the central executive. Most rationalistic experiments lend implicit support to institutionalization. The system was designed with input from academics and other experts, and every decade there was experimentation with some form of policy and budgeting and public administration initiative. In Moores's Cabinet Secretariat, for example, the Program Review and Development wing evaluated the efficiency and effectiveness of governmental programs. Wells took the New Public Managment, which had its origins in a mixture of social sciences, business, and ideological circles, and ran with it. The new Williams government has signalled its early intentions, through a program review exercise, to introduce more managerialist approaches.

Planning is a characteristic often associated with institutionalized cabinets. This is especially the case with provinces, such as Newfoundland, facing economic turbulence. Facing the results of little long-term planning, one of the first actions of the Moores government was to set up planning committees. Each successive government has had a Planning and Priorities Committee. This is not accidental. Peckford planned how to get resource rents and mitigate unemployment; Wells wanted a modern economy and a complementary social context; and Tobin and Grimes have had to plan and manage the installation of mega-projects of immense scale.

One endogenous explanation for the persistence of the institutionalized cabinet in Newfoundland and Labrador is that the power of the premier is tempered by what might be called the administration cycle, the analogue in a sense of the electoral cycle. Premiers are strong when first elected, and then their power wanes somewhat as other ministers begin to share in the pool. The premier is the prime decision-maker, but not the only major figure.

One senior official with long experience in the Newfoundland bureaucracy described the phenomenon in this way:

> Most governments when first elected are strong, and vice versa. In our [Newfoundland and Labrador] case, the leader leads the party in the polls. Wells consistently led the party in the polls. In fact, Wells, Peckford and Tobin were examples of this. This fact affects the committee system. It will leave the premier powerful in the policy system.
>
> This can't last, however. One example is the Wells Government. The ERC was brought in as something that was separate from other agencies. It was purely the creation of the premier. It came to grief because it did not have enough cabinet ministers on side.
>
> Premiers have to have the support of cabinet for things to move ahead

... [and] over time the support of the cabinet becomes relatively more important.

Tobin also led the party in terms of support – and also when he left. The normal pattern did not have the time to play itself out.

Something as simple as momentum can explain the persistence of institutionalization. Another senior official offered this explanation for the system's durability, simply that the cabinet system adopted in the early seventies had time to take root and mature:

There is a lot of amateurism, lack of stability, lack of depth in smaller jurisdictions. When a new administration if formed, there is a tendency to think that the Premier and advisors can 'reinvent everything.' One thing that may have helped [institutionalization last] is the relative lack of change in administrations in the province. Brian Peckford [who became Premier in 1979] was schooled in the 1973 system. Between 1973 and 1989 there was stability [with Conservative Governments in power].

It is interesting that Mr. Wells, who had strong ideas about public administration did not make more institutional changes. I would argue that he inherited the institutions and made them do what he wanted them to do. He was innovative in some things like the Economic Recovery Commission, but he expressed his desire to conduct public administration through other means.

Lastly, and most importantly, the institutionalized cabinet has lasted in Newfoundland because its premiers wanted it to. It has never been severely criticized by any premier in more than three decades. Sometimes, as in the days of Tobin and Grimes, it has been nursed back to health after some dysfunctionalities crept in. Moving away from institutionalization towards some other variant of cabinet machinery tends to leave idle hands. And in the bare-knuckle world of Newfoundland politics, idle hands are dangerous ones.

Chapter 4

Governing from the Centre in New Brunswick

STEWART HYSON

Interest in the role of premier or prime minister and cabinet in Canada, along with their politico-bureaucratic support structures, seems to have reached a peak in the early years of the twentieth-first century. We can only speculate whether this development is just a fad, or a more profound development that reflects a new or enhanced role being fulfilled by the executive branch. There have been previous flurries of interest with the role of the prime minister, cabinet, and support structures such as that during the 1970s.[1] Much of that interest concerned the executive's role in the policy process in terms of what was then the new thrust toward rationalization and coordination in policy-making. In addition, there was an unprecedented interest with associated matters relating to the first minister such as party leadership selection and the leader's role in electoral politics. It would neither be fair nor accurate to suggest that interest in these leadership concerns ever dissipated during the subsequent years; rather, it would be more precise to say that there has been a reinvigoration of interest in the first minister's role within the governing process in recent years.

Donald Savoie's *Governing from the Centre* on the prime minister in Ottawa, and Christopher Dunn's *The Institutionalized Cabinet* on the executive in the four western-most provinces have led the scholarly charge in this direction.[2] At the same time, Jeffrey Simpson's *The Friendly Dictatorship*,[3] which delivers a more journalistic account, has done much to alert the public to the broader political implications of the centralization of power in the position of prime minister. These recent works and the related public discourse have depicted the current structures and processes in the executive branch raising normative concerns elsewhere in Canada, but what can be said about the case of New Brunswick? Has there been a similar centralization of power, or has a distinctive style of governing evolved in the province?

On the one hand, there is reason to hypothesize from a constitutional perspective that the parameters and dynamics of the Westminster model of responsible parliamentary government as adapted in Canada are shared by the central and ten provincial governments, so as to warrant the same tendency toward centralization. This situation would be further reinforced by the tendency for governments in Canada to emulate each other (the diffusion theory of Canadian federalism), whereby an institution, practice, or policy that is pioneered and proven effective in one jurisdiction is frequently copied by other jurisdictions. Alternatively, it is equally valid to hypothesize that local factors – personalities, demographics, events, and issues – are sufficient to provide for particularistic variations in governing style. Hypothetically, therefore, there is reason to expect to find either of these tendencies in contemporary New Brunswick. However, rather than pursue a one-or-other position, it will be argued here that both tendencies have merged in the province so that governing is centred around the premier yet the current occupier of the premier's chair must never distance himself or herself too far from the populace. While this style of governing may not be unique in terms of being completely different from that found in other jurisdictions, it does definitely provide New Brunswick with a distinct style of governing.

Historical Perspective

Relative to other provinces, there is a dearth of research studies on the government and politics of contemporary New Brunswick. Admittedly, the situation is not as dire as that documented by Robert Young in his 1986 review of government and politics in the Maritime provinces,[4] although the literature on the executive's governing role in New Brunswick remains far from complete. Still, we can see signs of a rediscovery of the province in the unparalleled coverage by national news media of recent New Brunswick premiers. Between 1987 and 1997 Frank McKenna was acknowledged for his aggressive pursuit of policies to make the province more self-sufficient economically and to make the province friendly to business.[5] In the autumn of 2002, Bernard Lord was being touted as a future leader of the then federal Progressive Conservative party and again in early 2004 as a possible leader of the new Conservative party. There have also been a few light life-style and general biographies that have done much to focus public attention on former premiers Richard Hatfield and Frank McKenna: for instance, Richard Starr, and Michel Cormier and Achille Michaud have written on the former, and Philip Lee on the latter.[6] With all of this national attention on New Brunswick premiers, is there something going on in the province – a magic elixir on how to govern? In order to depict the style of governing in contemporary New Brunswick, we need to begin by sketching the province's background.

As one of the country's oldest political entities – first as a colony from 1784 to 1867 and then as a province since Confederation – New Brunswick has had a wealth of political experience. Since acquiring its status as a province, however, researchers have distinguished between the pre- and post-1960s, or between old-style and modern politics. This division is roughly based upon the premiership of Louis Robichaud (1960–70), particularly the wide-ranging reform measures initiated by his government's Program of Equal Opportunity.[7] Some of the modernizing trends that made this program possible may be traced to the 1940s and 1950s, including the establishment of the Civil Service Commission in 1943 and the subsequent gradual professionalization of the public service.[8] In addition, Mark Pedersen has observed two related developments that were unfolding almost unnoticed during the decades following the Second World War but became apparent by the 1960s and 1970s: first, there was a sharp decline of traditional patron-client politics centred around the local member of the legislature due to the growth of public bureaucracy in the dispensing of government services; and second, the rise of provincial mass media (newspapers, radio, and television) lessened the traditional communication role of the local member both during and between election campaigns.[9] Meanwhile, some initiatives associated with Robichaud did not come to fruition until subsequent years under the umbrella of other premiers, such as the implementation of the Official Languages Act, which made New Brunswick the only officially bilingual province in the country.[10]

Conditions were so different during the period following Confederation that it makes little sense to depict governing style then other than to mention a few relevant highlights. So, what was New Brunswick like during the old-style period, prior to the introduction of the Equal Opportunity program? In his 1983 collection of sketches of New

Brunswick's premiers, Arthur Doyle suggested that the earlier premiers had dictatorial powers partly because of the part-time nature of politics. Except for the three weeks or so when the Legislative Assembly was sitting, the premier and cabinet colleagues were seldom in the capital city of Fredericton and often were more preoccupied with the pursuit of their own professional careers and businesses than with their public duties; in fact, some of the premiers from Saint John in the 1920s and 1930s held cabinet meetings for convenience in their own home city. Likewise, the premier's staff in these early years usually consisted of one secretary, with the first full-time executive secretary only being appointed in 1935.[11] When it came to formulating the budget, detailed information is scarce to come by but one commentator has mentioned that the process was short and brief and that the number of political actors involved were few, even as late as the 1950s. Over the course of a few weeks, 'the premier, the provincial secretary treasurer and his deputy minister scrutinized submissions from all departments and agencies, struck a budget and sent their recommendations to full cabinet for final approval.'[12]

An examination of the province's political geography reveals that the major patterns of population settlement of the late 1700s and the 1800s had been around the coastal areas and the seven main watershed basins, with the different cultural groups living separately from each other.[13] This settlement pattern became the basis for the province's fifteen counties, which also served as the electoral constituencies of the Legislative Assembly. Starting with the first election to the legislature in 1785 until it was replaced with a system of single-member constituencies for the 1974 election, New Brunswick used a system of multi-member constituencies, with each being represented by two to five representatives in rough approximation to the size and diversity of the communities within each constituency.[14] Well into the 1900s, community and county economies were locally based and dominated by a few families in the form of a patron-client relationship. This system of clientelism also extended into politics, with the local economic elites or members of their family being elected generation after generation to the provincial legislature (and/or to the federal Parliament),[15] as if the constituency was their personal fiefdom. Politics in New Brunswick was thus very direct and personalized, in the sense of being based on a close, person-to-person, mutual dependency.

Besides the settlement pattern and the clientelism, it must also be stressed that political parties were slow to develop as disciplined organizations in New Brunswick; people voted more for individual candidates, who were loosely identified as being either with the government or the opposition party. The partisan leanings of these candidates were generally known (especially their attachments with the federal parties), but what really counted in gaining election provincially was the strength of each candidate's clientele network and his personal astuteness in distributing patronage. Besides the awarding of government contracts and services and the making of civil service appointments, there was also the practice of 'treating' on election day to buy votes. A curious part of New Brunswick's political history is that it was the only province that used the secret ballot as part of its electoral law regime when it entered confederation in 1867,[16] yet it relied upon each party to supply the ballots until an official ballot was introduced for the 1967 general election. It is impossible to say how much misuse there was with these party-made ballots through voter intimidation and buying of votes, due to these party ballots being identifiable; nevertheless, these party-made ballots did facilitate the use of patronage consistent with the clientele model of mutual dependency between MLAs and their supporters, and also contributed to other forms of corruption.[17] Thus, when it came to fashioning a cabinet and governing, political leaders had to be cognizant and respectful of the strength of localism – in other words, each MLA had won election in his own community mainly on his own terms, and would eventually depend on his own skills at patronage distribution to be re-elected at the next election.[18] So Doyle's earlier suggestion that New Brunswick premiers had dictatorial powers is misleading because the premier always had to listen to his legislative colleagues with respect and was expected to consult broadly members of society. The first minister was wise not to act arbitrarily or haughtily, or else suffer the consequence of either being defeated at the next election or being eased out between elections.

This pattern of localism was also reflected in the dominant role played by the elected county councils following their establishment in 1877.[19] Until their abolishment in 1967 under the Program of Equal Opportunity, these councils exercised considerable legislative and executive power in the province, which consequentially resulted in great inequalities in government services from county to county within the province. In fact, this program sought primarily to address this situation by standardizing services in the fields of health care, welfare, education, and administration of justice by shifting the decision-making responsibility to the provincial government in Fredericton. This shift of governmental responsibility from county to provincial government also coincided with major growth in fiscal transfers from the federal government to the provinces, and proactive expansion in the government's role in several policy fields. It could be argued that these changes were consistent with the notion of province-building and was thus similar to developments occurring at the same time in the rest of Canada in the 1960s,[20] but there were definitely elements particular to New Brunswick.

If there is to be any lesson learned from the pre-1960s period, it is that politics, including the role of the political executive in New Brunswick, was direct and personalized, with the premier and cabinet colleagues in close touch with their backbench MLAs, county councils, and constituents. This closeness was especially evident when many of the province's responsibilities under the Constitution Act of 1867 were decided upon and implemented primarily at the county government level, and when patronage and other forms of political corruption were widespread. With the advent of the era of modern politics, there was a definite shift in jurisdictional responsibility in several key policy fields, while other regulatory laws were adopted to curtail old-style patronage. But the need for the executive to remain in close touch with MLAs as well as the electorate remained the keystone of governing style in the province. A second lesson would be that there is no denying that the premier played the dominant role during the earlier period which continues to be the case today. Christopher Dunn's reference to the five P's of power – prerogative, Parliament, party, patronage, and press[21] – effectively captures the reality of the first minister's dominant position. These components have always been present, in both the earlier and contemporary periods; however, the scale and role of government have changed considerably so that the particulars of the premier's position are now more complex and more visible.

Contemporary Governing Style in New Brunswick

The modern period of New Brunswick politics has been dominated by four premiers: Louis Robichaud, 1960–70; Richard Hatfield, 1970–87; Frank McKenna, 1987–97; and Bernard Lord, since 1999. In addition, there have been two other premiers during this period who were in office for much shorter terms. Following McKenna's resignation in October 1997, he was replaced by an interim leader, Ray Frenette, who was a senior cabinet minister and longstanding member of the Legislative Assembly. Frenette was replaced by Camille Thériault who was chosen at a Liberal leadership convention in May 1998 to be the new party leader; Thériault then served as premier until defeated at the polls by Bernard Lord in the June 1999 election.

Although Hatfield was, and Lord is, a Progressive Conservative and the other premiers were Liberal, their particular differences in governing style have been based more on variation in personalities and orientation to the job than on partisan lines. Each premier has found it necessary to respond to the times, to the policy agenda before him, and to the current ideas pertaining to proper and effective governing (which is a situation probably not dissimilar to that found in other jurisdictions). This was perhaps most evident with the former Liberal premiers when Thériault asserted at the 1998 leadership convention that he would pursue a 'third wave of Liberalism' – the first being the social justice theme of Robichaud, the second McKenna's wave of fiscal responsibility, and his own, which was going to be a government with a human face. It is interesting how Thériault sought to associate himself and his new government with the legacy of the two 'greats' of the provincial Liberal party, while at the same time offering and legitimizing a new policy direction. This example also illustrates a major obstacle in trying to depict style of governing – that is, namely how do we distinguish minor changes and temporary points of emphasis from more fundamental or definitive structural attributes?

This is where Dunn's perspective of the sources of the first minister's base of power is of importance because it alerts us to the broad dimensions of the office. Dunn points out the fact that by constitutional convention only the premier is the link with the lieutenant-governor, decides who will be cabinet ministers, determines the cabinet decision-making structures and processes, and recommends when the legislature is to be dissolved and elections called. The premier also assumes the lead political role in setting the government's policy agenda, dispensing patronage, and presenting the governing party's position to the media, and through them to the public, both between and during elections.[22] These sources of power may be similar to those of all federal and provincial governments, but it is here that we can see the importance of personality, policy agenda, and setting as to how a premier chooses to govern.

A standard question asked in a university course on New Brunswick politics is: would any other premier but Robichaud have introduced the Equal Opportunity program? There were obviously similar province-building developments with other provincial governments in the 1960s; as well, the presence of proactive governments in Ottawa, especially in their promotion of transfer payments and social programs, affected all provinces. But it is impossible to overlook what Robichaud brought to the premiership, specifically being born and raised in one of the poorer parts of the province, his educational experiences in the late 1940s at Laval University's Faculty of Social Sciences, and his Acadian background.[23] Indeed, this last point is quite significant in its own right because Robichaud was the first Acadian to be elected as premier of the province; another Acadian (Peter Veniot) had served briefly as premier from the time that he replaced his predecessor who had resigned in 1923 until he lost the election of 1925. Unlike the pre-1960 era, however, when the province's bicultural identity was generally ignored in provincial politics and French was seldom heard in the corridors of power in Fredericton, official bilingualism in the 1960s was an issue whose time had come.[24]

Although Robichaud's government initiated the language legislation late in his last term of office (enacted in 1968 and proclaimed in 1969), it was left mainly to Hatfield, McKenna, and Lord to oversee the implementation of the legislation, including its subsequent entrenchment in Canada's constitution. Hugh Mellon has noted that 'sensitivity and support for Acadian aspirations' has characterized all governments in the province in the modern period, Liberal and Progressive Conservative, English-speaking or Acadian premier.[25] Related to the use of English and French in the public service, judicial courts, and legislature, it is now the norm for premiers to be more cognizant of the cultural-linguistic factor than ever before when making appointments to the cabinet in order to have a linguistic balance. While it is not a legal requirement for the premier to be fluently bilingual, it is at least necessary politically for the premier to make the effort to communicate in both languages and to include strong ministers from both language groups in the cabinet. Since most French-speaking MLAs in New Brunswick are bilingual, it is probably more of a political requirement for English-speaking premiers to include Acadian lieutenants in their cabinets. For instance, Hatfield relied heavily upon such French-speaking cabinet ministers as Jean-Maurice Simard and Jean Gauvin, while McKenna had a wider choice to draw upon, including Ray Frennette, Bernard Richard, and Aldéa Landry.[26] English is still the prime language used within the cabinet and at the executive poltico-bureaucratic level, but it is now not unusual to find that French is used by cabinet and staff members who are competent in that language. Being Canada's only officially bilingual province has thus left its mark on the style of governing in contemporary New Brunswick.

The Equal Opportunity program directly affected the policy process in two key areas: centralization and equalization. There was a centralization of power because the county councils were abolished and their responsibility for health, education, welfare, and administration of justice was shifted to Fredericton. In fact, this was one of the main reasons why an official languages law was necessitated because decisions affecting the delivery of public services to both language groups were now to be made centrally in the provincial capital. Equalization was clearly the ideological thrust behind the Equal Opportunity program, designed to standardize the quality of these services as well as the taxation rates from one county to the next. Together, centralization and equalization represented a radical change in orientation from the local community or county to a new sense of provincial identity, as well as in the governance of the province. The program was not introduced without bitter controversy, however, because there was no consensus on the need for change; in fact, the issue was so divisive that it even provided reason for the province's major industrialist, K.C. Irving, to make a rare public appearance in order to express his opposition before a legislative committee.[27]

The Equal Opportunity program was massive in scale, consisting of 130 legislative bills, that affected a wide range of policy matters and represented a radical departure with the past. So it is pertinent to note the stages by which Robichaud proceeded – that is, his style of governing. Governments in similar circumstances frequently call upon a royal commission in order to break with established thinking and practices, particularly those held by the permanent public service, and to pave the way for future change by offering alternative recommendations. In the case of New Brunswick, Robichaud appointed Edward G. Byrne in 1960 as chair of a royal commission on finances and municipal taxation, which reported in 1963, after consulting the public through hearings and commissioning its own research studies (some of which were prepared by consultants who came from outside the province). The commission's report was then studied by a cabinet committee of ministers and senior bureaucrats in 1964, which led to a government white paper being issued in March 1965, to be followed later that year by the introduction of bills in the Legislative Assembly. By the summer of 1965 the Robichaud government had also established the Office of

Government Organization as a secretariat to serve the cabinet committee in the preparation of the bills and related policy and administrative
documents, to fulfil a public relations and propaganda role, and to
facilitate the necessary changes once legislative approval had been
granted. When introduced in the Legislative Assembly, the bills
received extensive scrutiny by legislative committee, which received
interventions from concerned individuals and groups at public hearings, before being approved by mid-1966, and taking effect on 1 January 1967.[28]

Thus Robichaud cleverly relied upon new blood in the form of the
royal commission to formulate reform alternatives and the Office of
Government Organization to orchestrate the march forward, rather
than to rely upon the tradition-bound permanent public service. Similarly, in one of the more serendipitous events of Canadian politics,
Robichaud was able to recruit several talented bureaucrats from
Saskatchewan, following the Saskatchewan CCF government's defeat
by the Ross Thatcher Liberals in the 1964 general election, who were
instrumentally involved with the implementation of the Equal Opportunity program. To conclude, Robichaud was premier prior to the
advent of the administrative or welfare state in New Brunswick when
cabinet government was more like the traditional or unaided variety.
He was driven by a desire to reform the province, and was able to
choose ministers and advisers who shared his vision. At the same time,
the premier recognized the need to remain in close touch with the public through extensive consultations at both the royal commission and
legislative stages in order to win their support. Furthermore, the late
1950s and 1960s were the beginning of media politics in New Brunswick with elections based on province-wide advertising campaigns
centred on the party leader, and Robichaud spoke effectively on television directly to the people.[29]

While Richard Hatfield's tenure as premier was not dominated by
any particular ideological thrust or radical policy agenda, he won an
unprecedented four consecutive general elections and served as premier for seventeen years. To a significant extent, Hatfield pursued the
same policy agenda as Robichaud, especially in the areas of promoting
the language rights of Acadians, initiating reform of political and policy structures, and developing a cooperative working relationship with
the federal government.[30] Indeed, unlike previous Conservative premiers who came from the English-speaking part of the province, Hatfield brought a sensitivity for the French fact and cultivated electoral

support in French-speaking New Brunswick, and was primarily responsible for much of the initial implementation of the official languages act.[31] As the premier of a have-less province that was dependent upon the federal government for fiscal transfers, Hatfield found it strategically wise to work pragmatically with the federal government of Pierre Trudeau during most of his term as premier. In fact, Hatfield was one of Trudeau's staunchest supporters during the constitutional debates of the early 1980s, and was instrumental in having provisions protecting language rights (in respect to both the government of Canada and that of New Brunswick), and recognizing 'Equalization and Regional Disparities,' included in the Constitution Act of 1982.

Although Hatfield would never have been described as a rabble-rouser, especially when seen shopping leisurely on Saturday mornings at the Fredericton farmers' market, he did in his own quiet way prove to be a progressive reformer. Actually, it is interesting that while still opposition leader, Hatfield had played a key role in support of Premier Robichaud in creating the position of ombudsman in New Brunswick in 1967 – only the second province to do so.[32] Then as premier, Hatfield converted the province's two-centuries-old multi-member electoral constituencies to a system of single-member constituencies, introduced legislation regulating the political financing of candidates and parties, created the Advisory Council on the Status of Women, appointed the first New Brunswick woman (Brenda Robertson) to the cabinet, and actively promoted the notion of Maritime Union. He also initiated a complex cabinet committee system consisting of six cabinet committees and a comparable set of committees of senior public bureaucrats. A cabinet secretariat was also created in 1971, which developed the envelope budgeting system in 1974–75 that was later emulated by the federal government.[33] While this institutionalized cabinet system may appear to have been needlessly complex for such a small province (with a population of about seven hundred thousand at that time), Hatfield apparently was very much involved with the committee process, especially with the setting of the government's fiscal framework and the expenditure levels for the envelopes. He also took a keen interest in interviewing and selecting his deputy ministers, indicating a hands-on approach that perhaps belied the formal institutionalized arrangement. In any case, Hatfield did recruit talented staff from outside of the province, including both Marcel Massé as deputy finance minister and Lowell Murray as deputy minister in the Premier's Office in 1973.[34] His interest in politics, however, seemed to wane considerably during his last term as premier (1982–87), no doubt due to the cumulated weight of criticisms that came with being in public office for such a long time (especially in respect to his positions on bilingualism, constitutional reform, and the Bricklin car affair), as well as the more personal attacks (for his travels, lifestyle and RCMP investigation for marijuana possession). If Hatfield appeared as being quiet and non-confrontational, and perhaps somewhat hesitant, Frank McKenna was the polar opposite, with his abundant energy level, loquaciousness, and willingness to be 'in-your-face.' Part of McKenna's style was electorally motivated, such as his initial opposition to the Meech Lake Accord during the 1987 election campaign (when his Liberal party soundly defeated the Hatfield government by winning all of the legislative seats), and then later at the last moment accepted the accord (which was too late to save it).[35] Nevertheless, his style was more a reflection of his personality traits and was evident politically in his desire to make New Brunswick more self-reliant economically, and less a supplicant province dependent on the federal government's largesse. This was reflected in McKenna's policy agenda with its emphasis on 'economic diversification, a balanced budget, education reform, reductions in the size of the public service, a new approach to welfare ... and a better delivery of government services.'[36] While McKenna personally rejected the neo-conservative ideological label, he definitely set a business-friendly agenda. It was mentioned earlier that Camille Thériault described McKenna's term as the second wave of Liberalism with its emphasis on fiscal responsibility; others described it less charitably as ten years of economic tough love. His track record is still a matter of on-going debate in the province, but McKenna's assertiveness certainly did create a sense of provincial pride in being New Brunswickers.

Yet, while trying to reduce the size and cost of government in many areas, McKenna followed an aggressive hands-on approach to economic development, in part by providing incentives to businesses to set up in the province, going on trade missions abroad, establishing direct contacts with business leaders, and sometimes engaging in job poaching (or, in the minds of some other premiers, stealing established businesses from their provinces). A hallmark of the McKenna government was how quickly it got into the new field of information technology, which was especially evident with the call-centre industry that drew upon the combined strength of two of the province's most prized assets – the existing superior technology of the former New Brunswick Telephone Corporation and a large bilingual workforce.

This last point is interesting because it may suggest why McKenna changed his opposition to the Meech Lake Accord. He came to recognize the importance of official bilingualism in terms of economic development, and as a consequence his government (like those of Robichaud and Hatfield) actively promoted language rights. Also in a similar way, McKenna developed an effective and pragmatic working relationship with the federal government (with both prime ministers Mulroney and Chrétien), especially in the economic development sphere, including the twinning of the highway system, the harmonization of the federal and provincial sales taxes, and the role of the Atlantic Canada Opportunities Agency.

In terms of political reforms, the McKenna government created the province's first full-fledged independent electoral boundaries commission that established what was at the time the most egalitarian set of electoral constituencies in the country.[37] Some temporary adjustments had also been made following the 1987 election in order to allow the seatless opposition parties to have some say in criticizing government legislation.[38] There were also some moves in the areas of service delivery and public-private partnerships, such as in the case of the construction of the Wackenhut youth detention centre. Another controversial policy was the decision in 1989 to legalize video lottery terminal (VLT) gambling in the province by granting self-regulatory powers to those who had been previously illegally operating VLT machines, and by granting the industry a very large share of the gambling revenue – this decision was to haunt the McKenna government during its last few years in office and was to be a key factor in the defeat of the Thériault government in 1999.

As for his cabinet structure, McKenna scaled back Hatfield's six cabinet committees to just two: the Policy and Priorities Committee (PPC) chaired by the premier and the Board of Management Committee chaired by the minister of finance. This arrangement was later retained by the Lord government. By scaling back on the number of committees and the accompanying workload, McKenna seemed to be more personally out front than any of his predecessors, whether before the television cameras, promoting the province whether at home, across the country, and internationally in an effort to attract business investment. He also relied upon loyal and talented advisers whom he had appointed to key positions either in the premier's office or as deputy ministers – people like Fernand Landry, Francis McGuire, and Maurice Robichaud.[39] Advisory councils in several policy arenas were established to provide alternative sources of information input. At the same time, McKenna did not seem to mind it when a cabinet minister challenged him in private by criticizing his position on a policy matter.[40] Here we see at least the rudimentary elements of what Dunn and others would call the prime minister-centred cabinet.

It is understandable why Camille Thériault offered a third wave of Liberalism in the form of a government with a human face at his 1998 leadership convention victory. He (as well as many others) had realized that McKenna's emphasis on fiscal responsibility had begun to rub too many people the wrong way in such areas as health care, taxation policy, and VLT gambling. But Thériault was unable to tap effectively into this discontent; instead, it was Bernard Lord who did so as he led his Progressive Conservative party to victory with a large majority in the 1999 general election. However, after his first four years as premier, Premier Lord suffered a serious rebuke at the polls in June 2003 when his party was left with only a one-seat majority over the combined opposition parties.[41] Although it is still relatively early in his tenure as premier, it is possible to identify some discernible elements in Bernard Lord's style of governing.

As one backbench Progressive Conservative MLA noted when interviewed for this study, the Lord government is different from the McKenna government in its orientation to governing. That is, whereas McKenna had been more an activist in pursuing investment and economic growth, Lord has placed the emphasis on reducing taxes in hopes of making the province attractive for investment. It is interesting that both premiers have shared the common goal of being business-friendly, but they have differed sharply as to how best to achieve that goal. One key reason why Lord has followed this approach is that the Progressive Conservative caucus consists of an unusually high number (at least for New Brunswick) of MLAs with a small-business background.

Be that as it may, in other dimensions Premier Lord has been very similar to his predecessors in the modern period of politics in New Brunswick. For instance, Lord has emphasized official bilingualism, which is currently being extended to government services delivered by the larger municipalities. In regard to relations with the federal government, although there are the usual squabbles over funding levels, pragmatic cooperation is still emphasized by the Lord government. His Executive Council Office continues to fulfill a secretariat role to the premier and cabinets as has been the case with previous premiers. Nevertheless, there have been a few political reform initiatives that deserve to be noted.

First, as part of its 1999 election campaign, the Lord Progressive Conservatives, wishing to be more responsive to the public's concerns, had promised to hold a referendum on the touchy issue of VLT gambling. For a province with little experience with referendums or plebiscites, this was quite an innovative proposal. However, even though the referendum was held on 14 May 2001 (with the public deciding to keep VLTs), there is little reason to suggest that the Lord government is committed to the ideal of participatory democracy or that other referendums can be expected in the near future.[42] It is thus with baited breath that we wait to see if anything substantive results from the province's current study of citizen-centred democratic reform.

Second, Lord has stressed the need to develop meaningful consultation with the backbenchers of his party; indeed, there now seems to be greater use of caucus support committees to initiate ideas and channel input to the executive in the policy-making process. Furthermore, the premier has adopted an open-door position to hear the concerns of individual Progressive Conservative MLAs, including having breakfast in his office with five or so MLAs at a time, and, as might be expected in this electronically connected age, the premier's office keeps all of the party's MLAs regularly informed via e-mail of the latest political developments.

Third, besides the greater use of party caucus, there seems to be greater use of public hearings by legislative committees to consult the public, and the legislative sessions appear to be considerably longer under Lord's administration. Not surprisingly, Progressive Conservative MLAs maintain that this is a reflection on the part of the Lord government to consult and deliberate before making a decision, while opposition MLAs argue that it is a sign of uncertainty and/or delay on the part of the government.[43] In a related area, following the 2003 general election, Elizabeth Weir (the sole NDP MLA) was appointed to chair a legislative committee to report on the public or crown corporation model for automobile insurance in the province.[44] Whether this is a case of political opportunism or a serious commitment to legislative power-sharing reform remains to be seen.

Finally, at a time when there seems to be so much public concern throughout the country about ethics in government, the Lord government oversaw the proclamation of an act, stemming from a legislative committee report of December 1998 and enacted in March 1999, that created the Office of the Conflict of Interest Commissioner. All New Brunswick MLAs, and not just cabinet ministers, are now subject to this commissioner, who serves as an independent officer who reports only to the Legislative Assembly.

Concluding Thoughts

New Brunswick poses an interesting case study in respect to the question of the governing style of the provincial executive. On the one hand, as suggested by Dunn, the bases of the power exercised by the first minister are the same at least in terms of the constitutional conventions associated with the Westminster model of parliamentary government found in Canada. Yet societal and personality factors as well as the current policy agenda can always be expected to have a particularistic impact on how a first minister exercises his or her tools of power. In the case of New Brunswick, the patron-client relationship and county councils that used to dominate the province's politics are now a distant memory, as are the old styles of patronage and political corruption. The advent of media politics, the introduction of the Programme of Equal Opportunity and related reform measures of the 1960s, the bureaucratization and universalization of government programs, and the rise of the proactive state affected the province substantively. This is not to suggest that these developments were unique to New Brunswick, but only that they had a major impact on this province, including the role of the first minister.

Nevertheless, a lingering sense of localism (or, more specifically, down-to-earth neighbourliness) remains when it comes to governing in New Brunswick. This may be attributed in large part to the province's small population. New Brunswick is not dominated by a single major metropolitan centre and about 50 per cent of the people live in rural areas (in bedroom communities for the most part). In this type of setting, the premier and cabinet colleagues cannot be too pretentious, or else they will suffer the consequences at the next election, if not sooner. People expect their MLA to be part of their community, to see their premier at the farmers' market or walking to work, and to be able to contact their politicians when needed. This is the setting of New Brunswick politics that each premier has to always take into account. Although the job of premier is a full-time position with abundant support staff, with perks of office and daily media attention, he or she must seek new, more effective ways to consult and remain in touch with the public.

Chapter 5

Premierial Governance: The System of Executive Power in Nova Scotia

DAVID JOHNSON

Does the government of Nova Scotia possess a distinct administrative style? How are we to best characterize the nature and working of the system of executive governance in Nova Scotia? Has this province been witness to a centralization of power within the senior echelons of its government in a manner similar to what has been happening in Ottawa in recent decades? Have we been observing the rise of a Blue-nose 'premierial' style of government that borrows from and is derived from the dynamic of 'prime ministerial' government now found in Ottawa?

These are just a few of the basic questions that arise from a contemplation of Donald Savoie's work *Governing from the Centre* and the application of his analytical framework to provincial governments. Savoie challenges Canadians to confront the realities of power within governments and to probe how and why and to what ends political power is organized and exercised, manipulated and controlled, in this society. He admonishes us to pierce the veil of formalistic and conventional understandings of power relations within governments and, to borrow a phrase, to probe the 'real world of democracy.' Savoie's study of the evolution of power relations within the federal government over the past four decades is also highly suggestive of the type of research and analysis that is too seldom devoted to provincial politics and government in this country.[1]

In recent years, interest in the concepts of reinventing government and the practice of the New Public Management has led to growing awareness of the idea of an administrative style. In their works, authors such as Knill, Bekke, Perry and Toonen, and March and Olsen stress the importance of viewing political and governmental action through a variegated analytical lens allowing for a complex assessment of a complex world.[2] All polities will have an administrative style, and by definition, the contours of an administrative style are rooted in the political, social, cultural and institutional heritage of a polity, such that the past is of crucial importance to the present. Yet an administrative style is more than an historical artifact in that it is also infused with the leading ideas, values, attitudes and practices respecting politics and governance in and for the present and future. In this sense, an administrative style is vibrant and evolutionary. The contours of an administrative style will then be found both in people and what they have created. It will be found in institutions and the working of institutions; it will be found in political behaviour and the results of such behaviour. In short, an administrative style will be found in the complex reality of the political and governmental life of any society.

Administrative Style and Nova Scotia

In reflecting upon this theoretical understanding of administrative style in relation to the political evolution of Nova Scotia, certain questions present themselves. What are the roles of the premier and other leading ministerial officials within the government? What is the nature and working of cabinet government and what are the power relations between the premier, other cabinet colleagues, and senior governmental officials? Have Nova Scotian premiers been witness to an accretion of premierial authority? What is the structure of cabinet and of cabinet committees and to what extent have these structures been changing over recent years? What has been the role of senior public servants in this system of executive governance and has this role been subject to change? In short, can it be said that Nova Scotia has a distinct administrative style and, if so, what is it?

This paper will assert that there is a distinct administrative style that can be captured by the terms premierial, pragmatic, centrist, and traditional. Premierial in that the key overarching and defining figure in every Nova Scotian government has been and is the premier. Pragmatic in that the basic organizing principle of governmental structure in the province has always been one of practical effectiveness, simplicity, and past experience over theoretical rationalism. Centrist in that the fundamental policy objectives of Nova Scotian governments, the broad goals for which its governments are organized and operated, are essentially middle-of-the-road understandings of moderate reform-liberal socio-economic policies. And traditional in that within this system of governance there is a strong appeal to past methods and manners of action and organization, to past wisdom in how to govern the province, and a relative distrust of new and theoretically abstract approaches to governmental organization and policy direction deriving from the rest of the country.

The Nova Scotian Structure of Governance, 1867–1970s

In looking at the structure of executive governance in Nova Scotia, two basic dynamics stand in sharp relief. First, the province has always had a tradition of strong premierial leadership in which the premier was head of a government and governmental structure was noted for its relatively small scale, its cabinet departmentalization, and its lack of institutionalized structures of cabinet coordination. Second, over the past thirty years there has been a trajectory in which the Nova Scotian executive system has become more institutionalized, to use Christopher Dunn's term,[3] but any reference to such institutionalization must be qualified as limited.

In his cursory review of the Nova Scotian executive system, Rand Dyck writes that 'Nova Scotia was rather slow to reform cabinet operations but since the late 1970s, it has had a cabinet committee system.'[4] Prior to the late 1970s, Nova Scotia essentially offered the country a classic illustration of first a traditional and then a departmentalized cabinet system presided over by strong premiers. As Murray Beck suggests, successive Nova Scotian governments perceived their essential function as being providers of basic public services and infrastructure (roads, education, electricity) as well as being interlocutors for the province vis-a-vis the federal government with respect to taxation policy, trade, freight rates, fiscal benefits, regional development policies and, eventually, equalization policy.[5] The provincial government itself, however, was rarely perceived as having a distinct developmental role for the province which would require it to display progressive skills in policy and program leadership. In the absence of such a visionary perspective, provincial politics came to be defined not so much by debates respecting ideologies, policy options, and desired roles for the state as by concerns respecting frugal management, traditional political cleavages rooted to family and religious ties, and by the creative uses of patronage and the spoils systems as a means to building and maintaining the electoral advantages of governing parties.

In such a political system, governments were of small scale, cabinet organization was rudimentary, and the overarching feature of provincial political life was the prominence of the premier. In the years prior to the 1970s, Nova Scotia possessed a departmentalized cabinet structure. Provincial cabinets were relatively small by central Canadian standards, numbering in the teens,[6] and they were 'unaided.' There was no tradition of permanent standing committees of cabinet allowing ministers with related portfolios to collaborate on the assessment of policy priorities and the development of policy and program initiatives. Likewise there was no tradition of permanent central agencies providing policy and program advice to the premier and cabinet. In classic departmentalized fashion, cabinet decision-making was highly compartmentalized with each minister being responsible to the premier for his (rarely her) policy and program field, with departmental deputy ministers being the key sources of policy and administrative advice, and with the premier and his minister of finance being the critical developers, coordinators, and overseers of governmental initiatives.

Within this system of government, the role of premier was all important. 'One of the more notable aspects of politics in Atlantic Canada,' Adamson and Stewart argue, 'has been the prominence of the party leaders who swaggered across their small stage. Leaders dominated their parties, not only during election campaigns, but also in party programmes, in the legislature and, when in office, in defining government policy.'[7] In short, one cannot understand the political history of Atlantic Canada in general, and Nova Scotia in particular, without appreciating the pivotal importance of its premiers as the key leaders. Such leader dominance was derived from a number of factors. One was simply the longevity in office of particular parties and premiers. Nova Scotia is famous in Canada for certain of its political dynasties, notably of a Liberal hue. This party governed the province continuously from 1882 until 1923 and then again from 1933 until 1956. During the first Liberal dynasty, Premier George Murray served without interruption for twenty-seven years (1896–1923), the longest premiership in Canadian history. While the Nova Scotia Conservative party cannot claim such a record of success, they too have had their reigns and champions, particularly Robert Stanfield and G.I. Smith (1956–70) and the premiers of the Buchanan-Bacon-Cameron years (1978–93).

Such longevity in office gave these men a privileged status within

their parties and governments. They were generally undisputed leaders and, as such, brought their parties to office and kept them in the
'winners circle.' They were the ones who had forged the winning
teams, policies, and platforms that enabled their party and their government members to enjoy the greatest prizes of political life – the
sweet taste of victory and the heady realization of power. In the acid
test of political leadership they had been victorious and they claimed
their due – the direction of their parties and their governments, with
these organizations and governments very much being seen as the
reflections of the men who led them. Hence 'Murray's ministry,' or
'Angus L's government,' or the 'Buchanan Tories.'

While premierial power and authority was obviously entwined with
electoral victory, its roots ran much deeper than that. Premiers in
Atlantic Canada generally, and Nova Scotia in particular, were, and
still are, leaders in a political system that is leader-dominated, where
there is a relative absence of ideological or societal cleavages dividing
the two main political parties, and where governing caucuses and provincial administrations themselves were, and are, relatively small and
thus amenable to close oversight and direction by the 'man at the
helm.' In these circumstances, premiers would invariably be the undisputed leaders of their parties and the driving force within their
governments. They would control the shape of their ministries, their
memberships, and the number and nature of key administrative and
political advisory bodies to the premier and cabinet.

A final point has to do with scale. Nova Scotia is a relatively small
province. Metro Halifax and Sydney, for example, the two largest metropolitan areas of the province, are still rather small urban centres by
national standards and they are places where people pride themselves
in keeping and maintaining personal contacts and knowing 'who's
who.' The same dynamic is even truer in rural Nova Scotia. Politicians
know this; they are part of this culture, and they actively seek to cultivate local political connections. All politicians worthy of the name thus
become a part of a vibrant local political culture. And premiers are
obviously not excepted; on the contrary, they become the centre of
such local political elites. Similarly, the provincial government is a relatively small institution where it is perfectly possible and even expected
that senior bureaucratic actors will know of everyone who is a senior
player in their institutional community. In such a small world, a premier can expect to know everyone of consequence within the provincial political and governmental environment. And through such

connections a premier could expect to be fully in control of all major strategic policy and program initiatives of his government.[8] As Dyck and Beck have argued, premiers would pride themselves on being the key players in provincial policy-making and program development and would take ownership of all major issues as befitting pre-eminent leaders of their province.

The Era of Limited Institutionalization

The development of the modern institutionalized cabinet in this country can be traced to the Pearson and Trudeau governments of the mid to late 1960s. Over the 1970s most provincial governments generally followed the federal lead, as different governments sought the gain the perceived benefits of cabinet institutionalization: enhanced policy and program capacity, the enhanced role of elected ministers in collective cabinet decision-making, the relative curtailment of the power and influence of departmental deputy ministers (the perceived mandarins) in the development of government policy, the creation of a plurality of countervailing sources of political and bureaucratic advice for cabinet respecting policy and program options, and the overall systematization and rationalization of general governmental priority-setting and program initiation and management. As provincial governments experimented with and established systems of cabinet institutionalization, Nova Scotia was part of this phenomenon, though never a major player. Indeed, the history of Nova Scotian initiatives with systems of cabinet reform reveals a distinct distrust of the rationalist movement.

Nova Scotia's first undertakings toward cabinet institutionalization began in 1968 under Premier G.I. Smith's short-lived government. In a move to enhance his cabinet's decision-making capabilities as well as to modernize and rationalize his government's interactions with other governments (especially the federal government) and interest groups, Smith established a Cabinet Committee on Planning and Programs, to be aided by a Planning and Program Secretariat. The secretariat consciously adopted a systems approach to policy-making in keeping with the federal model and, over the next two years, devised programs in such fields as regional development, urban planning and public housing, and internal managerial development and training. This cabinet committee and its secretariat, however, were to be of short duration.

In 1970 there was a change of government with the Liberals coming to power under the leadership of Gerald Regan. In actions designed to put his stamp upon the government, Regan abolished the Planning and Programs Secretariat on the grounds that it had met with resistance from within the senior ranks of the public service while also having inappropriately mixed policy development with program administration. He also replaced the Cabinet Committee on Planning and Programs with a Cabinet Office designed to provide policy advice to the premier. By 1972, however, this office had been reduced to playing a clerical role in the life of the government, a mere keeper of cabinet documents and records rather than a body of policy analysis and advice. The sole standing committee of cabinet within the Regan government was the Treasury Board, designed to facilitate policy and program coordination respecting general financial management.[9] The Regan government clearly displayed a distrust of rationalism and institutionalized systems of cabinet organization and structured decision-making, preferring the more traditional systems of cabinet decision-making – that is, informal premierial leadership. By the mid-1970s Nova Scotia was noteworthy as being the only province in the country with no standing committees of cabinet save the Treasury Board. The provincial government also lacked any strong central agencies to provide policy advice and coordination. This informal, non-institutionalized system of decision-making was clearly derived from Premier Regan's preferred style of management. In commenting on Regan's approach to handling cabinet meetings, Peter Kavanagh has written that 'Regan's meetings seem to have resembled a troika being approached by supplicants. If a cabinet minister had not cleared a matter with [premierial advisers] Garnet Brown [or] Peter Nicholson or Gerald Regan beforehand, it was unlikely to go.'[10]

With the advent of a Conservative government in 1978 the new premier, John Buchanan, moved to systematize and institutionalize decision-making processes within the government in an effort to distinguish his new administration from the excessively informal and procedurally sloppy decision-making of his predecessor. Buchanan worked to enhance both the program control and policy development capabilities of the government. He established two standing committees of cabinet, a Management Board headed by the minister of finance, and a Policy Board chaired by the premier; Buchanan also created separate secretariats, as central coordinating agencies, for each board. This was the true beginning of permanent standing committees and central agencies of cabinet within Nova Scotia. These bodies would co-exist with the pre-established Executive Council Office, responsible for the general management of cabinet meetings and records, and the Premier's Office designed to provide exclusive policy and administrative support for the premier.

Despite the existence of a greater degree of institutionalization compared to his immediate predecessor, however, one should hesitate to assert that the Buchanan government practised the politics and management of institutionalized cabinet decision-making. Far from it. As Beck, Dyck, and Kavanagh have all argued, Buchanan was very much the heart and soul of his government, as well as being the key decision-maker. Regardless of his early attempts to distance his managerial style from that of Regan, over time his approach to decision-making and the exercise of power came to have more in common with his much criticized, excessively informal and idiosyncratic forebear. In his system of cabinet leadership, Buchanan would exert full control and decision-making authority over the government's strategic priorities just as he would keep close direction over the management of leading government files, be they the development of offshore oil and gas, the handling of the Michelin bill, or the overseeing of policy respecting the Sydney Steel Corporation. In all these and many other cases the premier would be the alpha and omega of governmental decision-making. In his assessment of Buchanan's leadership style, Kavanagh writes that the premier would dominate cabinet and that his most important advisers were not fellow ministers but key officials, hand-picked by the premier, who were 'unelected and secretive.' According to Kavanagh,

> His close advisors Joe Stewart, Don Ripley, Fred Dickson, Ian Thompson, Mavis [his wife], and a small group of others provide the premier with suggestions, feedback and a sense of how a decision, if made, might play and what might result from inaction. Buchanan then takes the pulse of the cabinet and seems to then ponder the matter in his own inestimable fashion. Getting through to the premier can be a difficult and often embarrassing proposition. Stories abound of cabinet ministers having to call Mavis to get the premier to meet with them privately or a minister having to travel to the Spryfield Mall on a Saturday morning to get John Buchanan to pay some personal attention to a matter of some urgency. If Buchanan is out of town then decisions just do not get made.

Structural Reforms and Policy Dynamics of the 1990s

This system of premierial leadership within a weak institutional cabinet structure lasted through the Buchanan years as well as through the shorter-lived Conservative governments of Roger Bacon (1990–1) and Donald Cameron (1991–3). The Cameron government was noteworthy, however, for the reforms it initiated respecting human resource management within the provincial public service. The patronage system has deep roots in the political culture of Nova Scotia, yet it has increasingly come under attack for being both a throwback to an earlier, more corrupt era, as well as an inefficient, uneconomic, and unjust system of personnel management within government. Concerns respecting the hiring, promotion, demotion, and removal of public servants date back to the colonial period; but while both leading parties would criticize the 'scandalous' hiring and firing decisions of their adversaries, each would continue the practice of partisan patronage once in office. The Macdonald government did establish a Civil Service Commission in 1935 but, as Aucoin argues, it was 'weak in several crucial respects: power of dismissal was retained as a prerogative of the government; numerous positions were not encompassed by the act; and several "loopholes" were provided in order to preserve a good measure of ministerial discretion.'[12]

Despite these weaknesses in the human resources system within the provincial government, a permanent public service slowly developed in Nova Scotia. Yet it was one that faced a large degree of partisan micro-management with respect to low-end casual employment (highway maintenance and transportation jobs), term positions, and high-end policy positions. The governments of Stanfield and Regan oversaw the growth of a permanent and professional public service in the province in keeping with personnel policy developments within the federal and other provincial governments, but neither premier felt capable of eliminating these enduring vestiges of the spoils system. In 1979 the Buchanan government transferred the Civil Service Commission to the new Management Board, thereby stripping it of formal institutional independence and placing all staffing decisions under the direct ambit of ministers. Though Aucoin stresses that this reform did not destroy the professionalism of the Nova Scotian public service and did not render the public service a 'hot-bed of patronage and inefficiency,' it did send negative signals throughout the province and abroad and, over time, the Buchanan government was implicated in a variety of patronage scandals that increasingly undermined its political credibility and electoral fortunes.[13]

When Donald Cameron replaced John Buchanan as premier, the new government launched a major reform initiative to both streamline the size of the public service through institutional reorganization and employee downsizing and to 'eradicate partisan intervention in the staffing process.'[14] To this latter end, Cameron promoted a career public servant as his deputy minister, advocated for a non-partisan approach to public sector management, and launched an undertaking to establish a new department of human resources that would be vested with responsibility for promoting the merit principle throughout the public service. Notwithstanding this reformist agenda, the Conservative party, in power since 1978, could not withstand the public desire for change and in 1993 they were defeated at the polls.

The Liberals returned to power under John Savage and, in a now familiar act, he promised to reform the system of cabinet decision-making so as to make it more systematic, coordinated, and capable of imposing fiscal prudence of a government facing a severe and growing deficit/debt problem. Gone were to be the days of highly informal and idiosyncratic premierial leadership undertaken at the expense of rational and collegial cabinet decision-making. By late 1994 the Nova Scotian system of executive governance had come to resemble that of most provinces. While maintaining the Premier's Office and the Executive Council Office, Savage eliminated the Management and Policy boards, stressing that the former had duplicated the functions of Finance while the latter was to be replaced by a new Priorities and Planning Committee, to be aided by a new secretariat. This committee would play the role of an inner cabinet of select ministers who would become the leading ministerial advisers to the premier with respect to the development of policy priorities and program implementation. The Priorities and Planning Secretariat, in turn, was to be the governments key policy and program advisory body while the Department of Finance would become the dominant institution with respect to provincial financial management. As a mark of the growing importance of financial management in the life of this government, the premier named his finance minister as head of the Priorities and Planning Committee. Savage also established a cabinet secretary/deputy minister of priorities and planning who would also be responsible for the Office of the Premier, with this official acting as a conduit between the premier and the Priorities and Planning Committee and secretariat.

And working alongside this official's more policy-oriented role was the clerk of the Executive Council, engaged in the coordination of government policy and interrelationships with the public service. As the final pieces of this rather elaborate executive infrastructure, Savage also created a chief of staff in his Premier's Office and, under this official, a communication director given the job of managing media relations.[15] The Savage structure of executive organization thus consisted of one cabinet committee – Priorities and Planning – assisted by four institutions fulfilling the roles of central agencies: the Premier's Office, the Executive Council Office, the Priorities and Planning Secretariat, and the Department of Finance.

This more elaborate system of cabinet institutionalization accentuated the heightened role of the minister of finance in policy development and program implementation, yet it did not alter the fundamental power relations within the government. John Savage remained the overarching figure in the government, being the key decision-maker with respect to government priorities, the development of major policies, and the management of leading government initiatives such as deficit and debt control, health policy reform, regional development programming and municipal amalgamation, and efforts to restrict, curtail and reform the management of patronage. All of these policy fields were to give Savage headaches over the mid-1990s but it was the last one, and his attempts to restrict the application of patronage appointments within his government, that engendered growing resistance to his leadership from within the ranks of his own party.

When Savage was first elected he sought to inherit the reformist, anti-patronage initiative launched by his immediate predecessor, Donald Cameron. To this end, he denounced the politics of patronage, promising to eradicate partisanship from public service hiring and firing. He established a Department of Human Resources, mandated to promote the professionalization of the public service, to advocate the merit principle, and to attack patronage. The new government purposively decided against sacking previous Conservative patronage appointees, especially those on the highway service, for example, but this decision quickly bred ill-will amongst rank-and-file members of the Liberal party who had obviously hoped that Savage's anti-patronage statements had been more campaign rhetoric than statements of actual government policy.

Coupled to this initiative to further the professionalization of the public service, the Savage government also sought to advance the reform of the public service through the adoption of a number of measures associated with the New Public Management principles. Initiatives were undertaken to reduce the size of the provincial state, to restrain provincial spending, to reduce the annual deficit, and to streamline, reorder, rationalize, and reconceptualize the nature of government services. Government was to be cut, the provision of public services were to be commercialized as much as possible, and public servants were to be made more accountable for the delivery of more economical and efficient, more streamlined and effective program delivery.

The Savage years witnessed significant change in the nature and working of the provincial public service. The politics of patronage was de-emphasized to a large degree, with the government stressing the importance of a professional and non-partisan public service. This was also a public service that was subjected to policies of restraint, reorganization, and retrenchment. Departments were amalgamated and downsized, the overall size of the public service was reduced by some two thousand persons, public spending was restricted, wage restraints became commonplace, and all government institutions were instructed to do more with less.[16]

These changes were significant, yet in a province with a strong sense of traditionalism in its political culture such developments were also controversial and contested, especially among members of the Liberal party themselves. Following three years of swallowing tough medicine, a majority of the rank and file of the Liberal party had had enough and a challenge to the premier's party leadership was inaugurated. Sensing he could not win this battle, Premier Savage resigned as party leader in March 1997, to be succeeded by Russell MacLellan.

Premier MacLellan essentially maintained the cabinet structure and system of executive governance that he inherited, while returning to a more traditional approach to the politics of patronage within the provincial public service. Entering power in the beginning of the fifth year of his party's legislative mandate, MacLellan had limited time for wide-scale structural reforms. Any interest in such reforms was further blunted by the Liberal party's razor-thin minority government victory in the provincial election of March 1998.

In the provincial election of July 1999, the MacLellan Liberals were defeated and the Conservatives returned to power under John Hamm. Once in office, Premier Hamm moved to simplify the structures and systems of executive governance in the province though, in truth, the

Hamm system differs little from that of Savage and MacLellan. With respect to cabinet committees Hamm abolished the Priorities and Planning Committee, replacing it with a new Treasury and Policy Board of Cabinet. Unlike the old Priorities and Planning Committee, this board is not designed to act as an inner cabinet but to be a plenary board of cabinet chaired by the premier. The core central agencies assisting the premier and cabinet are then five: the Premier's Office, consisting of a chief of staff, the deputy minister for the premier, a director of communications, and various policy analysts, the Executive Council Office, headed by the secretary to the Executive Council, the Treasury and Policy Board Secretariat, the Department of Finance with respect to budgetary and financial management issues, and a new Public Service Commission that replaced the Department of Human Resources in 2001. This commission has responsibility for personnel policy matters, collective bargaining, and staffing and the promotion of the merit principle. Alongside these core central agencies can now be added a new Department of Intergovernmental Affairs, headed by the premier, with responsibility for coordinating Nova Scotia's relations with the federal government, other provincial and territorial governments, and other national governments. The prime policy objective of this department, however, is clearly that of providing institutional and policy support in Nova Scotia's on-going battle to improve the quantity of equalization payments received by the provincial government as well as enhancing Nova Scotia's claim to the federal government for improved royalty payments for offshore resources.

Although the Hamm government has put its own stamp on the executive organization of the provincial government, it has nonetheless maintained the new public management initiatives of the Savage government, even engaging in its own variation of program review in 2000–01. Through these undertakings, the size of the provincial public service has been reduced still more, public policies with respect to regional development have been streamlined and curtailed, the policy fields of health, education, and social assistance have all confronted straitened fiscal circumstances, the Sydney Steel Corporation has been closed, the scope and utilization of user fees have been increased, and public service management is expected to be operated in as business-like a fashion as possible. By 2002, in response to such initiatives, the province finally recorded its first annual budgetary surplus in some three decades. Such results, however, did not translate into substantial political gains for the premier and his party.

Nova Scotians went to the polls in August 2003 and returned the Hamm Progressive Conservatives with a minority government, with the NDP becoming the official opposition, and the Liberals reduced to third place. This result illustrates a significant degree of public dissatisfaction with the government respecting cutbacks to health, education, and social policy spending during the previous four years as well as much public outrage at a $155 tax rebate cheque issued to most Nova Scotians just weeks before the calling of the election. Nevertheless, the Hamm government was returned, indicating that, notwithstanding strong media and opposition party criticism, the Progressive Conservatives retained a winning plurality of support from most Nova Scotians as the party considered best able to lead the province through tough economic times.

The Nova Scotian Administrative Style: Present and Past

At the outset of this paper it was asserted that the Nova Scotian administrative style could be captured by four key terms: premierial, pragmatic, centrist, and traditional. Each of these concepts now deserve closer scrutiny in light of the current working of the Hamm ministry and those of his predecessors.

Premierial Government

As we have seen, the premier has been and still is the essential lynchpin, the key figure and undisputed leader of all provincial governments. This was always the case with respect to administrations dating from confederation through the 1960s and it has remained the case through the past thirty years of relative cabinet institutionalization. In this sense Nova Scotia (as with all other Atlantic provinces) has always had premierial government,' a highly centralized form of top-down, command-and-control leadership emanating from the apex of political power within the province. It is interesting to reflect upon this in light of Savoie's findings respecting the evolution of such an administrative style within the federal government under the leaderships of Trudeau, Mulroney, and Chrétien. What is seen as a managerial and leadership development in Ottawa over the past thirty years has been standard operating procedure in Nova Scotia since Confederation.

The administrative operationalization of premierial governance within Nova Scotia has been generally uniform across differing governments and leaders. Senior officials knowledgeable about the Savage, MacLellan, and Hamm administrations have all described remarkably similar decision-making systems regarding the determination of policy priorities and the development of administrative means to turn these policies into realities. In all instances the vital decision-maker is the premier, acting in close concert with his senior advisors in the Premier's Office, the Executive Council Office, and his minister of finance. As one senior official remarked in reference to the Hamm government, the premier and his minister of finance are 'symbiotically linked.' The former needs a good, competent, prudent, and strong finance minister as an essential guardian of the public purse just as the latter needs the political support of the premier to enable him or her to be an effective manager of the province's fiscal resources. In other words, a weak premier will result in a weak finance minister, and vice-versa. Just as Savoie found a close operating and power relationship between prime ministers and their ministers of finance, so too do we see a similar dynamic in Nova Scotia.

With respect to actual policy and program decision-making, it is instructive to note the differentiation between strategic and standard policy and program matters, with the former, by definition the more politically important of governmental matters, being firmly in the decision-making environment of the premier. Once again, officials and commentators familiar with the Savage, MacLellan, and Hamm governments have all remarked on the bifurcated nature of governmental policy and program decision-making. Matters considered standard or routine, involving pre-established policy matters and the more or less standard implementation of set programs and the application of established programs to specific fact situations, would be devolved to line ministers and their departments. Such matters were to be left to the routine administration, implementation, and requisite managerial problem-solving of line officials down the hierarchy. The forces of the centre would only become involved in such files if they no longer became routine an account of problems arising in their policy or program implementation which necessitated the political intervention of the premier and his key advisers. Such intervention, however, was never desired by premiers for all the obvious reasons: it would indicate that a previously routine matter had ceased to be routine; that a line department and its minister had failed to adequately manage and control a file, that the government was taking political heat from the opposition, the media, various interest groups and the general public for such perceived mismanagement; and, most important of all, that the premier's personal policy and program agenda was being entrenched upon.

Each premier would have such agendas and they were, and are, generally uniform in their basic contours. During the legislative term of any government, a premier would normally take possession of four to six key policy and program initiatives as being the most important policy issues facing his government, and thereby being the essential ones upon which his premiership was to be judged. With Premier Hamm these priority issues in his first term were: balancing the budget; stabilizing and reforming the health care system; promoting off-shore oil and gas development; privatizing or liquidating the fiscal running sore of the Sydney Steel Corporation; negotiating a better fiscal and equalization relationship with the federal government; and providing general tax relief in the fourth year of his mandate. By means of comparison, Premier Savage's priority list was held as being: tighter fiscal management leading to a balanced budget; health care reform; the promotion of off-shore oil and gas development; municipal reform and amalgamation; and reducing the prevalence of patronage within the Nova Scotian government. While one can assess each government in light of its key priorities and its relative ability to deliver on these pledges, the essential point is that each premier will establish such a list of priorities and will then devote the majority of his time and attention to working on these policy and program files, delegating other non-priority or administrative and managerial matters to his line ministers and departments. Within the province, then, there is a strategic premiership dedicated to a select few policy and program fields with these matters very much being those upon which the premier and his government is to be judged and upon which the success of his leadership is to be determined.

Pragmatic Government

Premierial government in Nova Scotia has also been pragmatic government. Within the upper echelons of the Nova Scotian public service concern for policy and program pragmatism has always outweighed interest in abstract concepts of organizational theory and design, and the development of policy and program rationalism. The basic evidence of this is simply to be found in the history of cabinet institutionalization. Nova Scotian government were slow to embrace systems of cabinet institutionalization, with the concept of organizational rationalism and rational policy-making being generally viewed with a quite jaundiced eye. Interest in practical solutions to practical problems achieved, by and large, through traditional and long-established forms and institutions of governmental decision-making have long been the preferred approach to policy development and organizational management within Nova Scotia. As such, the Nova Scotian public service has seldom had a reputation for progressive policy initiation or managerial and administrative innovation. With the exception of human rights policy development in the 1960s and 1970s, the Nova Scotian public service has possessed a tradition of being a policy and program follower in this country rather than a leader and groundbreaker. This is not to suggest that the quality and capability of those active within the senior ranks of the Nova Scotian public service are less than those found in other provinces and the federal government, but that the Nova Scotian public service holds a different tradition of management – an administrative style that downplays theoretical innovation in favour of pragmatic responses designed to fit easily, and with little rancour or difficulty, within the Nova Scotian political tradition. Of course, there are drawbacks to such a pragmatic acceptance of past ways of doing governmental business, with one of the greatest being the province's long and problematic history with political patronage.

Centrist Government

The corollary to administrative pragmatism is the political and program dynamic of centrism within Nova Scotia. Just as with federal politics, electoral success in Nova Scotian politics has always been found by appealing to the broad centre of the Nova Scotian political spectrum. Authors such as Beck, Dyck, and Adamson and Stewart have all commented upon this dynamic, with its overall effect that parties in this province have less ideological differentiation than in other parts of the country. As Beck has argued, this has always been true of the Nova Scotian Liberal and Conservative parties, and it is also arguably the case with the provincial New Democratic party. Despite minor differences in policy positions, all of these parties essentially display moderate policy platforms that can best be characterized as 'reform liberal.' All parties in Nova Scotia have generally sought to achieve sound economic growth and prosperity while also advancing fair and just social-welfare policies designed to benefit all Nova Scotians but especially middle- and lower-income earners. All parties in Nova Scotia have endorsed policies supportive of a mixed economy in which the predominant role of the private sector in economic growth and development is recognized. Nevertheless, the state is called upon to play an important role in the social and economic life of the province, especially in relation to the promotion of economic infrastructure, regional economic development, the distribution of public service employment across the regions of the province, and the establishment and maintenance of basic elements of the social-welfare safety net.

Given the general congruence of thought amongst the three major parties as to desired socio-economic policy, it is not surprising that Nova Scotian governments have pursued generally moderate, centrist, and similar approaches to socio-economic management. All governing parties were supportive of the promotion of the social-welfare state in the 1950s and 1960s. They were all Keynesian when Keynesian policies were in fashion in the 1960s and 1970s and they are all, still, significantly Keynesian and reform liberal in a deep sense to this day. But all these parties and governments have been influenced by the rise of neoconservative thought in the 1980s and 1990s so that all Nova Scotian parties and governments over the past decade have endorsed the policies of fiscal restraint, deficit elimination, and debt reduction. Yet, in typical Nova Scotian fashion, the province and its parties and governments have never moved as far to the right as have other provincial governments in Ontario, Alberta, or British Columbia. Deficits here are to be fought more by increasing revenue than by cutting services. The debt is to be dealt with more by growing the economy than by taking monies from programs and directing it to debt payments. Tighter fiscal management is to be achieved while also protecting core social programs such as health care and education, and a smaller, more economical and efficient government is to be desired, yet one that continues to play a significant role in the social and economic life of the province. As such, the Nova Scotian experience has been more moderate and centrist than that found in other provinces. Even the current Conservative government of John Hamm is much more liberal in its socio-economic policies and its initiatives of deficit reduction than those found in its Conservative counterparts elsewhere in the country. This cleaving to the liberal centre is simply indicative of the broad liberal centrism that defines the political culture of this province and which, in turn, shapes and informs the development and administration of governmental policies and programs.

Traditional Government

The final defining characteristic of the Nova Scotian administrative style is its traditionalism. Given all the foregoing, this province is not one noted for its courageous breaks from past ways of doing things and for promoting a developing new and innovative approaches to policy and administration. In fact, quite the opposite is true. While the broad political culture of the province can be defined as being liberal, it is also true to say that the operating culture, the operational style of the government is situationally conservative in that traditional forms of behaviour and decision-making are preferred over newer, revised, and experimental forms. Hence the continued appeal of a highly central-ized premierial approach to political and governmental leadership, the general interest and support for institutionally pragmatic approaches to policy and administration over more theoretically innovative and rationalistic approaches, and the support for the maintenance of a broadly reform-liberal approach to socio-economic policy – all in keep-ing with the embedded political and governmental traditions of this province.

Institutional Government

Adamson and Stewart have long commented upon the traditionalism found within the socio-economic and political life of the Atlantic Cana-dian provinces and there is much truth in their findings. One cannot understand Nova Scotian politics and government without appreciat-ing the pull that traditional and deeply embedded patterns of political thought, organizational and managerial behaviour, and governmental approaches to policy and program operationalization have on the nature and working of governments. Of course, this is not to say that the province possesses a political and governmental culture that is stuck in amber. There have been significant reforms to the nature and working of the system of government in the province, as the develop-ments within the province's personnel management process indicate. There has been a professionalization of human resource management and a general move to the institutionalization of decision-making pro-cesses within the government. But this process of institutionalization has been limited. It may be possible to term the Nova Scotian executive system as post-institutional due to its premierial-centred nature but this perhaps places too much stress on a linear dynamic within the evolution of the province's administrative culture. Notwithstanding alterations over past decades, the administrative style of Nova Scotia was set well in the past. And as the province evolves, it does so slowly and cautiously, seeking to maintain the core features of a style that is premierial, pragmatic, centrist, and traditional.

Chapter 6

The Executive Administrative Style in Prince Edward Island: Managerial and Spoils Politics

PETER E. BUKER

Prince Edward Island's executive administrative style is driven primarily by socio-political rather than legal-institutional factors. Three interrelated aspects of this small province colour the choices and establish the constraints of provincial cabinet: the effects of small scale, in terms of geographic size and particularly population; the relative importance of federal government financial support; and a conservative island political culture that competes primarily over spoils rather than public policy.

The conceptual outcome of these three spheres of analysis is that neo-institutional interpretations have weak explanatory powers, and, despite an incremental modernization of the island's government, much of the executive's administrative style can be classified as traditional, as cabinet collectively seeks to aggregate province-wide interests while retaining some vestiges of the spirit of patronage-distribution or modified clientism. An informal subjectivism pervades executive actions, although changes are occurring over time that have created more neutral government structures while at the same time moving the executive towards a rational/managerial role in public policy.

Historical Precedents and Small Size

Prince Edward Island is by far the most densely populated Canadian province, with a population of 140,000 on an island that is only 224 kilometres long at its greatest distance. The island's Legislative Assembly has been in existence since 1773, achieving responsible government in 1851. The character of PEI's government was, from its inception, based upon a primal attachment to land, and the first half of the nineteenth century was coloured by bitter struggles with absentee landowners

In some sense, the governance of PEI is more analogous to local government than provincial government just because of this size. The flavour of this analogy to local governments is a consequence of a smallness that leads to subjective considerations in a political culture where the boundaries between public and private citizenship are often blurred and overshadow the objective considerations of institutional disinterestedness in governance and its institutional structures. The small-size phenomenon is so fundamental in PEI as to render models that are used elsewhere in this monograph to describe the executive styles of other Canadian provinces mostly irrelevant.

This being said, the experiences of most other provinces in their early days, when they were typified by small populations and primarily rural-based economies, also describe PEI's early experience. These archetypal patronage-ridden systems perhaps remained a part of the island governance structure for a longer period than in most other provincial jurisdictions, in part because the island's small size encouraged the dominance of personal and personality-related relationships.[1] Size was not just a function of *numbers* of citizens, but also a function of the *velocity* of interaction among citizens, and until the mid-twentieth century, even given the railway, movement on the island was often difficult and limited. Also, as in other provincial jurisdictions, 'Provincial cabinets [operated] on an informal trial-and-error basis until into the 1960s,'[2] in part in response to the clientist system, and in part because *planning* in its political-bureaucratic sense, was still in its infant stages in Canada. This clientist system included brokers and promoters of patronage – often party officials – who characteristically used their government connections to reward themselves, their families, and their friends. The aphorism, 'if it moves, pension it; if it doesn't move, pave it,' is still cynically remembered by many of PEI's older residents, as is vote-purchasing by payments of either liquor or money. A broader social concern has also always existed, however, and churches, especially the Roman Catholic Church, played an important backroom role in island politics. While there has, on the face of it, always been a dominant role of the premier in PEI politics, economic, religious, and social elites, including the churches, have held great sway through much of the island's history.

Size affects the style of PEI's executive's administration in part because it reduces the constraints of 'critical size'[3] normally found in larger provincial jurisdictions. Critical size is reached when information flowing up and down the organizational structure becomes too complex for good decisions; these diseconomies of scale are often dealt with by implementing institutional reforms that try to disentangle this complexity by substituting more objective divisions of organizational labour for the subjectivity of the push and pull of politics. By analogy, this is the reason for the phenomena of conglomerates, or the Catholic Church's use of subsidiarity. The executive branch of governments often deal with critical or inefficient size by a combination of centralizing power and implementing institutional and legal constraints on policy determinants in substitution for political determinants. This later phenomenon is what makes the neo-institutional approach to understanding administrative styles so useful in provincial jurisdictions that have reached a critical size.

The government of PEI, in contrast, is such that the organizational structure does not reach these critical junctures for most public-sector activities, and so most public policy can fall easily within the rubric of the existing provincial government's jurisdiction. This lack of criticality of size results in a clear jurisdictional concern of the provincial government for almost everything and limits inter-jurisdictional competition and dispute over appropriate levels of authority. A traditional structure of ministerial predominance – ministerial accountability and responsibility in the custom of Westminster-style government – can exist because of the small size of the population and territory, and the sub-critical size that avoids administrative diseconomies of scale.

That the cabinet has in recent years generally consisted of ten people and that there are only five cabinet committees – Treasury Board, Agenda and Priorities Committee, Strategic Planning Committee on Economic Policy, Strategic Planning Committee on Community and Social Policy, and the Legislative Review Committee – attests to the comparative simplicity of institutional structure. The small cabinet size and lack of cabinet committees compared with other provinces exist not because of any difference in the constitutionally determined scope of provincial jurisdiction – PEI's is the same as other provinces – but only that the executive does not administratively require more institutional structure given the size of the jurisdiction. Institutional structure can still be interpreted as a determinant of executive style, even if not in the neo-institutionalist conceptual framework, by the fact that it exerts relatively limited constraints on the provincial executive. Indeed, the extra-legislative position of ombudsman, found in all other provinces, has never existed, and PEI is notable for being the last province in Canada to proclaim a Freedom of Information and Protection of Privacy Act in 2002. The implication of small cabinet size and of simple institutional structure is that social and political factors are given freer play as compared with larger provinces and their constraining institutional structures. Thus, the broader basis of the island's political culture plays a far greater role in the executive's administrative style than it does in larger jurisdictions.

The size of PEI's jurisdiction, and the attendant thinness of insulating layers of organizational structure between the citizenry and their ministers, allow the cabinet's attention to be directed to a range of policy concerns, from the petty to the important, from the small to the great. The administrative style of the executive becomes one humbled by this amalgam of high and low politics; high politics is the realm of dramatic, big issues, typified by federal-provincial relations and public policies with island-wide implications, and low politics is about issues that, in the context of larger provincial jurisdictions, would be considered as either administrative or within the realm of private law. PEI's executive style includes a phenomenon that has been graphically described by one well-placed insider as the 'minister as *diddler*,' where ministers preoccupy themselves with low-politics concerns, in part because that is where their best capability lies, or because they are not adequate to the job of dealing with true public-policy issues.

Usually, low politics relies more on technical information than on social or ideological grounds for public policy decisions, and tends to affect either the citizenry unequally, or only a subgroup of the citizenry. Low politics tends to be less contestable in the public eye, and often involves public policy decisions for which general agreement is a given, or for which the proportion of the disaffected is small and generally non-vocal. Administrative politics is typically about low politics. In PEI, the bulk of government activity is low politics, and is, thereby, administrative; if PEI's cabinet wants to be seen to be doing something in terms of public policy, or if it is to use its public policy-making capacity, it must, perforce, do much of it in the realm of low politics. High politics, for the cabinet, almost always is about federal-provincial relations, and it is here that islanders tend to rally behind their premier and ministers to present a united front. This consensus of support by the voting public is both one of general self-interest as well as one of giving their support to the leadership in issues that are not easily understood by most people. The general lack of public debate about the province's relations with the federal government, and the acquiescence to PEI's executive in these issues give, from a provincial perspective, a bureaucratic-administrative rather than a political air to decisions of high politics.

It is telling that provincial high politics – issues of political manoeuvring in the interstices between the island and outside authority – are subsumed in an administrative realm within the province by the fact that relations between the four federal members of parliament, the four island senators, and the provincial government are almost always cordial and often mutually supportive, despite, in recent years, provincial and federal representatives being of different political parties. Granted, both provincial and federal elected representatives owe their electoral success to the same constituents, but the level of cooperation among them is uncanny, and suggests that, in the realm of off-island affairs the executive's administrative style is apolitical and conducted in a framework by which policy decisions are made in an administrative manner of bounded-rational decision making.

There is no denying that there is small-size consciousness continually in the minds of Prince Edward Island bureaucrats and politicians. This sense of smallness variously plays out as a tendency to look to bigger jurisdictions as somehow being more cumbersome because of their institutional complexity and their distance from their constituents. Comparison with larger jurisdictions contributes to both a pride in, and a defensiveness about, the 'Island Way' – a way that relies more heavily on personal initiative, personality, subjectivism, and common sense rather than a bureaucratic process-dependent, rule-oriented, objectivism of institutional decision making. Small size, therefore, simultaneously leads to copying, or more commonly adapting lessons learnt from bigger jurisdictions, while offering an excuse for not following the extant standards in other instances. Often the choice between these two rationales depends on pure instrumental opportunism. The fact that PEI has the second-lowest per capita income among Canada's provinces is commonly referred to when that portrayal is seen as an advantage, while PEI's high relative score in various quality-of-life indices is often cited in opposite circumstances.

Thus, the bureaucratic and political struggles throughout the late 1990s to eliminate the partisan-motivated turnover of provincial casual employees with each change of government party, and the whole issue of patronage offered by members of the Legislative Assembly (MLAs) to their riding's faithful, was really a traditional fight between the norms and standards of what a neutral civil service ought to be by Weberian standards, and pork-barrel politics. That in the 1990s MLAs were still unabashedly arguing that they were in a better position to reward their constituents with casual government jobs based on need because of their personal knowledge of individuals' situations is a telling comment upon how subjective these home-grown politicians can be compared with Weberian bureaucratic norms of impartiality.[4]

Political Culture: The Citizens

It is impossible to understand the nature of PEI's executive style without understanding the province's political culture, as the executive's ability to govern stems directly from the close and frequent interaction that they have with their citizenry. PEI's social culture is very traditional; the island is populated by multi-generational citizens of overwhelmingly British, particularly Irish and Scottish, descent, with some Acadian. The population size has been stable compared with most other provinces, and intergenerational and extended family connections are extremely strong. Until the provincial election of 1996, the legislature consisted of thirty-two members, each riding electing two representatives. Since 1996, a one-riding, one-vote structure has been in place, and the legislature has twenty-seven members. The island's private-sector economy is almost evenly divided, at least in income, between agriculture, fishing, and tourism; federal and provincial public-sector employment accounts for 11.5 per cent[5] of total island employment – greater than any other province.[6] There is also extensive reliance on federally administered employment insurance, and grants or subsidies to island industries. There is a strong sense of pride of place among the population, which makes for far more energetic public engagement than would be expected from the same-sized population without this geographic identity and borders.

It is against this background of heavy government involvement in the economic well-being of the island citizenry that the province's political culture has developed. PEI has the highest political participation rates at both the provincial and federal levels of any province; not only does it have the highest voter turnout of any other province, but membership in political parties is great, and a small but very active alternative system of pressure groups is continually present. This exceptional level of public attentiveness and participation in the political process has had great influence on the administrative style of the provincial government's executive. Contrary to a neo-institutional approach, factors affecting the public-policy decisions of cabinet, and the constraints under which it operates, are best described by the political culture of the island itself.

For a heterogeneous and geographically dispersed population used to the complexities of larger organizational structures in their day-to-day environment, issues of concern, complaint, or public input will be directed through hierarchical channels to the appropriate government official in the provincial bureaucracy. For citizens of PEI, however, the contact point is typically their MLA, or a minister. Indeed, there is a good chance that their MLA is a cabinet minister. Using an MLA as a general point of contact with government works in two ways: it tends to politicize administrative functions, and it tends to 'administrize' political functions. In both cases, the citizenry's inclination to contact their political representative instead of a member of the provincial public service fosters an administrative style in cabinet that tends to be administrative in a bureaucratic sense. Whatever the cause of this tendency to deal directly with government, there is no denying that it has become the preferred channel of government contact for many citizens. MLAs, cabinet ministers, and their political staffs welcome such contacts, because it gives them the chance to earn future votes. In a province where the provincial riding electorate number from 2,608 to 4,602, elections are fought and won vote-by-vote or family-by-family, based on an incumbent's performance. This whole system becomes self-perpetuating.

Political Culture: The Government

The communitarian antecedents of PEI's political culture within government are interesting and rich. Ever since the depression years of the 1930s, there has been in the province a tradition of grass-roots cooperative community building – the ideology of community economic development as it was known in later years.[7] At this time, inspired in part by the philosophies and individuals involved in the Antigonish Movement that had begun in the 1920s in Eastern Canada, cooperatives, credit unions, branch libraries, farm radio forums, and so on, blossomed. Adult education was taken to desperately impoverished rural communities, and the vigorous pioneering spirit of the island's people was rekindled. This vital time in PEI's history still has a notable influence on its political culture.

Many of PEI's current cabinet members, including the current premier, were influenced in their formative years by the Comprehensive Development Plan introduced in 1969 by the then-premier, Alex Campbell. This was an era of far-reaching government expansion throughout Canada, and in PEI enormous injections of money from Ottawa expanded the public social and physical infrastructure. This 'special' public policy was conducted in much the same manner as it had been in the late 1930s and early 1940s – by grass-roots consultation. The Comprehensive Development Plan – a fifteen-year plan eventually superseded by a succession of other regional economic development initiatives from Ottawa – not only introduced a cadre of outside administrators of the program to the island, but also coincided with a high demand by the provincial government to hire educated young islanders which the province met by recruiting its native-born who either had off-island higher education, or were in the process of getting it. What resulted was a progressive, communitarian, grass-roots approach to introducing modernization and change. Later influxes of federal development funding did two things: it reinforced the island population's dependency on the largess of the federal government, and it maintained political spoils at the grass-roots level. These were lessons learnt by the individuals involved in the restructuring program of the 1960s who went on to become important in the political and elite leadership of the province. As an example of the importance of this communitarian tradition, in the 1979 election campaign Angus McLean won the premiership on a platform of 'rural renaissance' inspired in part by E.F. Schumacher's influential book, *Small Is Beautiful*.

There has always existed a small, vocal radical fringe in PEI politics. Issues surrounding land, a fixed link to the mainland, and *independentiste* political causes have had perennial resurgences. For example, the self-styled Brothers and Sisters of Cornelius Howatt was a group initially inspired to counter the government-sponsored Centennial Commission's historical interpretation of PEI's entry into Confederation.[8] Extra-legislative political activities can be important; for example, in January 1988 the government of Joseph Ghiz held a plebiscite on the building of a fixed link to the mainland because of the passionate public debate surrounding the issue. Current extra-legislative groups characteristically focus on the substantive issues of the island's natural environment and on social policy. An annual *Alternative Budget* is published by a so-called radical coalition, and mailed to every household in PEI. Spontaneous coalitions have emerged in protest to specific government waste sites, the use of pesticides, and other issues of both local self-interest and general altruistic concern. Unlike legislative debate, these extra-legislative groups tend to combine politicized debate on substantive policy choices with the instruments of pressure and protest groups. The existence of this small but legitimate, consistent, and strong segment of island politics, dominated by a handful of well-known and dedicated social and environmental activists, can be construed as attesting to the sometimes apolitical administrative style of PEI's provincial cabinet, as substantive debates on public policy are, on occasion, conducted in the public realm instead of within the legislature.

Due to the high political attentiveness of the public in PEI, successful executive administrative style appears to lie at one of two extremes: either proactive and leading, or reactive and consensual. Historically, the governments of Walter R. Shaw (1959–66) and Alex B. Campbell (1966–78) were characteristically leading, while the current government of Pat Binns (1996–present) has been innocuously reactive in public policy. In a sense, there is only so much political 'space' to be occupied in terms of initiative; and with such an attentive public, the current executive has the opportunity to fulfill their role by following rather than leading their constituents. A following role has proven to be successful from an electoral standpoint, and there seems to be a preference on the part of islanders for governments that offer benign stability rather than innovative leadership. Indeed, this attitude is so accepted in PEI's current political landscape that, in the provincial election of 2000, the Conservative government returned for a third mandate, winning all but one seat, based on the campaign slogan, 'Let's Continue!' Whether this phenomenon represents a sustained historical change in executive style, or whether it is just an artifact of the good fortunes of the current government, returned for a fourth term in the autumn of 2003, where the economy has been buoyant and no major challenges have been faced, remains to be seen.

Indeed, one of the benefits of the administrative style that de-politicizes decision-making by forcing it into a rational or bureaucratic mode is that it provides no ready target for cynicism, and this relative lack of cynicism by islanders may be both a cause and an effect of this administrative style.

One of the striking components of the PEI executive's administrative style is that it goes to great length to augment public-policy debates by public consultation, which usually takes place in town-hall meeting settings. The executive style of going directly to the citizenry to engage in public consultation and debate contributes to the observation that the delivery of public policy becomes relatively apolitical and managerial-administrative once it arrives at the executive level. This strategy of public consultation also legitimizes prior administrative decisions by providing controlled public information in a cooperative setting. Quite apart from the real and useful input and ideas that can be gained about public opinion, the executive successfully uses public consultation as a kind of soft-sell for public policy.

The executive's administrative style fits very well into some of the more progressive elements in political and public administration norms. An increased reliance on public opinion polling, as in all developed democratic jurisdictions, as well as self-consciously adopted client-centred service delivery have, on the face of it, better allowed the PEI government to follow their electorate with accuracy and confidence; these things, as well as well-developed contemporary information technologies on the island, have provided a continual formal portal for elected representatives to know what their constituents think. Good public opinion information has transformed much of the public service and many executives in other, larger, jurisdictions; in PEI these innovations may have augmented, but not changed, an executive style that has always had a good grip on public opinion as a consequence of small scale and a politically attentive electorate.

Political Competition: Public Policy versus Spoils

In many respects, PEI's provincial politics is about old-style politics, where the robust push and shove of political activity is primarily concerned with gaining the spoils of power within an existing framework. PEI's provincial elections are fought very much like a sporting contest between the red and the blue teams[9]; it does not much matter to the abstraction of the public policy agenda which team forms the government, it only matters who gets to win. The issue is political in terms of winning the advantages of power, including the salaried job of MLA, and the opportunity, diminishing in recent years, to offer government patronage to one's friends. Elections and legislative debate are not, therefore, primarily about public policy – although this clearly remains a component and rhetorically important – but are mostly about gaining and keeping the spoils of power. This tends to divert the machinations of political activity towards competition for competition's sake, and away from substantive dissent about public policy itself. This is not to suggest that the system gives bad public policy; indeed, it may give better public policy as, at the end of the day, most public policy decisions are made on bounded-rational administrative criteria rather than on subjectively skewed political criteria. Political parties tend to be cooperative on substantive issues where the decision is rationally clear, and, like in other good team sports, tend to play cleanly and honestly over the issue of who wins or loses while tacitly agreeing on the general flavour of public policy. This subtle distinction makes for legislative debates that are disproportionately about patronage issues, and leaves the premier and his or her provincial cabinet looking very much like a chief executive officer and a board of governors, albeit one constrained by high public scrutiny. Existing artifacts of the Westminster-style of government – plurality electoral structures favouring majority governments, cabinet solidarity, ministerial accountability and responsibility, and executive control of the provincial public service – all underpin the bureaucratic administrative-style provincial cabinet by their very structure and nature. This leaves what remains of politics to the question of the spoils of power.

Internecine conflict within the ruling caucus and cabinet has historically been small, partly because distribution of the spoils has been the premier's prerogative, and partly because cabinet ministers generally 'owe' their electoral fortune to the premier's success. The general lack of internal competition tends to make for strong governments that habitually deal with policy issues through the use of bureaucratized administrative processes rather than politicized processes.

Indeed, in his study of the 1993 government reorganization under the Liberal government of Catherine Callbeck, John Crossley made the observation that 'The restructuring of the provincial government in P.E.I., then, seems to be driven by the political and bureaucratic elite ... The decision makers are united in their assumptions and goals and the public is compliant.'[10] The 1993 restructuring was itself an attempt to streamline and rationalize the organization of departments and autonomous provincial agencies. Central agencies remained at six, although two new ones were created and three combined, the number of departments shrank from a huge twenty-seven to eight, and autonomous provincial agencies decreased in number from sixteen to nine. This rejigging of institutional structures reflected what Crossley refers to as a decision of a 'united elite' as well as the luxury of increasing ministerial span of control consequent of small scale, lack of complexity, and general consensus in policy-making. The Premier's Office itself has tended to be small in terms of staff size, and the current office relies on a few close advisers for political advice, policy advice, and advice in intergovernmental affairs. It is clear that the small size of the enterprise of governing makes for mostly non-institutionalized and fluid structures in terms of issues, advice, and policy development. Because of the intimate connection between the premier, his or her caucus, and the public, PEI's cabinet tends to be one where the premier dominates, and neither challengers nor lame-duck leaders have ever been in much evidence.

As of 2004, there are seven legislative standing committees. One, the Standing Committee on the Constitution of Canada, is charged with matters concerning the constitution of Canada and is chaired by the premier, in keeping with the dominant role of the first minister with all off-island government interaction. The premier's role in federal-provincial relations is key, and dramatic increases in provincial and federal-provincial summitry since the original days of the patriation of the Canadian constitution have reinforced this standing, both in the eyes of the public, and in the realities of negotiation. Federal-provincial relations, the Council of Maritime Premiers (1972–2000), the Council of Atlantic Premiers (from May 2000), and the Conference of New England Governors and Eastern Canadian Premiers (NEG/ECP) are entirely the premier's bailiwick. The added historic fact that PEI has had long-serving premiers over the span of several electoral mandates, including the current premier, has lent diplomatic dignity and authority to the position. During the potato wart crisis of 2001–2, where potato exports to the United States were stopped by what were widely seen as protectionist measures by the Americans, all the Island's political elites, including the premier, the minister in charge of agriculture, federal members of Parliament (which, following tradition, included a federal cabinet minister), as well as agricultural industry leaders, rallied as one unified group to pressure both Ottawa and the Americans for a solution. From the provincial perspective, there was no need for substantive internal political debate, and the provincial executive's role was not about policy per se, but rather about management and political extra-provincial lobbying. The leadership shown by the premier and his executive was clearly different from the ability to make independent policy choices.

The Standing Committee on Public Accounts, charged with matters concerning the public accounts of the province and the annual report of the auditor general, is chaired by a member of the official opposition, which both limits government action to probity, and, in some sense offers institutionalized evidence of the administrative role of the legislature, and by implication, of the executive.

Only the Liberals and the Conservatives have historically formed governments in PEI, and they are widely thought of as interchangeable from a public-policy perspective. Indeed, when well-known island politician and former mayor of Charlottetown, Ian 'Tex' MacDonald switched his life-long party allegiance from the Conservatives to run for the leadership of the Liberals in 1996, he publicly stated in effect that 'there was no difference between the two parties anyway'; that he *said* this drew criticism, but the *fact* of it really did not. The Liberal and Conservative parties are quintessentially brokerage parties in PEI, and play to an ideologically homogeneous electorate. While they must attempt to differentiate themselves in public policy, particularly in electoral competitions, the primary underlying motive is to gain the spoils (which, as time goes by are increasingly limited) of governing. This leaves the business of public policy as mostly a managerial function. In instances where debate does occur about substantive public policy issues, the distance between the sides is proportionately smaller than is the case in most other jurisdictions. It is not uncommon, for example, for private members bills to be considered and passed by the legislature, although almost all bills remain government bills. It also appears that a tacit understanding exists between these two parties as to what is fair game in debates and political attacks, and what is not; it would seem that the object is to score political points without really damaging good governance – for which the politically attentive electorate would punish transgressors – and to avoid being too critical of privileges possessed by the executive because the opposition hopes one day to win these for themselves.

PEI has a relatively homogeneous demography and, arguably, a great consensus concerning public policy, so it is ironic that PEI has a very politically attentive public. Much of this participation can be explained by the disproportionately high number of full-time government employees in PEI, the many people with insecure part-time and seasonal jobs, and the past existence and current perception of overt provincial government patronage for scarce jobs, business grants, and the like. Again, politics is mostly fuelled by self-interest in allocating spoils and obtaining government largess rather than being about substantive public policy debate.

Changes of Administrative Style over Time

Historically, PEI's public service has tended to recruit from the province's small population, and has looked to the norms and standards developed locally and internally rather than those existing in other jurisdictions. Islanders have tended to distrust the centrist initiatives of the national government, and have relied a great deal on a tough, down-home pragmatism that some maintain derives from the poor rural roots of much of the island's population. An important external influence on provincial administrative styles comes from the interaction and cross-over recruitment between the provincial government and the federal government.

There have been two main incursions into the culture of the provincial public service that have shaped the administrative style of PEI's executive. These are the Comprehensive Development Plan and its federal regional development counterparts – currently the Atlantic Canada Opportunities Agency (ACOA) – and the decision in 1979 to move the Department of Veterans Affairs to Charlottetown. Both developments led to the introduction of off-island public administration norms to the provincial bureaucracy. The Prince Edward Island Federal Council (its antecedents that began forming in 1982), is composed of senior federal officials whose mandate is to provide leadership, collaborate on, and coordinate federal government initiatives in the context of PEI. This functionally-driven horizontal structure has spawned a multitude of other institutional contacts that bring together federal, provincial, and in some cases, municipal officials. For example, a recently created Managers' Network exists involving management from all three levels of government. As well, secondments and appointments across jurisdictional lines are increasingly common, and professional development activities are often shared. The 'parochialism which bordered on the xenophobic'[11] that was once used to describe PEI's political culture is now only slightly in evidence in the provincial public service, and PEI's executive style has, in some ways, followed the rationalization and professionalization that has occurred in the ranks of its own bureaucracy.

From a public administration point of view, PEI has benefited enormously from its small size and for its consequent desirability as a test site for various pilot projects. The province has in recent years, been used to evaluate a number of public-sector innovations, the result being that the character of the provincial public service has become an odd amalgam of the very traditional and the very avant garde. That there is a tradition of prominent grass-roots politics seems to have contributed to the happy marriage between these two characteristics.

Administrative styles of the provincial executives change as the expectations and constraints of the broader political environment change. One of the most striking evolutions in Canadian political culture over the last two decades has been what Neil Nevitte describes as a 'decline in deference.'[12] Deference to the leadership and authority of government have radically decreased everywhere in Canada. While a number of responses might be expected in terms of executive administrative styles among provinces, in PEI it is arguable that, either the deference for PEI's executive was never that high anyway, or that, if deference has declined, the administrative style of personalism fits it well in any event. In either case, it favours the continuation of informal interest mediation that has typified PEI's government.

Certainly, the deference to charismatic authority so prevalent in the days of René Lévesque's charm or Pierre Trudeau-as-Magus is gone, replaced by popular culture's cynicism regarding political leaders. Moral authority, based on ethical and ideological sentiments, has also gone the way of the end-of-ideology hypothesis of twentieth-century history. What is left is the authority of the manager, and administration qua administration. Indeed, the rise of the public manager in the rank and file of the public service may have permeated up the hierarchy to the ministerial level, as the corporate cultures of government departments in PEI have succumbed to the new public management processes of the early 1990s. In sum, there appears to be a change in public and public service taste away from traditional forms of authority and towards credentialism, expertise, and the organization man. To function successfully, in both electoral terms and in public opinion, PEI's executive has sought to present managerial competence with respect to public policy as the overriding virtue.

Centralism and the Premier's Role

A common hypothesis in Canadian politics is that the federal government has become more centralist over time, and that the provinces have been mimicking this trend. Donald Savoie has been a proponent of this theory; earlier work by Mancur Olson on the theory of collective action, and Michel's 'iron law of oligarchy' or Gunnar Myrdal's concept of 'cumulative causation,' where power begets more power, would all seem to support this centralist hypothesis.[13] Empirical evidence, however, does not maintain the centralist hypothesis in the case of PEI's executive, although it does sustain, to some degree, the hypothesis of a prime-minister-centred cabinet.

PEI's cabinet has, for the most part, functioned as a single unit. One argument is that the importance of federal funding and Ottawa's policies in the key sectors of agriculture and fisheries overlays any ministerial action with the politics of federal-provincial relations. This near-continual outside presence in provincial public policy-making forces a kind of cabinet solidarity where decisions must either be collegial or be subject to the premier's authority, in order to bring enough combined weight of expertise and political clout to bargain effectively with Ottawa. Indeed, Mancur Olson's theory of collective action would support this hypothesis; small numbers of high-stake interest parties, like PEI's cabinet, do indeed carry disproportionate power relative to the Canadian whole, and the benefits of cooperation at the provincial level are so obvious that a consensus may include the four federal MPs, the four senators, and, not infrequently, the official provincial opposition. While it is true that spirited adversarial politics occurs on the subsequent division of the federal pie, when competing for that pie, government, the opposition, and indeed, all of PEI's elites, tend to form a united coalition in support of the provincial executive.

That PEI's premier is the spokesperson for government policy, the focus of the public's attention in political debates, and chooses his or her cabinet, itself supports the idea of a prime-minister-centred cabinet. The premiers of PEI have varied considerably in terms of charismatic appeal, but, for reasons of political culture cited above, it is doubtful whether any could muster the power around his or her own office to unequivocally dominate public policy even though they were and are clearly bosses of their own cabinets. The province has had very powerful premiers with respect to their own executives, but it is unlikely that they could successfully exercise power in the manner of Newfoundland's Joey Smallwood's mercurial excesses, Ontario's Mike Harris's ideological excesses, or Alberta's Ralph Klein's personal excesses, and get away with it. PEI's premiers have always operated in a constrained, broader, political environment lying outside of cabinet and the Legislative Assembly; it is these broader factors that circumscribe the scope of their power, if not their power per se.

Indeed, the premier's personal staff has been too small to participate effectively in controlling the levers of power, and seems to concentrate on the premier's electoral and political interests. Nor can it be supported that PEI's is an institutional cabinet, where the premier's power lies in being the architect of the cabinet and departmental structures, or that PEI's departments act unaided and independent of either the premier or cabinet colleagues. Again, being a small province in a big federation forces a kind of pragmatic and rational collectivism on the provincial executive. Institutional structures of PEI's government have evolved, have been changed and modified over time, often by the initiative of premiers, but institutional structures have not been an instrument of a premier's power, nor have they determined the exercise of power.

Another constraint on the executive's power, and a factor in the creation of its low-key and sometimes apolitical style, is that PEI has a greater integration of elites across all sectors of society than would be the case in larger jurisdictions. The small number of people dictates that the social sphere and self-interests of business, educational, legal, and other elites are conjoined in multifaceted ways. That island elites are even more static in terms of emigration – those doing well in a society seldom choose to move – contributes even more to the old boy/girl phenomenon. The huge importance of government-sponsored spoils to all sectors of the island makes the stable elite network rewarding to its participants. In contrast, larger jurisdictions that rely less on government largesse and involve more people tend to have more autonomous elites. Such elites often tend to be adversarial to one another, and in this situation one would expect to find a more autonomous provincial executive exerting its power through one of the three administrative styles described in the Introduction.

As PEI's provincial executive is bound up in numerous ways to the society that it governs, the constraints in public policy-making tend to be political and social rather than institutional and structural. This is particularly true given that the two competing political parties have large, socially broad, active memberships. There is evidence that constituent interests are communicated and dealt with by that part of the government – often a minister himself or herself – who is most sympathetic to the individual involved, rather than by the official who is the most appropriate part of government in terms of expertise or departmental responsibility. All of these serve to make the administrative style of the executive one of *subjectivism* or *personalism*. Public policy in PEI is far less constrained by disinterested organizational structure than it is in most other provinces, and relies more heavily on pre-existing, nonstructural, subjective relationships organized around individual self-interest.

Subjectivism as a part of executive administrative style is also evident in the enforcement style of policy decisions. Enforcement tends to be by persuasion and negotiation, particularly in the latest government, rather than by coercion and legal processes. Since the introduction of the Canadian Charter of Rights and Freedoms, however, PEI, like the rest of Canada, has seen more legal challenges to government actions. Still, the benefits of a subjectivist relationship with the executive serve most of the island's elites. The major court challenges that have been launched based on the Charter have related to patronage. Remarkably, the underlying principle remains; these court challenges were about getting economic spoils, and not primarily about fairness, justice, or public policy, even though that is the rhetoric by which these challenges were launched.

The phenomenon of integrated elites in PEI is the reason that the interpretation of the province's executive style as clientism (described by S.J.R. Noel as 'a relationship between patron and client' that 'typically involve the bestowal of material rewards, advantages, security, or access to opportunities ... in return for his client's assumed reciprocal bestowal of loyalty or service ... and political support')[14] is only partly true. Certainly a relationship does exist between many islanders and their government's executive where favours are exchanged; yet these relationships have not the asymmetrical power structure of a patron and client. PEI's executive needs the support of the island's elite as well as the rank-and-file party members, and spoils politics is conducted in this rich arena of well-matched competitors rather than a typical patron-client relationship.

PEI's government has seen a historical incremental progression away from the more overt aspects of spoils politics and patronage; the probable explanation of this is that, over time, the norms of a Weberian bureaucracy, and a heightened demand for fairness among constituents, has made it less and less tenable to retain this aspect of traditional government. The managerial administrative style of PEI's executive, has, especially since the financial difficulties of the early 1990s, coupled with the introduction of the New Public Management, been supported by the institutionalization of many of the more controversial public decisions. The 7.5 per cent rollback of all provincial sector employees' salaries in 1994 – hugely unpopular among public service employees but applauded by much of the general electorate – also forced change and rationalization into the provincial bureaucracy. For example, many issues relating to the regulation of private interests are dealt with by the Island Regulatory and Appeals Commission (IRAC), which is a quasi-judicial arms-length body created in 1991 in place of a number of more specific regulatory boards. The replacement of the Civil Service Commission created in 1963 with the Staffing and Classi-fication Board in 1993, and then the Public Service Commission, an independent and impartial agency, in 1999, were those executives' attempts to tie their own hands with rational institutional structures. The same has been true with the introduction of arms-length public tendering processes through the Public Purchasing Act of 1985 affect-ing all government departments and some, but not all, agencies. Gen-erally only appointments to boards and commissions remain in the unfettered subjective control of the executive. The creation of bureau-cratized employment classifications is significant as it is an institu-tional attempt, through the use of law and organizational structure, to wrest control from sitting MLAs and somehow change the culture of patronage. The Freedom of Information and Protection of Privacy Act, passed in 2002 after many years of stonewalling governments, has pro-vided another nail in the coffin of subjectivism in provincial politics, and is likely to force the executive style even further away from spoils politics and informal interest mediation, as the protection of secrecy is lost.

Outside observers to PEI's government structure will be struck by its simplicity and its traditional hierarchies of authority. This is because legal-institutional factors do not drive decision-making; rather, depart-ments and the public service generally just act to fulfill their Weberian role of implementing executive decisions. Traditionally within the cab-inet, decisions are made consensually under the unchallenged leader-ship of the premier. There are no internal or institutional challenges to this top-down hierarchical power; rather, internal constraints to execu-tive decision making are almost entirely due to apolitical bounded-rational administrative considerations. External constraints are rigor-ous; a broadly consensual populace and a seamless single elite already define most major policy choices. Describing the relations between the premier, ministers, deputy-ministers, central agencies, and cabinet committees, in order to discover pockets of independent power and decision-making is fruitless; the values are broadly consensual, the relations are implicitly cooperative, and the decisions are mostly apo-litically bounded-rational administrative. This should not be surprising considering that premier, cabinet, and deputy ministers are all the products a broadly consensual population, and that the amount and complexity of public policy to be considered is well within the range and scope of the premier and his or her small cabinet. Rather than examining institutionalized groups or even positions within government to define decision-making power, an astute political observer would see that, given the small scale of governance on PEI, it would be more productive to look at individuals, their political and administrative abilities, and their friendliness to the premier and the cabinet. These idiosyncratic yet socially circumscribed personal attributes are the real keys to understanding executive decision-making in PEI, and not the legal-institutional structures themselves.

Conclusion

The administrative style of PEI's executive is, in many ways, unique to its small and sharply defined jurisdiction. The province's small size reduces organizational complexity to a point where the complexity itself does not engender a structural-institutional constraint. Thus, to try to apply models of neo-institutionalism, organizational process, or bureaucratic politics appropriate to the larger and more heterogeneous jurisdictions, such as to other provinces, is futile. The executive reflects a more seamless administrative relationship to its elites and citizenry than in other provinces, and consequently, its style is far more determined by socio-cultural factors than by structural and institutional factors. The dependence of this province on federal support has created a provincial political milieu that tends to support a communitarian viewpoint while simultaneously allowing for lively political competition motivated by spoils. The administrative style of cabinet, thereby, is managerial regarding public policy issues proper, is currently mostly reactive in its initiatives, and tends to pay conscious regard to spoils given to a broad elite and the government's grass-roots electoral support. Changes in government structure have incrementally increased the apolitical managerial function by diffusing some of the more controversial aspects of spoils politics. Historically, and into the future, it is clear that an overlay of informality, subjectivism, and personalism remain as the key factors of PEI's executive styles.

Chapter 7

Who Governs in Quebec?
Revolving Premiers and Reforms

LUC BERNIER

Who governs? In the Canadian tradition, the answer is supposed to be the cabinet. As has been suggested by other authors in this volume, this cabinet has in many jurisdictions in Canada been successively traditional, departmentalized, institutionalized and could be now 'post-institutionalized.' Not all provinces have completed this full cycle of development, however, and have not achieved a full measure of increased autonomy of the executive from the legislature. There are several reasons for these differences. Compared to the federal government Savoie has studied, for example, one would presume that provincial governments are easier to govern from the centre because they are smaller and easier to coordinate, not requiring the elaborate machinery of government that exists in Ottawa. It can also be said that attempts to improve coordination such as the use of strategic planning, have been more successful in some of the provinces than in Ottawa.[1] And, since the provinces are closer to the delivery of the services of the welfare state, focusing on health, social services, and education, consequently they have had to keep delivering services under increasing fiscal pressure. Unlike Ottawa, they cannot offload these duties very far, as even regional and municipal governments fall under provincial jurisdiction.

This chapter outlines the extent to which the organization of executive government in Quebec has followed the general pattern discussed by Savoie and Dunn. It will be seen that the traditional cabinet ended in Quebec with the death of Maurice Duplessis. A departmental cabinet gave birth to the Quiet Revolution under the Lesage Liberal regime, and the institutionalized cabinet rules to this day. The most important social and political transformation in Quebec over the last forty years has been the modernization of the state.[2] This modernization, coupled with the emergence of the Parti Québécois, challenged the legitimacy of the Canadian state.[3] This issue continues to influence all the other issues discussed below. From the modernization of the Quebec state comes the current administrative style as defined in the introductory chapter: 'a more or less consistent and long-term set of institutionalized patterns of politico-administrative relationships, norms and procedures.'

The short premiership of Lucien Bouchard involved probably the closest Quebec came to having a premier-centred cabinet, but for reasons developed later in this chapter, an institutionalized cabinet still governs. Although Quebec shares some features of the post-institutional model, such as centralization of communications in the Premier's Office, it lacks other aspects of this model. Most prominently, central agencies such as the Treasury do not work to serve the Premier's Office.

According to Savoie, premiers or prime ministers change but the institution of the central power continues. In the introduction to his book, *Governing from the Centre*, he argues that not only the Parliament but also the cabinet has lost power to the Premier's Office in recent years. Others, however, would argue that there have been two processes at work in Canadian executive government. The premier might have more power but also there has been more autonomy developed in the system of administration as a whole, because the implementation of policy has changed under the tenets of New Public Management, becoming much more manager-centric and autonomous. In Quebec, it is argued below, this second path has been followed. With the growing dissatisfaction with the state since the 1970s, executive power is now shared between the premier and the bureaucracy. New mechanisms have been developed within and around the margins of the state that makes the centralization of power in the hands of the premier unlikely.

The Early Cabinet System, the Quiet Revolution, and Its Aftermath

In the 1950s, though Quebec's society was evolving in a fashion similar to that of other parts of Canada or North America,[4] the development of its political structures and state apparatus was lagging behind. While Quebec had developed into an urban and industrial society, its political institutions remained very much modelled on those adopted in the previous century. Political and administrative development lagged far behind socio-economic transformations and caused considerable friction in Quebec society and government. Although strongly opposed to his Liberal predecessors Gouin and Taschereau, Duplessis's Union Nationale government maintained the same strong-leader model it had inherited from the Liberals. This is apparent in many of the formal institutions for controlling patronage in the civil service, for example. Quebec was the last province to establish a Civil Service Commission, in 1943, and it had only very limited powers until its reform under the Lesage Liberals in 1965.

The reform of the Civil Service Commission was only one of a number of reforms brought about during a period of accelerated political modernization and the transformation of the provincial state called the Quiet Revolution, which occurred in the early 1960s. The changes were triggered by the Duplessis's death in September 1959. His successor, Paul Sauvé, implemented the first reforms but died suddenly after only one hundred days in power. Under Jean Lesage, elected in 1960 against a third Union Nationale leader, Antonio Barrette, the pace of transformation accelerated. *Rattrapage*, or catching up with development elsewhere, became the motto. Looking at the gap between the needs and the limited possibilities of the antiquated provincial state, the Liberals increased their reformist efforts. Successive governments continued to make incremental reforms until the 1980 referendum results, the 1982 recession, and a dominant ideological movement toward liberalism in the 1980s put an end to the state-led reform efforts associated with the Quiet Revolution.

The Traditional Cabinet in Quebec: From Confederation to Duplessis

Maurice Duplessis's Union Nationale government's second term in office lasted from 1944 until his death in 1959. He was certainly the archetypal traditional leader of a government, operating with a state apparatus with no autonomy from politics and only very limited capacity to affect changes in society. As Gérard Pelletier once wrote, he had 'les idées courtes mais le bras long,'[5] a way of saying that his personal power was as strong as his lack of imagination.

Duplessis exercised far stronger control over the activities of the state than have any of his successors. After him began the two-terms tradition of electoral politics and rotating party leaders that has lasted to date. The Liberals were in power for six years starting in 1960, followed by the Union Nationale for one term under two premiers. Then came the first six years of Robert Bourassa's Liberal government, followed by nine years of the Parti Québécois under two different leaders. From 1985 Bourassa again served for two terms, although he was replaced by Daniel Johnson towards the end of his second term, and again was followed by two terms of the Parti Québécois under three different premiers. In 2003 the Liberals were again returned to office, this time under former federal Progressive Conservative party cabinet minister and leader, Jean Charest. Changing the government in office, and leader, has avoided the concentration of power that lasting prime ministers such as Pierre Trudeau or Jean Chrétien, and provincial premiers such as Duplessis, have enjoyed. Such turnover limits the capacity of any premier to increase his power vis-à-vis his cabinet and strengthens the ability of the administration to carve out a separate sphere of influence from the political executive.

The Departmental or Institutional Cabinet: From the Quiet Revolution to the Present Day

The term 'Quiet Revolution' encompasses three notions: the transformation of Quebec nationalism, the transfer of powers from civil society to the state, and the confrontation between the state and the traditional elites who dominated Quebec until then. General elections in most subsequent years, including the two most recent, in 1998 and 2003, have been run for the most part on what should be done about the inheritance of the Quiet Revolution. How much state is required in Quebec, and how it should be controlled, remain crucial issues in the province as a result of the inheritance of the Quiet Revolution.

Over the two decades following the Quiet Revolution, from 1960 to 1980, the Quebec government emerged as a mature and complex institution capable of governing in its own interests. This occurred through a process of what Young, Faucher, and Blais have defined as the best example of province-building or the use of the provincial state apparatus to lead the development of the economy and society of a province. Since the early days of the 1960s, the Quebec state became active in the economic sector with the creation of large and powerful public enterprises in key economic sectors. The nationalization of hydroelectric corporations and the creation of Hydro-Québec in 1966 is one such example. Another is the creation of the Caisse de dépôt et placement

Table 7.1   Reforms of the Public Sector in Quebec

Year	Project
1981	Rapport Bisaillon
1983	Loi de la Fonction Publique
1985	Pour une rénovation de l'administration publique
1986	Rapports Gobeil, Scowen, Fortier
1989	Politique d'évaluation des programmes
1991	Politique d'amélioration des services aux citoyens
1992	Opération Réalignement
1993	Loi sur l'Imputabilité des Sous-ministres et dirigeants d'organismes
1994	Unités autonomes de service et responsabilisation
1994	Politique de déréglementation (reprise en 1996)
1996	Loi anti-déficits
1997	Allegement réglementaire
1997	Loi sur les 'départs assistés'
1997	Rapport Facal
1998	GIRES, Inforoute gouvernementale
2000	Loi 82 sur la modernisation de l'administration publique
2003	Réingénierie de l'État

du Québec (Quebec Deposit and Investment Fund) created in 1965 to administer billions of dollars of government pension and insurance funds. Simard maintains that to understand what happened we should look at the number of agencies created and who they were confronting, and that state-building in this sense has been innovative in Quebec. McRoberts agrees, but has suggested that the ultimate result of the Quiet Revolution was not quantitative but qualitative, its essence being transfer of power to the state.[7]

This is not to say that all of the efforts and activities associated with the Quiet Revolution were successful. Some difficulties were encountered, since creating a large state apparatus cannot be simply improvised. As Table 7.1 illustrates, the number of reforms undertaken in Quebec in this period was necessary to correct earlier problems following from the Duplessis period. However, the post-Duplessis period of state-building in Quebec was less a planned, despite what some participants have said, than an iterative process that has led to interesting and sometimes unexpected results. The results of reforms in areas such as health, education, and economic policies were generally positive.

However, as will be discussed below, they were not good enough for an important part of the population and have engendered new problems for the Quebec state. Before we can move onto this discussion of contemporary problems, however, we will turn to the development of the institutionalized cabinet in Quebec.

There are not many documents about the activities of the 'centre of the state' in Quebec during the Quiet Revolution. Civil servants have not written much about their activities. Claude Morin is very much the exception in having written a personal account of the way the five premiers he served used to work, although this is limited by the fact that Morin's expertise lay in federal-provincial relations and not more direct province-building activities per se.[8] Only a few ministers have written their memoirs and these accounts are often quite self-serving, usually giving the authors more influence than they had in reality.

Nevertheless, it is fair to say that under Lesage, Quebec had the most classical, institutional cabinet the province has known. Lesage had a very strong cabinet with prominent and long-serving government ministers launching the reforms of the Quiet Revolution, with Lesage himself orchestrating the show.[9] His successor Union Nationale premiers, David Johnson and Jean Jacques Bertrand, had much weaker cabinets. The Liberal government of Robert Bourassa presided over the kind of state-building associated with contemporary Quebec, with a cabinet a bit stronger than his predecessor's, but it was only after 1976 under the leadership of ex-Lesage cabinet minister and Parti Québécois premier René Lévesque that the cabinet truly became fully institutionalized once again.

The first Lévesque cabinet was similar in strength to that of the Lesage years if we consider the quality of ministers assembled. The same cannot be said of the PQ's second 1981 cabinet, as Graham Fraser has noted.[10] The true originality of the first Lévesque cabinet was the creation of four super-ministers of state responsible for social development, economic development, land-use planning, and parliamentary reform. Finance Minister Jacques Parizeau and Intergovernmental Affairs Minister Claude Morin, who were then the only members-elect other than Lévesque with experience (as civil servants or advisers) at the cabinet level, did not want to be ministers of state, understanding how much power a minister derives from a real ministry. Nevertheless, the ministry of state idea was judged a success by later Quebec governments and since then ministers of state have existed in various forms. Immediately prior to the 2003 election, in the last PQ government,

Bernard Landry appointed both senior ministers and junior ministers of state to assist them.

The return of Bourassa in 1985 was an era of little management of the state. Bourassa's early efforts to be more business-oriented involved a reduction in the role of government in the Quebec economy and the failure of the Meech Lake Accord from 1987 to 1990 both ate up much of the time and attention of the provincial government and, ultimately, undermined Bourassa's legitimacy as provincial leader. His second mandate was certainly not an era of a strong leader. Daniel Johnson replaced Bourassa for a few months. Then, following the Liberal defeat at the polls, Jacques Parizeau was PQ premier for one year – a period almost exclusively used to prepare for the 1995 sovereignty referendum. He resigned following the narrow defeat of the yes side in that referendum and was replaced by former federal cabinet minister and Bloc Québécois founder Lucien Bouchard. The charismatic Bouchard did not enjoy the day-to-day operation of governing. He was at his best during the great ice storm of the late 1990s and during the referendum campaign. The Parti Québécois has always been a difficult party to manage for premiers and Bouchard, as Lévesque a decade before, had to deal with it. Unlike Lévesque, though, Bouchard had to cope with a governing party with whom he was not strongly associated. The possibility that, as the Union Nationale before it, the Parti Québécois might be a generational party[11] whose supporters failed to replace themselves, added to Bouchard's difficulty, creating a sense of emergency among supporters who felt the pressures of a seemingly inevitable demographic evolutionary slide. Bouchard, like Landry who followed in his footsteps, was caught between a population which did not want another referendum and party militants who wouldn't stay without one. Landry had stronger roots in the party and had a bit of an easier time with his party, but ultimately he could not reconcile its desires with those of the electorate.

The styles and charisma of premiers, however, were not the only elements that shaped administrative reforms and the development of an institutionalized cabinet in Quebec. The second Lévesque government was badly hurt by the 1982 recession, as the second Bourassa government was by the 1992 economic downturn. As elsewhere, the state in Quebec had to be transformed for a variety of reasons: because the state was strapped for cash, because the downsizing of the civil service left the state undermanned, because the image of government and of politicians had become tarnished over the years, because too many jurisdictional disputes persisted, because past reforms were not always successful, and because technology made it possible to alter some of the basic operations and configuration of the public service. These factors have been discussed elsewhere.[12] In this section we will explore the more specific transformation of the role of the state in Quebec, in particular the use of policy instruments that were not even considered previously, such as privatization, deregulation, outsourcing, and partnerships.[13]

In the 1970s the social forces in Quebec that had wrought the interventionist state began to crack and break apart. Social movements started criticizing technocratic management of public services, and union federations became more radical and grew disenchanted with the state. Meanwhile, the business community criticized state intervention in the daily operations of companies and called for a return to private enterprise. The economic crisis, rising unemployment, and increasing international competition were therefore accompanied by a wave of social criticism and a reconsideration of existing institutions. It became clear to all social actors that statism had exhausted its capacity to sustain economic recovery and maintain political support.

By the early 1980s the rise of the French-speaking bourgeoisie had ended the previous debate over who would control the future of the Quebec economy. Globalization also changed the terms of the debate on the province's political and economic future as it was clear that the Quebec state could no longer go it alone; it had to find partners. It had to be part of a broader system of continental and global governance. The limitations of the state/market tandem calls for a new form of regulation, which can take one of two routes. One is neoliberal regulation, which relies on the market as the explicit and exclusive regulatory instrument (at least in its discourse) and understands the general interest as the sum of individual interests. The alternative is not the approach of the 1960s but a form of regulation based on a new mixed economy and a style of governance that involves the public, the private sector, and the social economy. The migration of some functions of the state to the private sector, the social sector, cooperatives and so forth – in short, to civil society – is a significant trend today.

The Quebec model that emerged from the Quiet Revolution derived from a hierarchical approach, the limitations of which have become clear. Since the 1980s Quebec society has been searching for new ways of doing things. With less hierarchical government coordination, new economic experiments have been launched, focusing on consultation and partnership among social actors based on new relationships that promote quality, economies of variety, and worker participation: issue tables, industrial clusters, networked companies, partnership-based labour relations, social contracts. In 1979 the government had proposed a new economic strategy, under which the state shed its role as entrepreneur and organized economic summits, where all the players in the economy were brought together and asked to work with the government and build unity around economic recovery objectives. While there was widespread distrust, in the 1980s some players did sign on. For example, the Fédération des travailleurs du Québec (FTQ) founded the Solidarity Fund. Business associations also agreed to cooperate, but the influence of neoliberal discourse should not be discounted. It was evident in the debates on the deficit, on poverty reduction, and on globalization. The consultation process was racked by conflict and yielded compromise rather then consensus.[14]

The search for new ways of doing things was stepped up in the early 1990s. The state supported several strategic value-added sectors in order to capitalize on its integration into the global economy. The Quebec model therefore has its own identity, combining a strong interest in free trade, defence of Quebec's cultural distinctiveness, and promotion of social solidarity.[15] Quebec is making the transition from one form of governance to another. In such system, the role of the premier, the central agencies, and cabinet has changed. Decision-making has become more consensus-based.[16] The result of this evolution is the socio-economic summits that have taken place since the early 1980s. They constitute an institutional construction that is central to policy-making.

Figures 7.1 and 7.2 represent the organizational charts of the Ministry of the Executive Council and of the Treasury Board, respectively, under the last PQ government of Bernard Landry. The current system in Quebec includes six ministerial committees as shown in Figure 7.1. The official documents mention a committee of priorities but it does not appear on the official organizational chart. The efficiency of the former Priorities Committee has been questioned several times. For reasons of sensitivity, the Native Affairs Secretariat has been kept at the centre of the state as has Intergovernmental Affairs. The Treasury Board is an organization in charge of controlling the other parts of the state and in charge of drafting coordinating policies, while it is also supposed to support the departments in various ways. Initially, the Modernization Secretariat was at the Executive Council but was moved to the Treasury Board as one of its eight branches. The core of

Figure 7.1. Ministère du Conseil exécutif

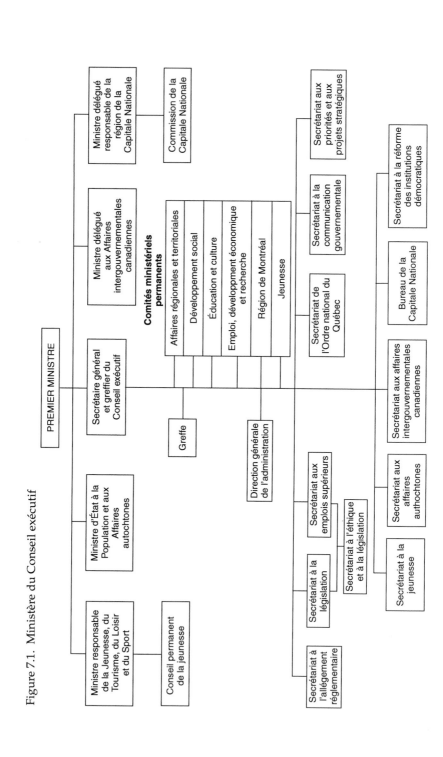

Figure 7.2. Secrétariat du Conseil du trésor Québec

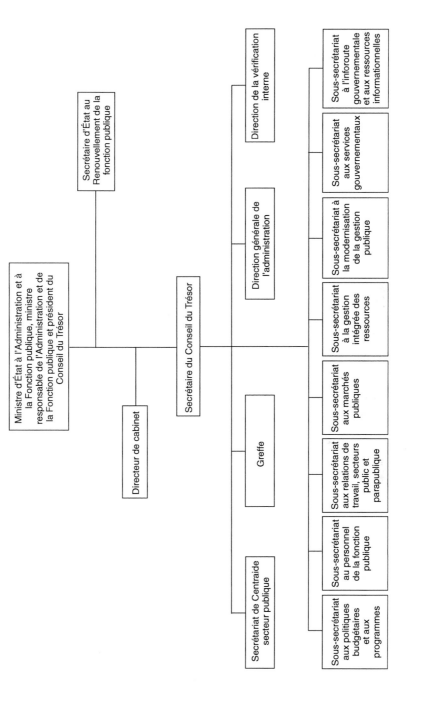

the Treasury Board remains the control of expenditures, although the management of all human resources is done here.

Revolving Premiers and Central Agencies

Why has the centralization of power been limited in Quebec? Why has the province continued to utilize an institutionalized cabinet system rather than move towards a post-institutional or premier-centred one, as has occurred, for example, in Ontario and British Columbia as well as at the federal level? The first thing that comes to mind when we think of the administrative style in Quebec is that only a few premiers had a lasting influence, simply because the others were in power for too short a period of time. Quebec has had thirteen premiers since 1944. Four of them held the position only a few months because of illness or because they were nominated at the end of a second term of a party in power. René Lévesque did not finish his mandate. Neither did Robert Bourassa nor Lucien Bouchard in the 1990s. Consequently, twice in a decade, the Quebec government was comatose. Even the charismatic Lucien Bouchard lacked legitimacy, ruling for three years without an election. His successor, Bernard Landry also did so for two years.

To the problems caused by the frequent turnover of leaders we can add the multiple reorganizations that short-term leaders have caused at the centre of government, reducing the ability of senior ministers to become entrenched in their ministries. Daniel Johnson, who replaced Robert Bourassa in 1993–94, reorganized the Quebec government severely, reducing the number of ministers. In order to win his referendum, Jacques Parizeau played again with the number of departments in order to promote more regionalization, a game Bouchard played again a year after the referendum. Parizeau did make one original move, keeping for himself the Cultural Affairs portfolio usually devoted in Quebec to a full-time minister. After the 1998 election, Bouchard reshuffled his cabinet without much continuity with the past. Landry in early 2002 expanded the number of ministers from twenty to thirty-six, a decision he admitted later was a mistake.

As a result of these turnovers and reorganizations, Quebec officials have become very good at writing policies that have seldom been put into operation. Central agencies have worked to launch a plethora of new reforms, as Table 7.1 illustrates. Reforms have been initiated without waiting for results, creating a culture of permanent change – a culture grounded in the necessity always to do more with less resources. Taken one by one, all these initiatives could be all seen as failures. Collectively, however, they have helped shaped a more efficient civil service, while undermining the ability of premiers and central agencies to control it. They also maintain the sense of urgency within the civil service of the Quiet Revolution, of the need to catch up with transformations elsewhere. It could be argued that the New Public Management movement caught the attention of officials in Quebec because the idea of launching a new revolution was appealing by reference to idealized period of change and transformation associated with the Quiet Revolution.

Despite this general tendency, some ministries in Quebec have nevertheless kept important powers. Before becoming premier, Bernard Landry was minister of finance, as was Jacques Parizeau. His former department has kept some of its autonomy and reputation. It has now integrated with its long-time rivals in the economic arena, the Department of Trade and Industry and the smaller Department of Research. Among various elements that make Finance important, one of the assistant deputy ministers there became secretary to the cabinet, following his minister to the Ministere du Conseil exécutif. Finance in Quebec has kept the 'fire department' mentality it has always had, never having integrated the policy planning mode now in vogue. An oddity in the Westminster tradition, there is a law in Quebec that has established the powers of Finance to be the equivalent of the Privy Council. Fiscal expenditures are the preferred Finance Department way of doing things, rather than the traditional mode of state intervention in the economy in Quebec.

The continued or rising importance of the Department of Finance has also been paralleled by the evolution of state-owned enterprises in Quebec away from their productivist origins. State-owned enterprises in the province have become more financial institutions than they were, leaving actual production activities to the private sector. They now intervene as shareholders in projects or guarantee loans to private companies. After the Michael Porter model, Quebec's government and state enterprises have moved to foster a particular type of hi-tech economic development strategy. The new economy has been specifically targeted: software companies and bio-tech enterprises have been helped by the venture capital institutions of the public and private sector but also by the trade unions. The best-known example is the Fonds de solidarité, which is a union fund that attracts pension money through generous tax deduction.[17] Money is invested for profit but also for considerations of indigenous economic development. Some economists, looking at the fact that the unemployment rate has remained higher than the Canadian average for a long period, argue that Quebec would be better off without so much state intervention in the economy. However, others argue that without such instruments, the Quebec economy would be even in worst shape. All this said, state intervention in the economy is likely to remain important. When asked how to reduce the size of the state, decision-makers in Quebec have a tendency to give examples from Europe where the welfare state is more developed and economic indicators are also very good.[18]

The Treasury Board has also managed to survive and prosper over the years of budgetary restraint; it currently enjoys greater power over expenditures than the entourage of the premier and the Conseil exécutif. Moreover in Quebec, Treasury Board has integrated the Office des ressources humaines, the equivalent of the Civil Service Commission, into its operations. On the other hand, although it is still a prestigious cabinet position, the Intergovernmental Affairs job is not what it used to be. This small office, located within the Conseil exécutif, in the Landry government at least, played a much less central role than it used too, simply because, due to the clash between the official party line upholding sovereignty and the reality or popular disapproval indicated by the polls, the government had no plan or possibility of doing much on the issue.

As in Ottawa, the office of the Quebec premier has to spend a lot of time doing damage control because of ministers who have been of rather 'provincial' quality. As Graham Fraser wrote about the Lévesque cabinet after 1981,[19] the Landry cabinet in Quebec was not particularly stellar. And it is not clear that the Conseil exécutif always recruited the best and the brightest. This is not to say that skilled and dedicated civil servants do not work there but that the aura of excellence of the Privy Council found in other Canadian jurisdictions does not exist in Quebec City. It also could be said that, as in Ottawa, specific policies should not be managed from the centre. For example, family policy in Quebec has suffered from its origin in the Priority Committee Secretariat because there was no minister pushing for its development in cabinet as is usually the case.

In Quebec, as elsewhere in Canada, the relations between politicians and civil servants have not always been easy over the last two decades. The low legitimacy of the state and in particular of politicians has forced reforms. At the same time, politicians have been able to gain political support by suggesting that they are able to control the bureaucracy. For budgetary reasons, in 1982 and in the 1990s governments have lost votes from the large number of civil servants in the province because salaries had to be cut. Early retirements in the civil service in general, but in particular among nurses, have made the day-to-day operations of many hospitals almost impossible. With the policy capacity at the party level remaining very limited, politicians still have to rely on civil servants for policy formulation. But such formulation is made more and more difficult because in Quebec, as in Ottawa, deputy ministers rotate more frequently. Reforming the state in Quebec in a more effective manner might mean that more stability is required, not less.

Reforming the State in Quebec

Despite, or perhaps because of, the rotation of governments, premiers, and ministers in office, the equivalent of program review has not taken place in Quebec. The government has attempted several times to diminish the number of agencies but without reviewing the programs first. The end result has been only a reduction of the least important government agencies.

From 1961 to the early 1980s the administrative machinery developed rapidly, creating new government departments and over one hundred agencies of all kinds. By September 1997, 204 agencies existed. The number of employees in the public and parapublic sectors[20] increased rapidly until the early 1980s, subsequently grew at the same pace as growth in the general population, and has gradually declined since 2000. From 350,000 FTEs (full-time equivalents or person years) in 1981–2, the overall number of FTEs rose to 379,000 in 1992–3, of which 65,000 were in the public service alone. In 1996–7, the total number fell to 356,500, with 54,000 FTEs in the public service. In an unprecedented effort to reduce government expenses over the long run, 30,000 employees and 1,900 managers accepted early retirement packages in 1997. Over 7,000 nurses also left. The capacity of the state to intervene in society and, in some cases, to deliver necessary public services such as health care, has consequently been diminished.

In 1985 the new Liberal government set up three committees to examine the administrative machinery that had developed over the preceding twenty-five years. The committee, chaired by Paul Gobeil, submitted a report that advised the abolition of a number of autonomous agencies, merging others or turning them over to the private sector. Another committee, chaired by MNA Reed Scowen, called for the streamlining of regulations controlling the activities of society at a time when regulatory expansion seemed impossible to curtail. A third committee, chaired by Pierre Fortier, a government minister, proposed the privatization of certain public enterprises according to six criteria that he claimed were pragmatic.

While the Gobeil Report did not initially result in significant changes in the system of Quebec public administration, it was the first broad attempt to re-examine its scope and continues to serve as a key reference. It also offered the government an opportunity to symbolically regain leadership over the administration after nine years in the opposition. The deregulation proposed by the Scowen committee, in keeping with what was happening elsewhere in North America, has yet to produce the anticipated results. It is noteworthy that Premier Bouchard deemed it necessary to announce the establishment of a Secrétariat à la déréglementation in the Ministère du Conseil exécutif at the Summit Conference on the Economy and Employment in the fall of 1996, thus reiterating the desire expressed by his predecessors while also acknowledging that their efforts had failed.

No one knows for sure currently how many organizations actually compose the state. If one looks at the public accounts, there are 105 public organizations. There are 171 according to the Treasury, 189 according to the Executive Council, 254 on the government web site, and 274 according to the auditor general.[21] This is not to mention the subsidiaries of the state-owned enterprises. The creation of these subsidiaries is a phenomenon that has existed for a number of years.[22] Such entities become extremely difficult to control from the centre. Consequently, the capacity of the centre to coordinate is weakened. Such a complicated web of organizations has created pressures to develop an improved central structure of coordinating agencies.

After the 1995 referendum, the Quebec government has embraced the New Public Management ideas.[23] This comes with an interesting twist. In Quebec, political parties can be differentiated using two axes: more or less nationalist or federalist, and more or less in favour of state intervention (or more business oriented). Over the long run, the Liberal party has traditionally been to the left of the Union Nationale. The Parti Québécois presented itself to the left of the Liberals who, with the disappearance of their former UN foe, have occupied all the right of the spectrum but at the same time has tried not to leave all the left to the PQ. In recent elections the newcomer has been the Action Democratique du Québec (ADQ), which has decided to be more right wing than the Liberals but also more nationalist in order to appeal to the PQ core support. After the Bourassa Liberals left a deficit of $6 billion to manage, fiscal austerity under the PQ became the norm, also undermining its core social-democratic constituency.

This said, the Parti Québécois decided to control the deficit and to use several of the principles of the New Public Management ideas. Under Lucien Bouchard, the deficit was gradually reduced to zero. This was done without abolishing key policy domains but rather through the reduction of availability of services everywhere. This comes after years of privatizations by the Liberals. Although there was no Klein or Harris revolution, and despite the social-democratic discourse, there has been a tendency to move toward the right. The current attempt at reforming the state under the Charest regime implies the use of new information technology (NIT), business planning, and managing by results. The few special operating agencies, called in Quebec unités autonomes de service, have been given as examples of what should be done for the entire civil service in the 'modernisation de l'administration publique,' which the Liberals continue with a change in vocabulary. Re-engineering has made a comeback as a catchword.

The new public management (NPM) is not a unified explanation of what ought to be done to improve the efficiency or functioning of public administrations. Most authors agree that NPM is the introduction of methods from the private sector or of market mechanisms, including a greater importance given to clients or customers and the diminution of the difference between the private and the public sectors. The emphasis is put on management rather than policy-making, on entrepreneurship rather than analysis, on flexibility and risk-taking rather than transparency, ethics, and stability. Although these elements could and have been debated, NPM also involves the use of policy instruments such as partnerships, subcontracting, and so on. This is an improvement over the traditional list that divided the instruments among exhortation, expenditures, regulation, and public enterprises.

All three parties had propositions on how to continue to reform the state. In short, the ADQ would cut everywhere, the Liberals would cut everywhere except in health and education. In its official electoral platform the PQ proclaims that services have to be improved before any further cuts take place, but the president of the Treasury Board under Landry had a plan ready to transform the state to fifteen departments and lower the number of state agencies.

The most important reform exercise in recent years has been the 'modernisation de l'administration publique' put forward by the Landry government. The general idea is to change the way policy is implemented in Quebec. The current law on modernization is made of four main elements: a declaration of services, or a charter on the British model, and strategic planning and increased accountability, followed by management by results.[24] The civil servants in Quebec consider that what makes this new reform different from past failed efforts is that a law has been passed to give it legitimacy. It is too early to tell whether the management by results that is supposed to emerge will work. The Charest government is still working on what the plan will be because of unfavourable poll results.

In Quebec, although there is still resistance to be to transparent, business planning is central to the current reforms. It is hoped that ministers can provide legislators with better information and so increase the confidence of the Public Accounts Committee. With the impact of NIT, business planning might lead to major corporate restructuring. This method also is necessary to managing by results, which should lead in theory to fewer central controls. The practice of the New Public Management has been proposed in Quebec as the way to reform the state. The pro-private sector origin, the efforts to plan rather than to react to crisis, and the necessity of transformations have all run counter to the statist tradition established since the 1960s. It is difficult to believe, however, that much change will be achieved before the baby-boom generation retires. The required cultural change is important, but in an aging civil service close to retirement bold transformations are unlikely.

Jean Charest's First Year in Power

In the election campaign of 2003, Jean Charest's election slogan was 'I am ready.' The aim was to erase the image left during the previous electoral duel when Lucien Bouchard took a majority of seats but slightly fewer votes. In 2003 the Liberals maintained the same percentage of the vote, but won a clear majority of seats because this time the number of PQ votes was lower. It must also be pointed out that a larger number of Quebeckers did not vote. The Canadian electoral system once again generated a clear majority government following a limited voter turnout.

In the British parliamentary system, when three parties instead of two go head-to-head, it is harder to interpret the results and render predictions using vote percentages that are quite random. Over the year leading up to the general elections in Quebec, each of the three parties had the lead at some point. When the election was called, Premier Landry thought he had a chance of winning. Twelve months before that, Mario Dumont of the Action Démocratique du Québec (ADQ) had been the front runner for the premier's job. Jean Charest won the day. He was capable of bringing together a team of star candidates who made his cabinet team interesting in the eyes of the electorate.

Two questions need to be asked given the electoral results. If the pre-election polls kept repeating that Quebeckers wanted change, what kind of change did they want? And if the government has a clear mandate, how should the state's upper hierarchy be organized to orchestrate this change?

Various considerations have an impact on the new government's program once the desire for change on the part of the electorate has been expressed. Both the Liberals and the ADQ could have carried this willingness for change. Tax cuts and smaller government are ideas that seem to please a certain proportion of the population, but the Liberals need to be careful not to leave too much room on the right if they want to dispose of the ADQ. The government has declared it wants to reorganize the way the Quebec government operates and refocus it on its priority missions.

Just as the new Ontario government realized when it took power, the Quebec government faced a deficit totalling several billion. Government expenses grew more quickly over the last two years of the former government than the gross domestic product. To keep public finances under control, the rate at which these expenses are growing must be reduced. This will be a difficult task given that the government said it will continue to invest in health care and will not make any budget cuts in education, the two most important areas of intervention for the provincial government, and that it would cut taxes despite the fact that economic growth is not occurring quickly.

The Charest government's inaugural speech proposed six major priority areas:

- Review of government structures and programs, under the responsibility of the chair of the Treasury Board
- Review of the government's means of intervention in the economy,
  under the responsibility of the minister of economic and regional
  development, in collaboration with the minister of employment,
  social solidarity and family
- Reorganization of health services, under the responsibility of the
  minister of health and social services
- Examination of decentralization and deconcentration options, under
  the responsibility of the minister of municipal affairs, sports and
  recreations and the minister responsible for regional development
  and tourism
- Refocusing of the education network on students, under the responsibility of the minister of education
- Simplification and easing of the tax burden, under the responsibility
  of the minister of finance

René Lévesque wrote an amusing chapter in his memoirs on the role
of a premier in the creation of his first cabinet. He told of how he had to
juggle a list of names and that, like Jean Lesage in 1960, he had no one
with ministerial experience. At the time, he was the only one who had
ever been a minister. He was also depending on former senior civil servants who had entered the political arena. Jean Charest was dealt a
similar hand in forming his first cabinet. The chair of the Treasury
Board, the minister of education, and the minister of industry and
regional development had experience as civil servants. The new minister of finance was briefly minister of revenue a decade ago. However, a
doctor who was a political neophyte was given the crucial Department
of Health and Social Services. Moreover, former minister Pierre Paradis
was excluded from the cabinet, which generated a great deal of talk,
more so than the list of twenty-five ministers chosen.

To help remedy the inexperience of his cabinet, Charest called upon a
civil servant with a long track record to be general secretary of the government. This choice has had an important symbolic value. Despite the
rhetoric for change and the reduction in the size of government, the
government decided to work with the public service, to place its trust
in it. The dismissal of deputy ministers has been rare and movements
from one department to another have remained within the usual limits.

After the original attempts to create structures that met the various
political considerations of his predecessors, the premier chose to ratio-

nalize the structures and return to a relatively classic model, both for the ministerial committees and the ministers' positions.

There are five ministerial committees for ensuring coherence of the whole: the Conseil du trésor (Treasury Board) which sees that the budget is respected; the Comité de legislation (Legislation Committee), which examines legislative bills; the Comité ministériel du développement social (Ministerial Committee on Social Development); the Comité ministériel de la prospérité économique et du développement durable (Ministerial Committee on Economic Prosperity and Sustainable Development); and the Comité ministériel de la citoyenneté et de la culture (Ministerial Committee on Citizenship and Culture).

Apart from the premier, the other ministers who took up their positions in January 2004 cover the usual fields of provincial jurisdiction: education, health, municipal affairs, agriculture, natural resources, transportation, and the environment. There is a minister separate from justice for public safety. Social and citizenship issues are assumed by the minister of employment, social solidarity and family, the minister of citizens' relations and immigration, and the minister of the environment. Economic issues are divided between the minister of finance, the minister of revenue, the chair of the Treasury Board (and minister of governmental administration), the minister of labour, the minister of tourism, and the minister of economic and regional development, the latter replacing the traditional minister of industry and commerce. As is customary in Quebec, there is a minister of culture and communications, a minister of international relations, and a minister of intergovernmental and aboriginal affairs. The cabinet team is completed with a minister responsible for the reform of democratic institutions.

Just as previous governments have had to learn the hard way, the Charest government has had to learn to govern. The first year in power has revealed that reorganizing the government is harder than expected. Recent surveys indicate that if the electorate wanted a change of government they do not want to see a reduction in government services and are no longer sure they chose the right party to govern them. In short, they want little change. The budget situation does not leave any room to operate in new directions. The classic problems of health care, the Aboriginal issue, and education reform have not found solutions. Overall coordination remains difficult in the system of ministerial responsibility as it exists and given the classic lines of cabinet composition. Certain beginner ministers have shown that they are not as ready to govern as their premier.

Conclusion

In Quebec the 1960s were a period of creation of institutions that became functional in the early 1970s, including a reformed cabinet structure and institutions of executive government. Until the early 1970s the budgetary and policy process in Quebec was one with only very limited central agency control. Since then, the concern has not been so much as to run the state like a private business but rather to maintain Quebec's competitiveness in the world economy. Successive Quebec governments have strongly believed in free trade. They have also tried to limit expenditures. Excluding pre-electoral budgets, once in power, the PQ and the Liberals have followed a similar logic over the years. The Parti Québécois launched a roll-back of public sector wages in 1982–3 and invoked back-to-work legislation on public sector unions that the Liberals continued once in power. Both faced a severe recession but, believing in the role of the state in the economy, they built the highest per capita debt of any province in Canada. It could be said that for most of the 1980s and 1990s the primary criterion for policy decisions was the fiscal reality.

The move toward more power to the premier, if there has been such a move at all in the province, has had to do with the personalities of individual premiers. After 1985, although he had some talent as a politician, Robert Bourassa was not as charismatic as some of his predecessors or successors have been and he had to spend time attempting to bolster his government against flagging electoral support. Jacques Parizeau also had a strong opinion on what his government ought to do: attain independence. His year as premier saw the organization of government for the sake of the referendum. Some of the difficult budgetary decisions of the years since then have had to do with correcting what was then decided in order to win votes in the referendum.

Lucien Bouchard was the ultimate charismatic leader, as described by Max Weber's ideal type. He had a limited knowledge of the state apparatus, did not seem to care, and was better in crises than in day-to-day operations. He was not considered either as coming from within the party or within government and was thus insulated from his ministers. According to several people within the party ranks and assistants to ministers, he never had good relations with either of them. The ice storm episode was the best example of his style. Forced by a crisis, without worries about other issues, his popularity rose during that period and forced a change of opposition leader. He left power explaining that what he wanted to achieve was not possible in the foreseeable future. His successor thought for a while he would do better. Landry had more experience of the state but he also had to deal with strong regional ministers who carried support from constituencies in the party and who were and remain potential leadership candidates.

Administrative styles can be studied from various angles. One could focus on cabinet transformations but, in Quebec, such changes are of limited significance. Most changes of the last decade have had to do with the personalities of ministers or their difficulties in getting elected. For example, Jean Rochon became minister of research in 1998 less because of the idea of a new ministry but because he was waiting for the election results for his riding. The last cabinet of Bernard Landry, with thirty-five ministers, was an electoral idea proven wrong by the electorate.

Rather, in Quebec, there is an institutionalized pattern of state-building over the last forty years inherited from the Quiet Revolution. It is easier to change the state incrementally than to do so radically, as the Action Démocratique du Québec has discovered to its chagrin. At the same time, in order to preserve the state, new ways of doing things have to be found. The junction of these two trends helps explain the popularity of the New Public Management ideas in Quebec, despite the neo-liberal overtones that come with it.

In this chapter we have described the basic characteristics of Quebec's executive system and its capacity to change. As we have shown, unlike at the federal level but in a fashion similar to many of the other provinces, civil servants need a clear and consistent political direction that only the prime minister can give. Such a line has been elusive in Quebec. Premiers in Quebec do not have the presidential power a Canadian prime minister has. On one side, premiers such as Lesage and Lévesque could be presented as strong leaders who for varying periods of time controlled the agenda and policy-making. On the other, both Johnsons, Bertrand, and Bourassa were talented politicians but were not as much concerned with policy-making. Under their premiership, ministers and departments were able to maintain their autonomy.

Hence the shift of power from the Parliament to the cabinet to the premier is not yet completed. Prime ministerial power is diffused in Quebec for several reasons. First, governments have not lasted for more than two terms since 1960. Second, being premier has been a rather unstable job since 1959. Third, because of fiscal pressure, Finance and Treasury have been able to hold their ground. Fourth, when the Parti Québécois is in power, the premier has to deal with an ideological party that cannot be taken for granted. Fifth, because of growing discontent with the state, new mechanisms of relations with economic and social actors have been developed. The new governance is about sharing power with other actors in society.[25] Sixth, the new policy instruments have created a movement of devolution of power. Agencies, partnerships, and such like involve less central control. Finally, the current modernization of the state apparatus creates an era of uncertainty while management by results is not yet fully implemented and the accountability mechanisms are established. The Quebec case leaves a few questions unanswered that could be interesting to pursue in a comparative study.

Chapter 8

Politics, Personality, and History in Ontario's Administrative Style

TED GLENN

Introduction

In June 1995 Mike Harris led his Progressive Conservative party out of the political hinterlands to claim victory in Ontario's thirty-seventh general election. Shortly after, the new premier introduced a number of radical changes to the structure and process of the Ontario government, most visibly a number aimed at the province's cabinet decision-making machinery. These included the elimination of the cabinet policy committee system in place since the early 1970s, the abolition of one of two financial decision-making bodies, and a massive reduction in central agency resources. Nine months later, in May 1996, the premier began to reinstitutionalize the cabinet decision-making process by creating a number of ad hoc policy committees and enhancing central agency resources.

In June 1999 Mike Harris led his party to a second electoral victory and then promptly introduced further reforms to Ontario's cabinet decision-making machinery: a full, formalized policy committee system; a new committee responsible for capital allocations and privatization initiatives; and additional central agency responsibilities and resources. In many ways, the new system resembled its institutionalized predecessors – except that it did not last for two decades. Taking a page from his first year in power, in November 2001 Harris partially dismantled the reinstitutionalized structure and replaced it with the relatively unaided version (see below) that he first set up in June 1995. This structure remained in place until March 2002 when Harris stepped down.

What do these dramatic changes say about the Ontario's administrative style?[1] In more elaborate terms, what do the changes in Ontario's cabinet decision-making machinery between 1995 and 2002 reveal about the formal system of constraints and incentives that define and structure the behaviour of Ontario's key state actors? Literature on the subject suggests that representational imperatives (i.e., region, language, and gender), the need for managerial capacity and collegiality in complex organizations, and particular governments' fiscal and policy programs are key determinants behind the design of cabinet decision-making systems.[2] These studies do not, however, pay sufficient attention to how much cabinet decision-making systems reflect and extend the political instincts, personal aptitudes, and governing experience of the first ministers who dominate them. This chapter attempts to understand Ontario's administrative style under Mike Harris from precisely this perspective: how did his sense of the government's mandate, his personal approach to decision-making, and the practical lessons learned over the government's time in office influence the design of Ontario's cabinet decision-making system between 1995 and 2002?

To appreciate the context for these reforms, this chapter begins with a short history of cabinet decision-making designs in Ontario, focusing on the period from 1968 to 1995. It then provides details of reforms introduced between 1995 and 2002 and highlights how Premier Harris's political instincts, personal aptitudes, and governing experience influenced these reforms. The chapter concludes with some thoughts on the centrality of first ministers to cabinet decision-making systems specifically and to Canadian administrative styles in general.

A Short History of Cabinet Decision-Making in Ontario

There has been an established pattern in the development of central executive (or cabinet) decision-making systems in Canadian provincial and federal governments.[3] Prior to the 1960s, most cabinets were largely 'unaided,' in that there were few institutional resources (i.e., professional staff in central agencies) available to support the comparatively few decisions cabinet had to make around the annual budget exercise. In this system, the first minister tended to dominate the decision-making process, with the advice and contributions of a few key ministerial confidantes. Ontario's cabinet was largely unaided until 1972.[4]

With the postwar boom, the 'range, complexity and interdependence'[5] of Canadian government decisions grew and forced governments to create decision-making systems that would enable them to manage their workloads effectively. Key features of these so-called institutionalized cabinets include a formal cabinet committee structure, with committees dedicated to planning and priorities, policy considerations, and finances, and central agencies to support both the non-partisan and partisan components of cabinet decision-making. The institutionalization of Ontario's cabinet began with the appointment of the Committee on Government Productivity (COGP) in 1969.

Appointed by Premier John Robarts, the COGP was to 'improve the efficiency and effectiveness of the Government of Ontario.'[6] Part of the COGP's recommendations involved a radical restructuring of Ontario's cabinet decision-making system in order to improve its 'organizational capacity to assist ministers in policy development, internal management and control, priority setting, and policy coordination.' And despite some modifications and minor reorganizations, the three key structures, the financial decision-making process, and the four central agency supports recommended by the COGP and established by Premier Bill Davis in 1972 have remained in place to the present day.

The first key structure recommended by the COGP was a Policy and Priorities Board (P&P), a central decision-making body designed for determining the government's medium- to long-term priorities and setting out the strategic directions for achieving them. Despite some modifications to address overload problems in the past decade, P&P has formed the heart of cabinet decision-making in Ontario for the past thirty years. In 1989, for example, Premier David Peterson created an agenda committee to assist P&P in reviewing future agendas strategically, evaluating committee reports to full cabinet for readiness, and approving urgent or late items for cabinet. In 1999, Harris expanded P&P's mandate to include communications planning, as discussed in more detail below.

The second key structure recommended by the COGP was a policy committee system. As in other provinces, Ontario's policy committees have, in various forms since 1972, been used to ensure that new policy proposals are consistent with the government's strategic directions and priorities, improve policy coordination, and ensure that proposals are fully developed before proceeding to cabinet. Initially, Premier Davis created new positions called provincial secretaries to chair the three policy committees.[7] These positions were essentially ministers without portfolios assigned the task of coordinating and integrating the work of the committees with the support of small secretariats. Peterson put his stamp on the policy committees by adding seven new ones to the system between 1985 and 1989,[8] but Premier Bob Rae eliminated Peterson's agenda committee and reduced the number of policy committees to four.[9] Harris did not use the policy committee system at all during his first term in office, although he did create a number of P&P subcommittees to perform essentially the same function.

The third key structure retained since the COGP reforms is a Legislation & Regulations Committee (Legs and Regs) to ensure that new statutory instruments implement the government's policy and fiscal directions.

With respect to financial decision-making, the COGP recommended consolidation of the government's traditional estimates process under the direction of a new Management Board Secretariat (MBS) and the Ministry of Treasury, Economics and Intergovernmental Affairs (the Ministry of Finance after 1993). As per COGP recommendations, MBS prepared annual base expenditure forecasts and Treasury prepared macro-economic projections of government revenues in late summer.[10] Both of these reports, together with a wish list of ministry proposals, were then submitted to P&P for consideration in early fall. Following P&P direction, central agencies (MBS, Treasury, and Cabinet Office) prepared a detailed fiscal strategy for each ministry, outlining operating and capital expenditure allocations, staffing levels, and program costs and pressures. These projections, known as preliminary allocations, would then return to cabinet in late fall via the three policy committees which would consider them against government priorities. Following cabinet approval, MBS would work with individual ministries over the winter to draft detailed expenditure estimates, which were then submitted to cabinet for approval in early spring and eventually tabled as estimates in the legislature as part of the budget in late spring.[11]

In 1991 Premier Rae altered this process substantially by creating a new cabinet committee, Treasury Board of Cabinet (TBC), and a corresponding secretariat (TBS) to address what he perceived to be fragmentation in financial decision-making.[12] In the midst of the worst economic recession in half a century, Rae felt that the more detailed budget responsibilities should be dovetailed with managing the government's overall fiscal plan in order to create a single, integrated financial manager within the Ontario government. This was Treasury Board's new role. MBS was left with responsibility for corporate administrative and human resources management policy, including acting as the government's collective bargaining agent, which became a significant task with the advent of social contract bargaining in 1993.[13] Harris abolished Treasury Board in 1995 and returned Management Board to its pre-1991 status.

The four central agencies established in the wake of the COGP recommendations have similarly been retained since 1972, despite some minor reorganizations. The Office of the Premier continues to provide political advice and support to the premier and overall political direction to cabinet and ministers' offices. Cabinet Office manages the cabinet decision-making process and provides non-partisan advice and critical analysis to the premier and cabinet. Cabinet Office also helps ministries translate the government's objectives into practical directions.[14] MBS is responsible for management of government resources (people, money, technology, information, land, buildings, and gaming),[15] and Ministry of Finance is responsible for revenue and overall planning, monitoring, and management of Ontario's fiscal plan.[16]

Spring: The Revolutionary Cabinet

Upon the Progressive Conservatives' election to office in June 1995, Premier Harris restructured Ontario's cabinet decision-making system as bequeathed to him by Premier Rae. Reminiscent of the unaided cabinets that preceded the COGP reforms, Harris pared cabinet down to nineteen members, abolished the policy committee system together with Treasury Board and its secretariat,[17] and returned the responsibility for in-year expenditure management to Management Board of Cabinet and its secretariat. When the dust settled, only three cabinet committees remained: Policy and Priorities (PPB), Management Board of Cabinet, and Legislation and Regulations.

For Harris, an elaborate, institutionalized cabinet decision-making system was not immediately required in this 'spring' period. As Cameron and White explain, 'The 1995 election meant that the policies of the Conservatives had been approved by the electorate and now implementation could begin. There was no need for policy committees of Cabinet, no need for papers presenting options or exploring the costs and benefits of alternative courses of action, apparently no significant issue for decision which had not been pre-figured and pre-determined by the CSR [Common Sense Revolution] policy framework. Action was what was required; public servants were simply to get on with the job, and politicians were there to see the job was done.'[18]

Central control over financial decision-making was similarly stream-lined and consolidated within a new business planning process, im-plementation of which occurred in three stages.[19] First, the 1996–7 esti-mates cycle was expanded to require ministries to develop and submit to MBC individual business plans that defined ministry vision, core businesses, key strategies, and related performance measures. Second, business plans were integrated with estimates in 1997–8 so that capital and operating resource allocation decisions were aligned with business planning and government priorities. Third, with all major components of business planning in place by 1998–9, MBC began the process of refinement with new requirements for ministries to identify policy and financial risk factors and cost drivers, and incorporate information technology (IT), office space and facilities, and human resources plan-ning in their business plans. At this time, ministries' legislative respon-sibilities to publish annual reports of their activities were incorporated into the publication of business plans as well.[21]

Although business planning may have made the Ontario govern-ment run more like a business, its introduction also imposed a rigid uniformity into financial decision-making across government. This uniformity, in turn, granted the centre (i.e., the premier and his advis-ers) an effective tool to manage how individual ministries made finan-cial decisions, in general, and to reduce government expenditures, in particular, over the course of the Conservatives' first mandate.

Summer: Mid-term Reinstitutionalization

By mid-1996 many of the commitments made in the Common Sense Revolution were either implemented or well on their way. The premier and his government had moved quickly to reduce social assistance rates by 20 per cent, reduce provincial government expenditures by roughly $5 billion, reduce the size of the Ontario Public Service (OPS) by 15 per cent, and repeal the NDP's Bill 40 labour legislation, among other things.[22] The outstanding commitments left from the 1995 election, such as education and health care reform, 'workfare,' and pro-vincial-municipal disentanglement, were far more complex, and exten-sive consideration of these issues threatened to subsume P&P as it was originally constituted. To relieve P&P of potential overload and allow it to retain focus on setting the government's priorities and strategic agenda, Premier Harris created five subcommittees of P&P in May 1996, thereby ushering in the 'summer' period.[23] These became the decision-making forums for such policies as workfare, primary and secondary school curriculum reforms, and a host of initiatives under the rubric of provincial-municipal disentanglement, including the amalgamation of six cities formerly within the old Metropolitan Toronto structure into a single City of Toronto.[24]

As the Conservative government began implementing these more complex policy changes in 1996 and 1997, it began running into difficulties on the communications front as well. As Ibbitson notes, 'the Tories had completely lost control of the agenda' during the Toronto amalgamation debate in early 1997 because they had failed to 'construct a communications strategy, to craft a long-term approach to selling the government's agenda, as the party had done so successfully with the Common Sense Revolution.'[25] Structurally, Premier Harris and his advisers responded to this problem by enhancing the capacity of Cabinet Office to provide strategic communications direction for the government across OPS. This was done by creating a new deputy minister of communications position within Cabinet Office (together with three new assistant deputy ministers) and reorganizing each ministry's communications resources into single communications branches.[26] Changes in 1998 also required each ministry's director of communications to report to the Cabinet Office's deputy minister of communications as well as to his or her home ministry's deputy minister. This new structure and reporting relationship gave the Office of the Premier and Cabinet Office the power to approve all communications initiatives, including news releases, advertising campaigns, and market research, and to coordinate all communications roll-outs. The new structure represents the most significant institutional recognition of the key role of communications in the process of governance in the history of Ontario.[27]

The reinstitutionalized cabinet decision-making system that began to emerge in mid-1996 illustrates some key elements of Mike Harris's personal approach to decision-making. Harris liked to sign off on all proposals coming forward to full cabinet – from strategic policy approvals, to financial and legislative details, to communications strategies – and his role as chair of P&P ensured that he could do so. With the volume and complexity of issues coming to cabinet in the second half of the mandate, though, the premier seemed to recognize the scarcity of his own time and the need to be strategic in his interventions. Thus the creation of the five P&P sub-committees and the enhanced advisory capacity of Cabinet Office. Ibbitson best describes Premier

Harris's personal approach to decision-making in this system as 'a combination traffic cop and judge.'[28]

As a prelude to the 1999 reforms, then, the initial centralization of Cabinet decision-making authority in P&P, together with the consolidation of financial decision-making under the business planning process, gave Premier Harris and his advisers firm control over the government's agenda and operations. But as the Conservative government moved away from implementation of the programmatic Common Sense Revolution commitments towards more complex public sector reforms, the simplified cabinet structure introduced in the spring period did not have sufficient capacity to accommodate the scope and implications of these reforms – especially related to communications – in an effective and timely manner.[29]

It is interesting to note that Ontario's return to a more institutionalized cabinet after a nine-month flirtation with a relatively unaided structure is not unprecedented. At the provincial level, newly elected premiers Lyon and Thatcher of Manitoba and Saskatchewan respectively dismantled many key features of the institutionalized cabinet systems bequeathed to them in order to focus on implementing relatively prescriptive, neo-conservative electoral mandates. At the federal level, Prime Minister Jean Chrétien streamlined the federal cabinet committee system upon election to office in 1993 before embarking upon a small-c conservative electoral agenda as well. While the federal cabinet remained relatively streamlined at the time of Chrétien's retirement in December 2003,[29] both premiers who followed Lyon and Thatcher into office (Pawley and Blakeney) re-established many of the key features of the institutionalized cabinets that their predecessors had dismantled. In this context, the modifications made to Ontario's cabinet system beginning in May 1996 with the creation of P&P subcommittees and expansion of the communications capacity of Cabinet Office should be seen as a prelude to the more significant reforms introduced in 1999.

Fall: The 1999 Reforms

In June 1999 Ontario voters returned Premier Harris and the Progressive Conservative party to office with a mandate significantly different from that of 1995. Compared with the Common Sense Revolution, the Conservatives' 1999 platform, Blueprint, set out strategic directions and goals for the coming term far more than it prescribed specific courses of policy action.[30] The urgency of fiscal restraint had lessened considerably, as well, with a balanced budget imminent in 2000–1. This was reflected in such Blueprint commitments as partnering with the private sector to spend $20 billion on public capital infrastructure projects by 2005.

The transition from governance in an era of restraint to governance in an era of choice (the 'fall' period) set the political backdrop for Harris's reform of the cabinet decision-making system in September 1999. As in 1972, a system was needed to allow the premier, his advisers, and Cabinet colleagues to provide strategic direction on a broad policy and communications program, ensure that new policy proposals were evaluated against existing government commitments, and retain effective control over finances. The system also needed to address critical lessons learned in the Conservatives' first term in office, particularly regarding the importance of sufficient systemic decision-making capacity and the need for strategic communications direction.

The heart of the new system was the Priorities, Policy, and Communications Board (PPCB), which replaced P&P. In addition to continuing to have a mandate for providing high-level direction on significant issues and initiatives across government (as P&P did), PPCB had increased emphasis on integrating policy, legislation, communications, and finances at the earliest stages of development. As with P&P, the premier chaired PPCB.

To help PPCB achieve this integration, four new policy committees were initially created: Education, Justice and Intergovernmental, Economic and Resource, and Health and Social Services. These committees received strategic direction from PPCB and reported directly to cabinet on their recommendations. To ensure integration of financial decision-making, all policy committee chairs sat on PPCB and all vice-chairs were members of MBC. As well, all policy committee chairs had ministerial portfolios that were not the main business of their respective committees – a nod to the role provincial secretaries played on policy committees established in the early 1970s.

In addition to these new policy committees, a new Committee on Privatization and Superbuild (CCOPS) was designed to implement the government's partnership-based approach to infrastructure planning and investment. Beginning in 2000, all capital and/or privatization decisions had first to proceed through CCOPS instead of Management Board before going to cabinet.[31]

Finally, a new Statutory Business Committee (SBC) replaced Legs

and Regs as the primary cabinet forum for dealing with statutory decisions. As Legs and Regs did, SBC reviewed the draft legislation and
regulations against cabinet's directions. SBC was also given the added
responsibility of reviewing orders-in-council that were not related to
appointments and that did not have significant financial or resource
implications.

Decision routing in the fall period was as follows. PPCB, with the
premier as chair, established the government's medium- to long-term
policy, and financial, communications, and legislative agendas. Line
ministers brought policy proposals to support this agenda to one of
the four policy committees, the chairs of which reported to cabinet
(not PPCB) on the committee's recommendations. All financial and
resource decisions, including financial supports to policy initiatives
approved at policy committees, proceeded to MBC before going to cabinet. To ensure linkages between policy proposals and their financial
implications, the vice-chairs of policy committees sat on Management
Board. The financial and resource decisions that went to Management
Board did not include capital or privatization decisions, which went to
CCOPS and then cabinet. All draft legislation and regulations went to
SBC and then cabinet, along with petitions and non-appointment
orders-in-council.

In support of the new cabinet decision-making system, a number of
enhancements were made to central agencies. In Cabinet Office, a new
deputy minister in charge of policy and strategic planning was created
in June 1999, along with nine additional policy staff, to play a leadership role in the policy development process by providing enhanced
service to the new policy committees and SBC. To support CCOPS, a
new forty-person Ontario SuperBuild Corporation (SuperBuild) was
established to lead the capital planning and allocations process and to
pursue investment partnerships, innovative financing, and privatization and commercialization opportunities with the private and other
parts of the public sectors.[32]

In addition to providing sufficient decision-making capacity and strategic communications direction, the 1999 reforms bear the mark of
Premier Harris's personal approach to decision-making. His role as
chair of PPCB allowed him to play traffic cop in an increasingly complex
decision-making system, and the enhanced advisory capacity of central
agencies provided additional support to him in his role as judge.

Beginning in 2001, a number of minor revisions were made to the
fall period reforms. First, a new policy committee, the Cabinet Com-

mittee on Environment Policy, was created to implement recommendations from a report entitled *Managing the Environment*. This report had been commissioned as part of the Conservatives' commitment to improve the government's environmental management capacity in the wake of the Walkerton water tragedy.[33] The committee was chaired by the minister of the environment and reported directly to cabinet. The ad hoc Special Cabinet Committee on Health was created in February 2001, but it met only a few times. In addition to these committees, membership on PPCB was expanded, from eight to eleven members, to include additional environment and economics perspectives.

Winter: Back to the Future

On 16 October 2002 Mike Harris announced that he would resign as Ontario's twenty-second premier following a leadership vote by Conservative party membership sometime in spring 2002. This announcement caught everyone by surprise. The premier stated that he wanted to spend more time with his two teenage sons and that he had accomplished all that he had wanted to as premier – well, almost all. Until the leadership vote, he intended to focus his energies on completing a number of the key initiatives launched under his tenure, such as the privatization of the province's electricity industry, pressuring the federal government for more health care funding, protecting the Oak Ridges moraine, and implementation of the GO Transit transfer funding from municipalities to the province. Implementation, rather than deliberation, was all that was required of cabinet decision-making machinery for the remainder of Harris's time in office. To that end, on 8 November, the secretary of cabinet notified ministers that the five policy committees established in June 1999 would be suspended until further notice. Meetings of the full cabinet, PPCB, MBC, CCOPS, and SBC were to continue as scheduled.

The premier's sense of political priorities was not the only reason for the return of the 'cabinet built for speed.' The state of the economy must also have been a consideration. In summer 2001 indicators were signalling an economic slowdown, including declining numbers of new jobs created, the slumping dot.com industry, and steep volume declines in stock market trading. The tragic events of 11 September and their economic fallout added strength to the trend.

This triggered a review of the government's fiscal position in October 2001 which culminated with the Fall Economic Statement of

6 November. The minister of finance revised his six-month-old projections for economic growth in 2001 from 2.2 per cent to 1.3 per cent. On the expenditure side, the minister declared that the government could avoid a deficit in 2001–2 by dipping into its $1 billion reserve fund and imposing a freeze on all discretionary spending for the remainder of the fiscal year. This left little room for new policy initiatives. The few new initiatives that were introduced in the 6 November statement, like protection of the Oak Ridges moraine and transfer of responsibility for GO Transit from municipalities to the province, had been in the works before the events of 11 September.

As in 1995, the economic situation in the fall of 2001 was crucial to defining just how much latitude the Conservative government felt it had in its policy agenda: the government's few priorities were clear and no further deliberations regarding alternatives appeared to be required. This suited Premier Harris's personal agenda as well.

Conclusion

This chapter highlights the significance of first ministers in the design and operation of Canadian systems of executive decision-making. First ministers are responsible for a number of key activities in governments, including hiring and firing ministers and deputy ministers; creating, reorganizing, and dismantling government departments; providing final approval for the pace and content of legislation, regulations, and policies; determining the pace and content of communications; and making appointments to a myriad of agencies, boards, and commissions. It is in the design of cabinet decision-making systems, however, that the centrality of first ministers is perhaps most conspicuous.

Premier Mike Harris's political instincts regarding the provincial economy and the government's deficit were critical to how Ontario's cabinet decision-making machinery was structured and restructured between June 1995 and March 2002. Whenever economic growth appeared limited or there was a deficit, cabinet machinery was reduced to bare bones. In both the spring and winter periods of Harris's tenure (June 1995 to May 1996 and November 2001 to March 2002), this meant full cabinet plus Management Board to make financial and resource decisions, Policy and Priorities Communications Board to make broad strategic decisions, and Statutory Business Committee to process the legislative and regulatory business of government. During these two periods, the message to ministers and public servants was that the government's priorities were set and all that was required of cabinet and the public service was to implement them.

This unaided, instrumental version of cabinet also reflected the premier's – and Progressive Conservative party's – ideology and resulting political priorities. In 1995 the newly elected premier obviously felt the government's mandate, as laid out in the Common Sense Revolution, was very clear: all policy discussions were subservient to the goal of deficit elimination. The unaided cabinet system subsequently became less a forum for deliberation than a mechanism to ensure implementation of the Common Sense Revolution.

As the initial period of restraint gave way to economic growth and increased demands upon the provincial government in the summer and fall periods (May 1996 to May 1999 and June 1999 to November 2001), the need for increased decision-making capacity grew. During the summer period, in particular, the complexity of the government's mandate grew exponentially, with such things as local service realignment, hospital restructuring, education reforms, and municipal amalgamation at the fore. Harris's initial response was to create five P&P subcommittees in the summer period. This was done to relieve P&P of these more complex policy-oriented and programmatic decisions and allow it to retain its focus on setting the government's priorities and strategic agenda. Harris later expanded the communications capacity of Cabinet Office to address perceived weaknesses in his government's ability to sell the government's proposals. The changes introduced in this summer period established important precedents for the 1999 reforms, in particular the expansion of P&P's responsibilities to include communications planning, the creation of policy committees, and the enhanced capacity of Cabinet Office to support policy and strategic planning.

The suspension of policy committees in November 2001 marked the return of the 'cabinet built for speed' put in place in the initial spring period. As in 1995, the prospects for economic growth in the winter period were slim and the possibility of the government running a deficit was very real. The premier translated this into constraint upon his government's policy flexibility, resulting in the pursuit of only a few critical initiatives that had long been in the works. The 'cabinet built for speed,' not surprisingly, became the cabinet decision-making machinery design of choice to carry the government through the winter period until the premier's resignation became effective.

The changes to Ontario's cabinet system also reflect Mike Harris's personal traffic cop or judge approach to decision-making. In the spring and winter periods, the premier became more the judge, determining the government's agenda outside of the formal cabinet decision-making process. In the summer and fall periods, he appeared more willing to temper the judge persona with that of the traffic cop. During summer and fall, Harris and his most trusted ministers set the government's broad policy, fiscal, legislative, and communications agenda at P&P/PPCB. Policy committees would then evaluate specific policy proposals against these priorities and make recommendations back to cabinet, where the premier had final say. MBC, CCOPS, and SBC then approved the implementation details, with Harris again having final approval at cabinet. In this connection, it is interesting to note that in his later years in office, Premier Davis only used policy committees 'in a fashion that was responsive to his own personal agenda and to the agenda that he believed, with Cabinet, was essential to his government.' For Davis, as for Harris, this often meant that major policy and budgetary items proceeded directly to cabinet without consideration by a policy committee or Management Board.[34]

What do the changes to Ontario's cabinet system of decision-making during Premier Harris's tenure ultimately say about the province's administrative style? This chapter suggests that Ontario's administrative style between 1995 and 2002 was highly reflective of the personal aptitudes, experience, and political instincts of the premier. It was, in short, premierial, to use David Johnson's description applied elsewhere in this collection. Before this observation can be applied to other periods, however, further research needs to be conducted to gauge whether Ontario's premiers, both past and present, made as indelible an imprint on the rest of Ontario's public administration as Premier Mike Harris did upon Ontario's machinery of cabinet decision-making between 1995 and 2002.

Postscript

When Mike Harris retired as premier in April 2002, the Progressive Conservatives governed Ontario for another nineteen months under the leadership of Ernie Eves, Harris's former finance minister and deputy premier. For the most part, the Eves cabinet and its decision-making processes were not much different from Harris's. Both cabinets included twenty-five members and the Eves cabinet included only three members who had not served under Harris. The Harris decision-making machinery created in 1999 and modified in February 2001 (i.e., the addition of the Environment Policy Committee) was left intact.

Eves, as premier, did introduce two innovations worth noting. One was the expansion of the number of associate ministers from one under Premier Harris to five.[35] Much like parliamentary assistants, associate ministers were responsible for making official ministry announcements, assuming ministry-related duties in the legislature, and helping to manage stakeholder relations. The second, more substantial innovation was the inclusion of two to three parliamentary assistants on all cabinet committees except PPCB, echoing a trend documented elsewhere in this collection of efforts to integrate the governing caucus with cabinet. Eves's initiative most closely resembles British Columbia's model where caucus members are appointed to existing committees of cabinet. This model, in turn, was based on an earlier Alberta reform that saw cabinet policy committees replaced with less-powerful standing policy committees whose membership included both caucus and cabinet.

Premier Eves's caucus-cabinet integration innovation seems to have set an important precedent for Ontario's new Liberal government. In the general election held on 2 October 2003, Dalton McGuinty and the Liberal party of won 72 of the legislature's 103 seats. In addition to promises of balancing the provincial budget and reversing the Conservative's plan to privatize the provincial electricity transmission and generation system, the Liberal platform included a commitment to 'reform government and renew trust in our democratic institutions.' Premier McGuinty has expanded upon Eves's integration reform in his early efforts to give effect to this commitment.

At his official swearing-in ceremony McGuinty announced the composition of his new, twenty-three-member cabinet and the supporting decision-making machinery.[36] The machinery includes a mixture of traditional committees (Management Board), renamed committees (Planning and Priorities Board), and new committees (Community Affairs).

The Liberal reforms go considerably further towards integrating cabinet with caucus than Eves had attempted. (They arguably go further than Premier Campbell attempted in British Columbia or Premier Klein in Alberta, for that matter.) The most significant point of integration lies in the appointment of the government caucus chair to the PPB as a full member. In no other jurisdiction does a non-cabinet member, let alone the caucus chair, sit on the inner cabinet. In terms of committee membership, backbenchers and parliamentary assistants outnumber ministers on three of the five policy committees and equal their number on a fourth, and two parliamentary assistants also sit on Management Board of Cabinet as advisers.[37]

Committee leadership also highlights the newfound prominence of caucus members in the Liberal cabinet decision-making process. Under the new system, a parliamentary assistant and a backbench member of the provincial parliament rather than a cabinet minister chair and co-chair the policy committees and the Legs and Regs committee respectively. And similar to Ontario's provincial secretaries of the 1970s, the committee chairs' areas of responsibility are not directly related to their committee's mandate. For example, Mike Brown, parliamentary assistant to the minister of natural resources, is chair of the Education Committee. Committee chairs are responsible for leading cabinet discussions on committee resolutions, not the ministers responsible for those items. This procedure should prove interesting with respect to the fourteen-member Federal, Provincial, and Municipal Affairs Committee, on which the premier sits.[38]

The Liberal reforms appear to challenge some of the basic tenets of Ontario's administrative style as it developed under Premier Harris. In periods of limited economic growth and government deficit, this chapter showed that the Harris style was to adopt lean, implementation-oriented decision-making machinery, in the belief that the government's policy options were severely circumscribed. Shortly after their election to office in 2003, the Liberals 'discovered' that the province's books were not balanced, as promised in the Conservatives' 2003 budget – but were in the red by $5.6 billion. Under Harris, this news would likely have signalled retrenchment. McGuinty, however, seems to perceive considerably more flexibility in his government's options and seems more committed to using cabinet, its committees, and caucus as a deliberative forum in which to debate the government's strategy on moving forward. It will be interesting to see whether McGuinty's personal commitment to broader participation in the inner workings of government can weather the political realities of governance and leave as clear a mark on Ontario's administrative culture as Premier Harris did.

Chapter 9

Cabinet Structure and Executive Style in Manitoba

JOAN GRACE

On 21 September 1999, Manitobans elected the New Democratic party (NDP) led by Gary Doer, a signal perhaps that voters were ready for a change.[1] Indeed, since 1988 Manitoba had been governed by the Progressive Conservative party under the leadership of Gary Filmon. Just prior to the election, however, some political observers were questioning whether the NDP government would be any different from its predecessor. As one analyst pointed out, social democratic political parties around the world were increasingly 'coming to terms with the political reality' that to be elected, a pragmatic, turn-to-the-right politics was a necessity. Furthermore, the NDP's first speech from the throne largely reflected the government's desire carry forward the previous administration's political agenda by holding the course in order to ensure economic continuity, while also addressing pressing policy challenges, such as health care, urban revitalization, and northern development. As the government saw it, 'The people of Manitoba have made it clear that they expect their government to live within its means. This is not an unrealistic expectation, however. In the recent election, Manitobans voted for a set of commitments that is focussed and achievable. They voted for improvements in the basic services that government provides and for sustainable tax reduction.'[2]

The NDP were re-elected in June 2003, capturing a few extra seats with a slightly higher percentage of the vote. In light of the party's electoral success, it is appropriate to analyse executive decision-making and cabinet design with an eye to teasing out similarities and differences between past cabinet structures and the Doer era. The first section of this chapter discusses the socioeconomic context at the time of the September 1999 election to discern some of the forces that influenced cabinet design under the newly elected government. We then move into a review and analysis of the actors, institutions, and processes at the central level, along with how policy development and decision-making are integrated with the NDP caucus. The final section analyses cabinet design and executive style in historical context. This chapter argues that the cabinet structure put in place by the NDP premier is not a post-institutionized system per se, given the presence of four cabinet committees – Treasury Board, Community and Economic Development, Healthy Child, and Aboriginal Issues – along with central agency units and processes that have facilitated the centralization of decision-making. Although the cabinet committee structure was streamlined under the Doer administration, it is best described as a hierarchical, institutionalized cabinet, given its emphasis 'on collegiality and extensive support of cabinet decision-making through specialized central agencies.'[3]

Election 1999: The Socioeconomic Context

The Filmon government implemented a two-prong economic strategy: deficit reduction and encouraging export markets that were now more open under the Canada–U.S. Free Trade Agreement. This export-driven economic strategy, which also included a low-wage policy, tax increases for business, and tax reductions for individuals to increase income levels, transformed Manitoba away from its historic position as the 'Gateway to the West' into the 'Gateway to the South.'[4] These policies were components of the Conservative government's overall neoliberal policy agenda, representing a shift away from Keynesianism to an economic strategy distinguished by 'fiscal orthodoxy, attention to market competitiveness, deregulation, and privatization.'[5] However, as the Canadian Centre for Policy Alternatives (CCPA) has pointed out, the downside of this economic strategy was having Manitoba's economic fortunes tied to the U.S. economy, making it vulnerable to factors out of its control. Indeed, CCPA reported that from 1988 to 1997 exports of manufactured goods to American markets increased by 152.5 per cent, while imports of manufactured goods increased by 192.9 per cent. Although gross domestic product (GDP) grew from 2.7 per cent in 1998 to 3.8 per cent in 1999, other problems beset the economy.[6] For example, although agriculture output rose by an estimated

2.1 per cent in 1998, low commodity prices seriously decreased farm income by more than half in that year, to $83 million, in contrast to a record high of $491 million in 1996.[7] Economic realities such as these, of course, also need to be considered in light of Manitoba's status as a have-not province, where federal transfers have become crucial to Manitoba's continued economic success. In 2001–2 major federal transfers totalled $2.4 billion, which accounted for 35 per cent of Manitoba's estimated revenue.

As to the social side of Manitoba's political economy in the mid- to late 1990s, CCPA also expressed a deep concern that the economic strategy in place would accentuate rather than alleviate Manitoba's serious problem of poverty.[8] And they were not alone. The Social Planning Council of Winnipeg reported that the child poverty rate in Manitoba in 1999 was 23.7 per cent. That year Manitoba had the third highest child poverty rate of all provinces, behind Newfoundland and Nova Scotia.[9] Moreover, Aboriginal poverty rates, especially in Winnipeg's inner city, were incredibly high, with Aboriginal child poverty twice that for all children.[10] Almost two-thirds of all Aboriginal households in Winnipeg, 64.7 per cent, had incomes below the poverty line. These poverty rates were, in part, a product of very high unemployment among Aboriginal peoples in Manitoba. Census data from 1996 indicated that 24.6 per cent of Aboriginal youths in Winnipeg were unemployed.[11] As might be expected, unemployment in northern communities was even higher. Manitoba's overall unemployment rate in 1999 was 5.6 per cent, well below the national average of 7.6 per cent. In part, this low level of unemployment had been attributed to the 'Manitoba Advantage,' the elements of which included:

- A diverse economy, often touted as one of the most diverse in Canada, home to a number of major industries including aerospace, bus manufacturing, food processing, health products and research, financial services, and transportation
- Location – at the northern end of the mid-continental trade corridor, as well at the mid-junction of Canada's east-west transportation system which has provided the province with the opportunity to expand trade and transportation links
- Hydroelectricity rates that are among the lowest in the world, and the lowest in North America
- An abundance of natural resources including zinc, copper, and gold, along with well-established forestry and agricultural industries

- An advanced telecommunications network
- A skilled, multilingual workforce

Under the NDP government, budget restraints continued. In September 1999 the new Minister of Finance Greg Selinger announced that a private-sector management consultant had been commissioned to conduct an independent review of the province's finances. In a preliminary report to government, Deloitte and Touche indicated that over $315 million in unbudgeted expenditures had been committed by the Filmon government prior to the changeover. As a consequence, during the estimates review process in 2000–1, departments were directed to draw up their budget proposals keeping the findings of the review in mind. Presumably, this underpinned the Doer government's resolve to implement a number of fiscal restraint measures, such as consolidating administrative functions, along with reducing the number of ministers and departments. The expected savings were approximately $1 million per year.[12]

Cabinet Structure and Central Agencies: Actors, Institutions, and Processes

According to Christopher Dunn, there are a number of endogenous and exogenous factors that can typically influence and sustain the institutionalized cabinet. Some endogenous factors are ideology, the influence of the premier, emulation of predecessors, cabinet's quest for financial and political control, and the so-called internal logic of structural reforms. Exogenous factors include policy coherence in relation to other governments and making a policy concern known.[13]

In Manitoba, the Progressive Conservative government of Premier Duff Roblin (1958–67), laid the foundation for the development of an institutionalized cabinet system. Premier Walter Weir's Conservative government (1967–9) and Premier Edward Schreyer's NDP government (1967–77), to a certain extent, emulated the previous governments' cabinet design while also expanding central units and processes, particularly under Schreyer. Dunn contends that cabinet institutionalization under Schreyer is attributable also to a Co-operative Commonweath Federation (CCF, and later, NDP) ideology rooted in a tradition of central planning, which was public sector oriented and focused on sectoral planning. As a result, multiple cabinet committees were created, along with two main anchor committees of cabinet that had existed under the Weir administration: Priorities and Planning (P&P) and Management.[14] Moreover, the number of ministers and ministries expanded. During Roblin's administration, there were twelve ministers and sixteen ministries. By 1977 the number of ministers was seventeen, while the number of ministries was 18. Conservative Premier Sterling Lyon (1977–81) preferred a somewhat unaided cabinet decision-making structure and style, which was reflected in his dismantling of many of the cabinet committees and central planning processes established by Schreyer. NDP premier Howard Pawley (1981–8) expanded the 'thin institutionalization' of the Lyon era, in part by re-establishing a P&P Committee that had not been in place since 1973.[15] By his second term in government, however, Pawley felt the need to reassert political control and streamline cabinet structures and decision-making processes in part because of a number of scandals. Arguably, this was also because of a shift in the overall political context in Canada, which at the provincial level was now based on ideas of smaller government and fiscal restraint.

The socioeconomic context influenced the design of the cabinet committee system under Gary Doer's newly elected NDP government in 1999. Promoting trade and fostering the so-called Manitoba Advantage, particularly within an economic strategy underpinned by continentalism, would mean keeping a keen eye on the economy, while also implementing the party's policy platform and election promises.

During the election campaign the NDP was clear on its policy platform and vision for Manitoba. The party offered five commitments to voters: restoration of health care; improvement of educational opportunities for young people; safer communities; no privatizations of Crown corporations; and finally, implementation of balanced budget legislation as passed by the previous government. This political direction reflected the NDP's perspective that pragmatic idealism could and should be implemented based on concrete policies that directly affect people's lives, such as ending so-called hallway medicine or maintaining tax reductions, while also giving Manitobans a political party to vote for rather than merely against a right-wing alternative.[16] According to Gary Doer, policy, not ideology, was the desired focus.

A second factor that influenced the shape of cabinet related to the first, was the size of the province. Given the relatively small size of the Manitoba government, radical restructuring of institutions and processes was not considered appropriate, nor required by the incoming NDP.[17] This was perhaps because dramatic public sector downsizing had been undertaken by the previous (Conservative) government, and certainly gone were the days of progressive expansion of the government and cabinet structures that took place during the 1970s under Howard Pawley were long gone. It may also have been because the new executive was led by a person with relatively long experience in Manitoba politics. Gary Doer was first elected to the Legislative Assembly in 1986. He was immediately appointed to cabinet by Howard Pawley as minister of urban affairs, a key portfolio given Winnipeg's size and importance as an economic engine in the province. He became leader of the NDP in March 1988 and, after the 1990 provincial election, the leader of the official opposition. As premier he brought with him a wealth of experience to the office and a persona well known to many Manitobans. As such, Doer has been the dominant politician and central architect of the new government, and in many ways, the familiar face of the provincial government since 1999.

During transition, the new government weighed its options on how to stay the course – that is, not implementing radical change – while also ensuring that the vision of the political party and the government had pride of place. In this vein, much of the central agency bureaucracy was maintained, although there was a significant change to the cabinet committee system.

The Doer Cabinet

The new premier reduced the cabinet from eighteen to fifteen members, a move that won some praise from both business and unions. This was done by merging the Ministry of Natural Resources and Ministry of Environment into the Ministry of Conservation, while the previous Ministry of Rural Development, along with Urban Affairs, was replaced with the Ministry of Intergovernmental Affairs (now Intergovernmental Affairs and Trade). The cabinet was comprised of persons representing all of the major regions of Manitoba, as well as the highest number of women that had ever been in the provincial cabinet.

Also in 1999 the cabinet committee system was substantially streamlined, or deinstitutionalized. Under the Filmon government, there had been eight cabinet committees (Economic Development Board, Human Services, Legislative and Regulatory Review, Multicultural Affairs, Provincial Land Use, Sustainable Development, Treasury Board Committee, and Urban Affairs). After some months in office, the NDP government had established only two new cabinet committees

(Community and Economic Development, and Healthy Child) and retained Treasury Board. Following the events of 11 September, a Homeland Security Committee was also struck, for a total of four cabinet committees.[18]

Treasury Board Committee (TBC) is a staple in the cabinet of any provincial government. Under Premier Doer it continued to be responsible for the overall fiscal management of public funds to meet government objectives. Under the Filmon government, secretary of TBC (Julian Benson) had been a political appointee; arguably, this reflected the Conservative government's preference to oversee the implementation of the deficit reduction strategy and to exert political and financial control over the bureaucracy.[19] Under the NDP government a career civil servant was given this appointment.

The new Community and Economic Development Committee (CEDC) was to be the 'focal point for the government's efforts to stimulate positive economic activity and strengthen communities.'[20] It replaced the Economic Development Board (EDB), which had been the key economic development committee under Filmon. CEDC is officially chaired by the premier, although in practice it is often chaired by the industry minister in the premier's absence. CEDC membership includes the ministers of Industry, Trade and Mines; Intergovernmental Affairs; Education and Training; Agriculture and Food; and Aboriginal and Northern Affairs. Working closely with the financial and business communities in Manitoba, CEDC is specifically charged with training and retraining, Aboriginal and northern affairs, information technology and research, and urban and rural Manitoba. This committee has become significant in the overall decision-making process of cabinet, given its responsibility for planning and coordinating the government's economic development strategy. CEDC also directly responds to economic crises and politically sensitive economic development projects. For example, the committee took a lead role in negotiating with Motor Coach Industries, a bus manufacturing company, which had threatened to leave Manitoba to relocate to a more business-friendly environment south of the Manitoba border. CEDC was involved in the discussions with the City of Winnipeg regarding the funding and development of a new arena scheduled to be located in the downtown area, as well as a number of key community economic development initiatives, such as the Northern Development Strategy (NDS). NDS, administered by Aboriginal and Northern Affairs, is a long-term strategy to develop human and natural resources in the north.

The Deputy Ministers Committee (DMC), mirroring the portfolios of the CEDC, exists alongside CEDC. This subcommittee meets approximately once a month; it was designed to support the work of CEDC by facilitating information, promoting discussion of the implementation of CEDC decisions, and identifying emerging issues. The subcommittee is officially chaired by the clerk of the Executive Council (Jim Eldridge), but often it has been chaired by the secretary to CEDC Eugene Kostyra, former finance minister in Pawley's NDP government.[21]

CEDC is supported by a secretariat (chaired by the secretary to CEDC) that includes nine project managers and three administrative support staff. CEDC is further supported by an Interdepartmental Working Committee (IWC), which officially reports to the Deputy Ministers Committee (DMC) of the CEDC. Composed of various department and agency public servants, one of the key mandates of IWC is to create awareness across government about the community economic development approach to policy development.

The third cabinet committee, Healthy Child, was established in March 2000. It was charged with directing the government's Healthy Child Manitoba (HCM) initiative as part of the Healthy Child Plan. It is chaired by the minister of family services, and it also includes the ministers of Aboriginal and northern affairs; culture, heritage, and tourism; education, training, and youth; health; justice; and the minister responsible for the status of women. The mandate of the Healthy Child Manitoba initiative is to facilitate community-based approaches for the well-being of children and families, with a focus on the early years. HCM's core elements include funding parent-child centres, and programs about nutrition, prevention of adolescent pregnancy, and prevention of fetal alcohol syndrome. Although Healthy Child has a rather narrow social policy mandate, it nonetheless speaks to the government's desire to address some of the pressing problems associated with social exclusion, such as the recent direction of funds to the Inner-City Youth Leadership Program in Winnipeg, a geographical centre of steep poverty among the Aboriginal community.[22]

In September 2002 Premier Doer announced the creation of a new Department of Energy, Science and Technology. The cabinet remained the same size, with the Ministry of Consumer and Corporate Affairs becoming a new division in Finance. As expected, after re-election in June 2003, a cabinet shuffle took place. A new Department of Water Stewardship was established, as well as a first-ever minister for healthy living (working within the existing Department of Health). Also, a new cabinet committee on Aboriginal Issues was created, arguably in recognition of the growing Aboriginal population in Winnipeg and the importance of addressing key issues in this community. These additions put the total number of cabinet committees at four and the total number of cabinet ministers at eighteen, back to the original number under the Filmon government.

Central Agency Support

Although changes to the organization of the cabinet system were made by Premier Doer, central agency support in the Office of the Premier was not substantially altered from what it was under the previous administration. Indeed, even the number of central agency staff remained the same. Currently, the key individuals and agencies are the clerk of the Executive Council and the Policy Management Secretariat. (There are also central agency units and staff for Cabinet Communications and the premier's chief of staff; these are not detailed in this chapter.) Clerk of the Executive Council Jim Eldridge was appointed by Doer when he assumed office, and he is both head of the civil service and secretary to cabinet. The current clerk also has a lead role as adviser on federal-provincial relations, working closely with the premier. In effect, the clerk is the 'institutionalized interlocutor between the premier, the cabinet and the bureaucracy.'[23] As clerk, he is responsible for taking minutes of cabinet meetings (which are also attended by central agency staff), managing cabinet decision-making procedures, and interacting with departments in policy planning. In many respects, the roles and functions of the clerk emulate those under the previous government.[24]

The Policy Management Secretariat (PMS), a key central agency, provides immediate advice to policy analysts in departments, as well as reviewing, on a weekly basis, departmental and ministerial proposals for cabinet consideration. If ministers want their policy proposal to 'remain alive' through the system, they are well advised to consult with PMS as well, passing their proposal by Treasury Board for financial analysis. Again, the roles and functions of this group are very much like what they were under the previous government.

Apart from the PMS, no cabinet committee vets departmental or ministerial submissions or proposals for cabinet consideration. This was not the case under the Filmon government, where the Legislative Review Committee (LRC), a cabinet-caucus committee created in 1990, was established to review policy documents sponsored by ministers. In the words of the former LRC secretary, the thinking behind the creation of the committee was that it would act as a 'substantive reality check for ministers, as their policy briefs were expected to be detailed and concise.'[25]

Overall, the structure of Premier Doer's cabinet is relatively steamlined compared with the cabinet design of the previous governments. It is, however, hierarchical in that the CEDC and TBC are at the apex of the central decision-making structure, headed by the premier, who is the final arbiter and decision-maker. This is not to say that government caucus members are marginalized from the decision-making process. Indeed, there are three avenues in which caucus members have voice and influence on the overall policy agenda of the government, and on executive decision-making, to some degree.

Cabinet-Caucus Integration

The Legislative Review Committee (LRC) continued under the Doer administration, if under a different guise, in that it is no longer a cabinet-caucus committee. Under the NDP, the LRC was transformed into one of three government caucus committees (GCCs) designed to integrate caucus members into the process of policy development and decision-making. The other two other GCCs are Health and Humanities and Sustainable Development. During the Filmon administration the LRC comprised members from the caucus, and central government, as well as policy analysts and departmental officials which, according Christopher Dunn, gave caucus members the opportunity to be involved in what was normally considered to be strictly cabinet business.[26] In its current form, the LRC is caucus-centred and therefore removed from cabinet.

Membership on all three GCCs is self-selecting. Each is headed by an elected chair, and any member of the government who does not officially sit on a GCC can attend meetings at any time. In essence, the Heath and Humanities and Sustainable Development committees are avenues for caucus members to review and evaluate policy issues and become better informed about the policy sector. To that end, members of these committees may request the presence of public servants from specific departmental units to answer questions about the policy sector or to provide details on a particular aspect of policy. Staff from the Policy Management Secretariat, from time to time, may also be asked to attend a GCC meeting.

LRC is different from the other two committees in that it is charged with reading and evaluating, line by line, all legislation before it is introduced into the Legislative Assembly. Indeed, it is practice for all ministers to submit draft bills to LRC where they are dissected. At this time, the responsible minister may be questioned, if clarification is required, or public servants in the various departments may be called on for elaboration or clarification. LRC can either approve a bill for introduction by the minister in the Legislative Assembly or send it back to the department for changes.

There are a number of legislative assistants appointed by the premier to assist ministers in the exercise of their duties, provide policy advice to the minister, as appropriate, and also to act as contact person with Manitobans. This second avenue is often thought of as preparation for potential future cabinet promotions. Third, all government caucus members have an opportunity to voice their opinions and ideas regarding the government's policy direction during the annual caucus retreat. Furthermore, members of government, along with opposition members, also sit on legislative committees to review bills after second reading, although this activity is not directly linked to decision-making at the centre.

Cabinet Structure and Executive Style in Manitoba

Graham White has suggested that provincial cabinets tend to be large, even though they are drawn from relatively small caucuses.[27] In Manitoba the typical size of cabinet has ranged from twelve ministers and ministries to eighteen. Since the Roblin era, cabinet structures also have changed from time to time, being either thinly or substantially institutionalized. Overall, there has been some reliance on three cabinet committees, a Treasury Board, an economic development committee, and a social policy committee. We see this basic pattern in the current cabinet committee system given the presence of the Treasury Board, Community and Economic Development committee, Healthy Child, and Aboriginal Issues committees. As for central agencies, the Doer administration emulated the basic structure and staff compliment of the previous Filmon government.

A smaller cabinet system reflected Gary Doer's preference that ministers not be burdened with too many cabinet meetings, while also facilitating a measure of ministerial autonomy. There is also indication that the premier wanted to make certain that the full cabinet would not become a rubber stamp. However, although there is no inner cabinet per se, of the four cabinet committees, CEDC appears to be the most important, given its high visibility and its wide reach across government policy and project priorities.

The transition from a Conservative to NDP government provided Premier Doer the opportunity to shape the cabinet to meet his particular preferences regarding policy priorities and decision-making processes. A streamlined system of cabinet committees also has a practical purpose. As they say, once in power, it is always easier to create new institutions and rather more difficult to disband existing ones. Doer's new government considered it wise to start small and allow for adjustments along the way. And this is exactly what transpired when the premier expanded the cabinet by creating a new ministry in 2002 and two new ministers (but only one new ministry) in November 2003.

The design of the cabinet system reflects the priorities of the government and its executive decision-making style. Doer did not re-establish a Priorities and Planning Committee of Cabinet to suppress the emergence of an inner cabinet and thereby foster a measure of collegiality among ministers. It has been previously argued that collegiality is underpinned in the Manitoba case given that most ministers and deputy ministers offices are located under one roof in the legislative building. White has suggested that this also encourages the availability of ministers for impromptu meetings – something not easily possible in larger jurisdictions such as Ontario.[28] Furthermore, the structure of the system of cabinet ensured that the new administration could be distinguished from the Filmon government, while also signalling to the business community (and other sectors of the attentive public) that a measure of stability would be promoted and maintained. A similar strategy was taken by Pawley when he assumed office in 1981 after defeating the Conservative government.[29] Another priority was to focus on economic development issues to foster and maintain the Manitoba's Advantage. This required the flexibility needed to promote domestic economic development initiatives and international trade, as well as the capacity to respond quickly to perceived economic crises. A smaller, deinstitutionalized structure of cabinet committees and executive decision-making provides this flexibility. Social inclusion was a priority, too, specifically linked to particular social policy agendas. To this end, the Healthy Child and, more recently, Aboriginal Issues committees of cabinet were established.

Although caucus members have a role as members of government caucus committees and as legislative assistants, the premier's cabinet design put in place a system and process of executive decision-making that ultimately facilitated the concentration of power at the centre. This was realized by the development of a streamlined, hierarchical cabinet system, together with an active and well-established central agency bureaucracy, at the apex of which is the premier.[30] While there are some key differences between the system of cabinet committees under Doer and Filmon, the processes of policy development and decision-making at the central level remain much the same.

Conclusion

Christopher Dunn once wrote that provincial government is cabinet government or, sometimes, 'premier's government.'[31] Although he reminds us that this is more of a historical rather than contemporary fact, we nonetheless see in Manitoba a government that is clearly centred around the premier. As head of government, the premier is the most prominent politician, chairs the most important cabinet committee, and is also the minister of federal-provincial relations. However, there is more to discover here. To fully understand and appreciate the details and nuances as to the degree of centralization of decision-making at the executive level, it is well advised to analyse particular policy issues in conjunction with the role and input of the minister heading the department. These two factors alone point to the need for further study.

Chapter 10

Saskatchewan's Executive Decision-Making Style: The Centrality of Planning

KEN RASMUSSEN AND
GREGORY P. MARCHILDON

Executive Decision-Making in Saskatchewan

Saskatchewan was the first province in Canada to create a system of cabinet committees supported by central agencies and departments – a development for which Christopher Dunn coined the term 'institutionalized cabinet.'[1] In so doing, Saskatachewan paralleled developments at the federal level at roughly the same time and for the same basic reason – to facilitate government planning on a major scale. In the case of the federal government, planning was essential to the war effort in the 1940s.[2] In the case of Saskatchewan, planning was a necessary complement to an ambitious agenda of social change as befitted the first democratically elected socialist government in North America, an agenda that involved a major role for government in both economic and social policy.

In this, Saskatchewan preceded similar developments in other provinces by almost two decades. Not until the reforms of the Quiet Revolution at the beginning of the 1960s, when the Quebec government succeeded the Church in directing education and social welfare and became a direct player in the Quebec economy through organizations such as Hydro-Québec, did another provincial government adopt similar reforms. This process of modernizing the provincial state was repeated in New Brunswick with the election of Louis Robichaud, who brought in a number of senior civil servants from Saskatchewan to help design and administer his new cabinet committee and planning systems. Many of them left the province immediately following defeat of the Co-operative Commonwealth Federation (CCF) in 1964.[3] Other provinces followed suit, so that by the end of 1970s, cabinet committees and government planning processes supported by central agencies had become the norm rather than the exception in Canada.

While the ideological explanation goes far to explain why Saskatchewan was such an early mover in introducing the institutionalized cabinet, it is hardly sufficient. Other factors also influenced this outcome. Although not unique to Saskatchewan, the Great Depression hit Saskatchewan far harder than it did other provinces, and as a consequence, loss of confidence in laissez-faire capitalism was correspondingly deeper in Saskatchewan. And while there was a general ideological predisposition towards more activist government by the new CCF administration, there was considerable focus on one particular policy: the party had campaigned on a platform of introducing public health care insurance. To ensure that this promise would be carried out, after the election Premier Tommy Douglas appointed himself as minister of health. Limited means, however, forced the government to implement this election promise in incremental steps. It also required careful budget planning using the newest techniques and the setting up of a new organization loosely patterned on the Bureau of the Budget in the United States.

The new planning paradigm reflected a new relationship between politicians and the civil service. At the most senior level, able and committed individuals were attracted into the civil service because of their basic agreement with the new government's philosophy and the excitement of being path-breakers. George Cadbury, Tommy MacLeod, Allan Blakeney, Al Johnson, and Tommy Shoyama were among the more prominent of these individuals. They constituted, however, a very small minority and a majority of civil servants were not so identified with the government of the day.[4] But the rules under which the majority operated changed dramatically under the CCF, in particular with the introduction of a new Civil Service Act. This act eliminated the practice of wholesale patronage in government departments and with it, the idea that patronage was a legitimate means by which governments could influence public policy outcomes. Indeed, as noted by one public administration scholar, the law was 'so thorough that its basic form remains to this day, and despite amendments, no political party that has formed a government has done away with it.'[5] The law was given meaning through protection by collective agreements negotiated under the new Trade Union Act, the establishment of a strong

Public Service Commission, and a new emphasis on training, development, and continuing education that encouraged public servants to see themselves as professionals.

The Civil Service Act had three major consequences. First, it limited the ability of the Douglas and subsequent governments in Saskatchewan to stack the public service with partisan individuals to achieve their political objectives. Second, it increased the provincial government's dependence on key senior bureaucrats, who were appointed outside the regular civil service process. Third, it put a premium on planning processes to ensure that the government's political agenda would be translated into policy action and that civil servants would be constructive participants in the design and implementation of these policies. Furthermore, it freed public servants from party control and created a permanent career structure in which appointments were made on more objective criteria and career paths could be established within the government.

Well in advance of similar developments in other provinces, this modern professional public service helped shape an administrative style whereby both politicians and civil servants regarded (and still regard) cabinet committee and planning processes as a way of bringing greater rigour, rationality, and coordination to cabinet decision-making. It also created generations of public servants who have great confidence in the capacity of the institutionalized cabinet and the importance of their role within it. Indeed, decision-making in Saskatchewan has often been thought of by senior public servants as a partnership between the civil service and elected members of cabinet.

The final aspect of this style is the affinity of successive CCF-NDP governments to planning. Although most explicit during the administrations of Tommy Douglas and Woodrow Lloyd – because of their strong ideological identification with the Fabian socialist literature on central planning – the emphasis on planning continued through the Blakeney and Romanow administrations, in part because of Blakeney's own function as a bureaucratic planner in the Douglas administration and Romanow's long apprenticeship in the Blakeney government.[6] What is important about the way planning evolved is that it was not merely a technocratic exercise, nor a part of an administrative reform initiative; rather it was, and remains, a key element in the process of translating a political vision into government policies and programs. Planning characterizes the Douglas government's administrative and social reforms that were required to create a more just society, the Blakeney government's economic diversification and province-building based on resources in the 1970s, and the Romanow government's aggressive management of the debt crisis of the 1990s.

Not surprisingly, the two governments elected between 1944 and the present that were not CCF-NDP did not have a similar belief in the centrality of planning. The Thatcher Liberals (1964–71) would go furthest in attempting to break with this administrative style, and while the Devine Conservatives (1982–91) kept many of the structures in place, they adopted a more transactional and project-oriented methodology in their decision-making.[7] That said, the planning tradition was entrenched deeply enough in the civil service that it readily sprang back into action upon the re-election of NDP administrations. Because those governments most shaped the planning approach in Saskatchewan, this chapter focuses on planning through cabinet structures in successive CCF-NDP administrations – the governing party for roughly four of the decades since the Second World War. Implementation of the planning paradigm and its longevity depended upon at least three interrelated factors: a professional public service operating in the manner of a Westminster-style bureaucracy; an elaborate institutionalized machinery available to coordinate planning and decision-making in the service of cabinet's political agenda; and the ideological affinity of successive CCF-NDP governments to planning.

The Douglas and Lloyd Governments, 1944–64

The Douglas administration soon found that the decision-making machinery of the Saskatchewan government was extremely rudimentary. There was no position of cabinet secretary and little resembling an office of Executive Council.[8] There was a clerk of Executive Council, who was quite literally a clerk, but no other staff support for either the premier or cabinet. The decision-making structure was so disaggregated that the only information provided to cabinet came from individual ministers. During the first four years of the CCF government, the minister of education, Woodrow Lloyd, served as an informal cabinet secretary, partly because the new government did not want any public servants in the cabinet room.

This 'unaided' cabinet (see Figure 10.1) led to some serious administrative problems that imperilled the CCF's ambitious reform agenda, as is described most clearly by Tommy McLeod, one of Douglas's closest advisers: 'After a year in office the premier could see the root

Figure 10.1. Saskatchewan's unaided cabinet, 1944

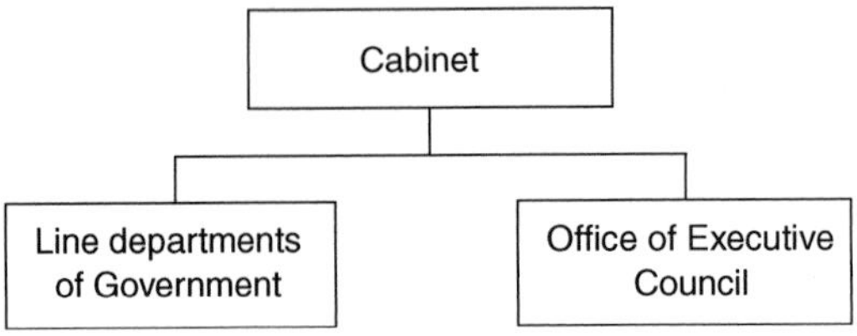

```
                    ┌──────────────────┐
                    │     Cabinet      │
                    └──────────────────┘
              ┌────────────┴────────────┐
    ┌──────────────────┐      ┌──────────────────┐
    │ Line departments │      │ Office of Executive │
    │  of Government   │      │     Council      │
    └──────────────────┘      └──────────────────┘
```

causes of what were not obvious mistakes. All of them were related to poor planning, a shortage of trained managers and an ignorance of management methods. Douglas has a philosophical commitment to planning, but until 1944 he had not been required to put it into operation. Now he was confronted with the need to put words into deed ... [A]ll the cabinet ministers were coming forward with new programs and new ideas and there was no mechanism for meshing them together."[9]

With its administrative and decision-making shortcomings apparent, the CCF began to pioneer the development of institutional support for cabinet planning.[10] The first response came with the formation of what amounted to Saskatchewan's first cabinet committee, called the Economic Advisory and Planning Board (EAPB), in late 1945. The creation of the Planning Board also began the Saskatchewan tradition of combining decision-making structures with planning processes. The Planning Board, in turn, spun off two new cabinet committees and associated central support agencies – the Government Finance Office (GFO) and the Treasury Board (TB) committees. The former was supported by a full-time staff within the new GFO and the latter by a new unit called the Budget Bureau, soon to be located within the Department of the Provincial Treasury. These committees and their staff support structures became a classic administrative troika that would define the institutionalized cabinet in Saskatchewan for the next half century (see Figure 10.2).

The Planning Board quickly took a prominent role, with the support of a permanent secretariat within the Department of Executive Council that also provided advice directly to the premier. The Planning Board examined all subjects that came before cabinet, but focused particularly on those items related to economic development and diversification. It was described by George Cadbury, its bureaucratic architect, as

Figure 10.2. Douglas-Lloyd governments, 1948–1964

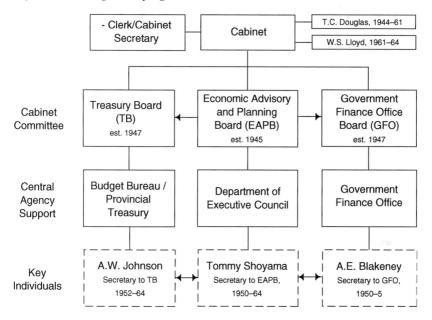

'marriage of the politician and the technician ... with a chairman who combined business experience with economic training.'[11] Initially, this board was composed of four cabinet ministers and three senior officials who sat as members. Indeed its role at first was to advise the premier on all economic, industrial, and commercial matters affecting the province, coordinate all existing and future planning efforts, and provide studies and research relating to the government's existing or proposed participation in the economic, industrial, and commercial fields in the province. The Planning Board and its secretariat were also responsible for preparing the fall planning conferences involving all of cabinet. These took place over a three-day period and focused on the longer-term policies of the government as well as the priorities that would be reflected in the following year's budget.[12] These cabinet planning conferences have remained a constant feature of the Saskatchewan government since that time.

The staff of the Planning Board continued to grow during the Douglas administration and directly employed some twelve to fifteen research officers and policy analysts. The Planning Board's staff, however, was soon divided into two parts, one responsible for government policy and the evaluation of government policy, and another responsible for the oversight of Crown corporations. In 1947 the latter became the Government Finance Office (GFO), which would be reconstituted as the Crown Investments Corporation (CIC) Inc. in 1978. George Cadbury, of the famous English chocolate family, was initially appointed executive director of the GFO. Recruited directly by Premier Douglas, Cadbury had been the leading light behind the Planning Board, having brought with him to Canada a strong belief in Fabian-style socialist planning.[13] By 1950 the secretary of the GFO was Allan Blakeney, a young lawyer and Rhodes scholar who had moved to Saskatchewan from Nova Scotia. Taking over from George Tamaki, the originator and first secretary of the GFO, Blakeney would expand and improve the operations of the office so that it would become a permanent fixture of the Saskatchewan system.

Key to the articulation of a planning regime was the Budget Bureau, established in November 1947 by the Planning Board Secretariat and moved to the Provincial Treasury Department the following year. The Budget Bureau had two arms, one concerned with financial control and budgetary analysis and the other with the systematic organizational review of all government departments and agencies. Thus was inaugurated a long tradition in Saskatchewan of budgeting as a crucial instrument of fiscal and economic planning. In this respect, the Budget Bureau performed the following tasks:

1 Advised the department in drafting departmental programs and budgets in light of the government's overall policy
2 Scrutinized proposed legislation as it related to the expenditure of funds
3 Evaluated departmental programs to advise the government regarding the drafting of the annual budget
4 Analysed expenditures as to rate and effectiveness
5 Advised the government on budgetary techniques

Rational planning became centred on a budget process that became a year-round activity, starting with a set of objectives and broad priorities set by the provincial cabinet during its annual planning retreat.[14] This annual planning cycle, beginning with the setting of priorities by cabinet, moving its way through calls for estimates from the departments, review by Treasury Board, and then finalization by cabinet, has become a constant feature of the Saskatchewan cabinet decision-making process.

These three cabinet committees – the Planning Board, the Government Finance Office, and the Treasury Board – and their central agency support structures, formed a planning troika that has remained an enduring feature of the Saskatchewan system. While the committees and their secretariats have been renamed and even restructured over time, they have nonetheless performed remarkably constant roles.

Direct central agency support for cabinet was also established, with the creation of a modern cabinet secretariat within the Department of Executive Council in 1948. The cabinet secretariat's chief purpose was to record and disseminate Cabinet decisions to ministers. Depending on available time and personnel, however, it was also to provide follow-up to decisions and arrange for specialized advice to cabinet before final decisions were taken. Before this change, the clerk (who never attended cabinet meetings) had to record decisions after cabinet meetings on the advice of the premier or a cabinet minister designated by the premier. However, as planning become more precise, written records of cabinet decisions were needed to communicate them to key members of the bureaucracy, and before long a formal cabinet secretariat was established under a former staff member of the Planning Board. The introduction of a cabinet secretariat greatly enhanced the functioning of cabinet. Essentially, it now required ministers to give notice of their intention to introduce a matter in cabinet which allowed all ministers a chance to be prepared to discuss it.

Another aspect of the structure of decision-making involved the more systematic use of ad hoc cabinet committees in addition to the permanent committees discussed above. Sometimes these committees were established to deal with areas of social policy, such as health care, that were outside the central focus of the EAPB. At other times they were used to compensate for the perceived weaknesses of a given minister or government department. Finally, they were used to deal with major problems or issues of concern to all members of cabinet.[15]

It was clear from the outset that this structure had the potential to increase the power of the premier in relation to other participants in the decision-making system, and some of the architects of this structure were alert to this danger. George Cadbury noted at the time that the objective was to create cabinet decision-making structures that would make cabinet 'supreme without making a dictator out of T.C. Douglas,' while ensuring that cabinet and the premier were being 'serviced competently by an organization that did not interfere with the regular operation of departments.'[16] The delicate balancing act between the premier, cabinet, and departments is fraught with tensions, but as the machinery became more elaborate it brought with it an increasing role for the premier at the apex of this system. This culminated in Saskatchewan, as in all other provinces, with the growth of the premier's own department – the Department of Executive Council – and its dual role as a focus for government-wide planning and coordination and a focus for more partisan political advice to the premier and cabinet.

These new structures of decision-making established a planning regime that continually reassessed government's policies and evaluated proposals coming to cabinet from ministers. Improved central analytical and organizational capacity had implications for departments as well. Inadequacies in departmental planning became clear and the Budget Bureau initiated reviews of departmental organizations and consistently proposed planning branches in line departments, foreshadowing the growth of 'policy shops' in all government departments during the 1970s.

The Thatcher Break, 1964–1971

While the basic structure described above survived the defeat of the CCF government in 1964, it had to face a premier who clearly wanted to exercise more personal control and was more comfortable with transactional decision-making than with more comprehensive and long-term planning processes.[17] Often described as having an autocratic style, Ross Thatcher neither believed in cabinet committees nor made much use of them, in part because he preferred to reserve what he regarded as the most important decisions of government to himself. He also disliked a great deal of the CCF government's approach to governing and did much to dismantle and change the relationships between the premier and cabinet and also between the government and the civil service.[18] Departing from the general practice of collective decision-making, Thatcher simply did not believe in the team approach of the CCF government that had preceded him.[18] Thus the Thatcher years saw less reliance on cabinet committees and a reduction in the resources devoted to the machinery of cabinet decision-making.

Thatcher used Treasury Board in a highly idiosyncratic way. Members were often not invited to meetings. Instead, they were expected to sign the minutes of decisions made by Thatcher in concert with the deputy provincial treasurer and his officials from the Budget Bureau. When it came to the management of government, it was clear that Thatcher did not accept the institutionalized cabinet version of planning and budgeting that was made available to him. Equally, he was of the firm opinion that the aim of budgeting was merely financial control. He therefore rejected both past practice and recommendations that favoured the expansion of the purposes of the budgeting process to include planning.[19]

Perhaps the most significant change in the institutionalized decision-making structure came with the reduction of the role of the GFO. While it was not officially disbanded as a Crown corporation, it was almost completely sidelined during the Thatcher years. Ministers who continued to serve as the chairs of the individual crowns were not obliged to participate in GFO board meetings. At one point all the GFO staff were moved to the Provincial Treasury. Although there was no privatization of Crown corporations at this time, there was a decrease in the level of coordination and planning that had previously been associated with the CCF government and its relations with the Crown sector.[20]

The Blakeney Years, 1971–1982

When the NDP re-assumed power in 1971 they were clearly the bearers of a strong tradition of extensive planning within a system of institutionalized cabinet decision-making.[21] This tradition included the troika of cabinet committees and its associated central agency support. However, over time, the planning system during the Blakeney era became even more structured than it had been under the Douglas and Lloyd administrations. One of the first changes was the creation of a new Cabinet Planning Committee, the successor to the old Planning Board. Responsible for most long-term policy planning, including social policy, the Cabinet Planning Committee also had a coordinating role in departmental program development even though policy-making itself remained with line departments (see Figure 10.3).[22]

The Blakeney administration created the Cabinet Planning Secretariat, made up of ten to twenty senior policy advisers and housed in the Department of Executive Council. Like the old Planning Board Secretariat, the Cabinet Planning Secretariat coordinated policy and planning throughout the bureaucracy and directly supported the Cabinet Planning Committee as a cabinet committee. It was also instrumental

Figure 10.3. Blakeney government, 1971–1977

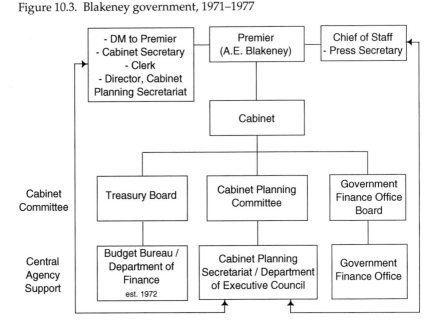

in helping to build (or rebuild) policy capacity in individual line departments so that they were capable of originating policy themselves. From time to time, members of the secretariat also assisted cabinet directly on the major issues of the day as they developed, including the expropriation of much of the potash industry to form the Potash Corporation of Saskatchewan, as well as smaller crisis-type issues.[23] Reflecting the importance of this position, the director of the Cabinet Planning Secretariat was secretary to the Cabinet Planning Committee and treated as a full deputy minister within the system.

Allan Blakeney, as the former provincial treasurer in the Lloyd administration, took a direct interest in finance and budgeting. Once again ministerial members of the Treasury Board played a direct and influential role in setting the government's fiscal policy. The Budget Bureau was given back its dual role of providing advice not only on finance and budgeting but also on machinery of government. In 1972 the Department of Provincial Treasury changed its name to the Department of Finance, in keeping with similar name changes in the rest of Canada, but no major changes were made in terms of its role in the system.

As the former civil servant at the head of the GFO, Blakeney quickly moved to restore that central agency's powers and responsibilities. This was necessitated, in part, because of the government's new emphasis on province-building through its control and ownership of natural resources including oil, natural gas, potash, uranium, and other minerals. The GFO's board was made up of senior cabinet ministers who ensured that the government agenda was translated into action. Many new expert staff, some of whom were highly supportive of the government's philosophy, were brought into the GFO during this expansionist era.

In addition to these changes, the Blakeney government also increased the power and coordinating ability of the Premier's Office. Two developments are important in this regard. First, Blakeney took on the responsibility of directly appointing all deputy ministers.[24] Before this time, deputy ministers had been appointed directly by ministers through order-in-council. Although Blakeney rarely interfered in these relationships between individual ministers and their deputies, the fact remained that the first loyalty of deputies shifted to the premier and the officials in the Premier's Office. Naturally, this development increased the power of the premier relative to the other ministers of cabinet.

The second change came in response to an external development. With the growing role of television and the intense media focus on the premier as the focal point for the government, an increase in the size of the political staff within Executive Council occurred. There was a new emphasis on communications, which would grow with time and become a necessary part of managing government. Essentially, the influence of the media meant that all governments were in a process of continuous electioneering, and this required much greater sophistication in the control of government communications from the centre. This also meant the growth of the role of the press secretary or director of communications, a position that has been labelled in many ways in successive administrations. During the Romanow administration, the premier's chief of staff occupied this position for a time, after which a new position of deputy chief of staff was created for the individual hired to perform this role. Whatever the label, however, the role has consistently been to be the chief communications strategist for the premier and cabinet as well as the functional head of the unit in the Department of Executive Council responsible for the coordination of communications in the government as a whole. As has been the case in other Canadian governments, the press secretary or director of com-

Figure 10.4. Blakeney government, 1978–1982

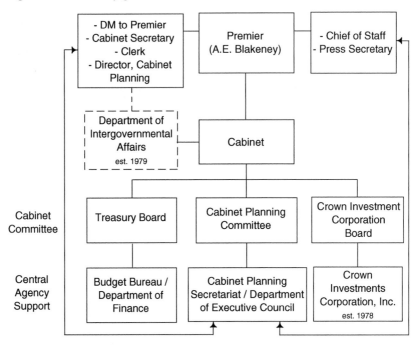

munications, as shaper and guardian of the government's public messaging, has arguably become the third most powerful non-elected official, after the deputy minister to the premier and the chief of staff (occasionally known as the principal secretary). Indeed, departments and ministers in many provinces, including Saskatchewan, rarely communicate with the media until after the message has been approved by this individual. The emergence of this new role also greatly enhanced the power of the premier in relation to his cabinet colleagues.

Both of these developments resulted in the growth in the complexity and number of branches in the Department of Executive Council, all of which from their inception reported to the premier. The growth of the communications functions within the department had the added advantage of being, to some extent, a partisan activity funded by taxpayer dollars, and this practice was continued by all subsequent premiers (see Figure 10.4).

The Blakeney administration both depended on and broadened other central agency support to cabinet and its troika of subcommittees. The first change involved the GFO. From the early 1970s, considerable efforts were made to create a holding company structure that would have significant tasks beyond that of political control. This, combined with the growing investment portfolio of the GFO, led to transformation of the GFO into the Crown Investments Corporation Inc. in 1978.[25]

The second change involved the creation of the Department of Intergovernmental Affairs in 1979. This new central agency was established in response to the increasing time and effort that Saskatchewan was devoting to constitutional negotiations among the provinces and with Ottawa, and their importance to the province's future. The minister placed in charge of the new department was Roy Romanow, Blakeney's deputy premier and attorney general. Not attached to a cabinet committee, the new department supported cabinet as a whole and Romanow and Blakeney in particular in strategic planning and negotiating on a host of intergovernmental files.[26]

The Devine Interregnum

In 1982, after the defeat of the Blakeney government, Grant Devine's Conservative administration wanted to distance itself from the practice and ideology of the NDP. The Department of Intergovernmental Affairs, which was visibly identified with the NDP government's preoccupation with the constitution, was immediately disbanded, although some of its functions were simply moved to Executive Council. Despite this, the Devine government maintained some of the characteristics of the Blakeney cabinet system. Because he was new to government, Devine found some aspects of CCF-NDP planning convenient even if he had less belief in planning per se. The Cabinet Planning Committee continued to function, although it engaged in less long-term planning and priority setting, and more on developing discrete policy and project proposals for cabinet. The Treasury Board and its bureaucratic support continued much as it had under the NDP administration.

The major transformation in the classic pattern of institutionalization came with the changing role of the Crown Investments Corporation Board. Because of their hostility to the NDP's family of crown corporations, the Conservatives were interested in bringing about changes to this aspect of the decision-making structure. Of all the cabinet committees in existence in 1982, CIC Inc. was clearly the most closely associated with the NDP. Thus the government instituted a number of changes following the recommendations of a commission of inquiry.[27] The CIC Board was renamed the Crown Management Board (CMB), but retained its supervisory and coordination functions. The government appointed three citizens to the board, but it was still dominated by the eight cabinet ministers who were on the boards of individual crown corporations. But, as noted by Stevens, 'Cabinet ministers by virtue of being members of the board of directors of the holding company – a Cabinet committee – as well as vice-chairmen of individual corporations boards, continued to be linked to the Crown-corporation instrument by conventions of collective and individual ministerial responsibility.'[28] Thus, as much as the Devine government wanted to change its relationship with the crown sector, it never managed to succeed at this aim and continued to have a cabinet level committee involved in this key sector. This was particularly true during the Conservative government's second term when the issue of privatizing both the crown-owned utilities and commercial enterprises was high on the political agenda.

As a whole, however, there remained an emphasis on the structures of planning as well as the institutionalized cabinet during the Devine era. Indeed, the persistence of institutionalization during this period prompted Dunn to conclude that it 'ended the automatic identification of structured cabinets in Saskatchewan with the CCF-NDP approach to governing'[29]

The Institutionalized Cabinet and Planning during the Romanow Years, 1991–2001

When Roy Romanow became premier in 1991, he resurrected the paradigm of planning that had become relatively dormant during the Devine years using a structure that was largely still in place. Having been a minister as well as deputy premier in the government of Allan Blakeney, Romanow reinstituted aspects of the Blakeney model which, in turn, had its origins in the Douglas-Lloyd era. At its core, this meant re-creating a policy coordination function within the Department of Executive Council that would support a committee of cabinet ministers especially assigned to the task of longer-term policy planning for the government. That was accomplished through the creation of the

Figure 10.5. Romanow government, 1991–1997

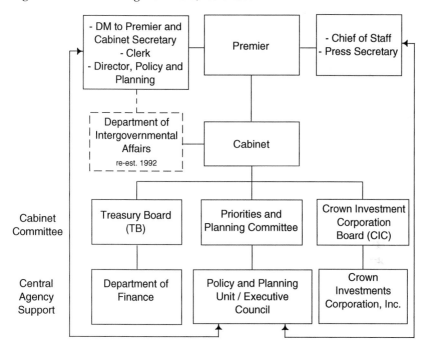

Planning and Priorities Committee of cabinet shortly after the election, along with the Policy and Planning Secretariat within the Department of Executive Council to support both cabinet and its Planning and Priorities Committee.

The second major change was the reconstruction of the Crown Investments Corporation, both as a full committee of cabinet and as an expert secretariat of civil servants servicing the committee. Unfortunately, the name CIC was applied to both the cabinet committee and the agency supporting it, and this has caused much confusion in the secondary literature. To avoid this, the former is referred to as the CIC board and the latter as CIC Inc. In addition to servicing its committee of cabinet, CIC Inc.'s day-to-day task involved administrating a diverse range of investments as well as performing holding company functions for various crown corporations, the largest of which included SaskPower, SaskTel, SGI (Saskatchewan Government Insurance) and SaskEnergy (see Figure 10.5).

Since Treasury Board as well its support secretariat from the Department of Finance was kept intact during the Devine era, they easily fit into the resurrected troika that had been the foundation of the Saskatchewan model, and despite changes in name over time, the three main poles of decision-making influence and fundamental policy direction rested with the three long-term policy, Treasury, and Crown Corporation cabinet committees along with their respective secretariats in the departments of Executive Council, Finance, and the Crown Investments Corporation.[30]

The next major change was to give intergovernmental affairs a higher priority in government planning and decision-making. Initially, through the Department of Provincial Secretary, Romanow reconstituted Intergovernmental Affairs as a separate central agency, with its own specialized staff covering federal-provincial, constitutional, and intergovernmental relations. Although a minister was formally put in charge of the department, the deputy minister in effect reported to both premier and minister. Similar to the Blakeney approach, Romanow initially chose his deputy premier to be minister of the new department but, unlike Blakeney, Romanow played a central role in most intergovernmental issues, and these came directly to cabinet rather than through any existing cabinet committee.

In keeping with the management style of earlier CCF-NDP administrations, all final decisions on cabinet committee matters in the Romanow government were taken in full cabinet. At no time was the federal system of confirming cabinet committee decisions without discussion by cabinet adopted.[31] Instead, each recommendation from the relevant cabinet committee was put before the cabinet for discussion. In most cases, the political and policy pre-digestion of the issue by the subcommittee of cabinet would facilitate reaching a final decision in cabinet and thereby save considerable time, but in some cases, cabinet would re-examine the fundamentals and reconsider even the assumptions buried in the cabinet committee's recommendation. As a consequence, the once-a-week cabinet meetings often went much longer than the anticipated four to five hours. While such an approach may be impossible at the federal level where so many more decisions are taken each week, it is feasible for a relatively small provincial government to review all cabinet committee recommendations within a single cabinet day. Moreover, the approach created greater cabinet identification with, and ultimate support of, the major decisions of government. It also served to emphasize the collective nature of the decision-making process, encouraging ministers to think beyond their departmental interests and make decisions on behalf of government as a whole which, in turn, buttressed the planning paradigm as a whole.

Such a cabinet planning system also puts a premium on central agency support and coordination. The support was taken care of by attracting and training key personnel to work in the secretariats attached to the Priorities and Planning, Treasury, and CIC cabinet committees. As Figure 10.6 illustrates, some changes were made during the Romanow administration to enhance coordination. Priorities and Planning was originally an all-purpose policy committee with little definition attached to its mandate. This was not a problem for social policy development which the government displayed considerable ability in coordinating. This fact, along with the fact that Romanow's personal interests and expertise in federal-provincial relations led to the creation of an intergovernmental affairs central agency, allowed the Saskatchewan government to take a lead role in the social union negotiations that led to the National Child Benefit and the Social Union Framework Agreement (SUFA).[32]

Economic policy was another matter entirely. The lack of precision with respect to the Priorities and Planning Committee's mandate generated some competition and conflict with both Treasury Board and CIC that was exacerbated when yet another cabinet committee on economic development (with secretariat support from the Department of Economic Development) was created in the mid-1990s. At that time, economic policy was divided among the CIC-based Crown corporations, Treasury Board Crown agencies, new public-private enterprises such as Tourism Saskatchewan, and the Saskatchewan Trade and Export Partnership (STEP) as well as a myriad of line departments and agencies including Agriculture and Food, Finance, Environment and Resource Management, Energy and Mines, and of course, Economic Development. From the perspective of cabinet, the Committee on Economic Development was too focused on the promotion and development efforts of the supporting department to be effective in integrating economic policy overall.

As part of a series of cabinet committee changes in 1998, both the Economic Development and Priorities and Planning committees were replaced by two new policy cabinet committees with more focused policy mandates – the Cabinet Committee on the Economy and the Cabinet Committee on Social Development (see Figure 10.6). Both pol-

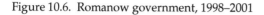

Figure 10.6. Romanow government, 1998–2001

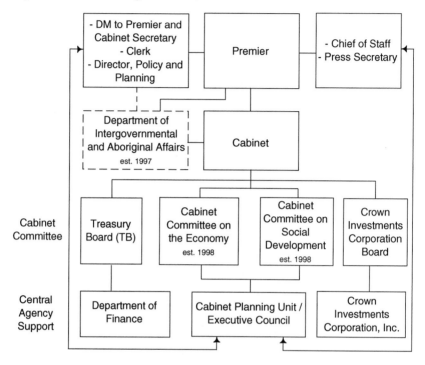

icy committees were redesigned to be supported by an enlarged Cabinet Planning Unit in Executive Council with economic and financial capacity in addition to its already considerable social policy capacity. The one danger in the new structure was that the cabinet committees would artificially segregate long-term social and economic policy. This was addressed in part through having a single secretariat in Executive Council with the onus on the senior policy analysts as well as the head of the Cabinet Planning Unit (who acted as secretary to both cabinet committees and as associate deputy minister to the premier) to draw the linkages between the two.

These changes built upon previous reforms aimed at improving coordination among central agencies but were also a response to coordinating policy issues that increasingly spilled across departmental lines. These included regularly scheduled Monday morning meetings involving the deputy minister to the premier and cabinet secretary and all cabinet committee secretaries plus central agency deputy ministers. These one-hour meetings allowed for a review of all upcoming cabinet items, traffic control in terms of ensuring items were moving through the appropriate committees, and discussion of the cabinet's corporate policy agenda. These discussions were a time-effective means of allowing the most senior officials in the government to keep the complex decision-making process of a highly institutionalized cabinet system on track. Another change involved circulating all minutes of cabinet decisions to affected deputy ministers. Prior to this, it had been customary to minute the relevant minister only. It was found, however, that these decisions were occasionally communicated in an irregular way to deputies. The end result was that deputies would (occasionally) misinterpret cabinet direction at the implementation stage. Initially, this change ran some risk of breaching cabinet confidentiality, but the risk was more than outweighed by the greater understanding of cabinet direction displayed by the deputies after the change.

In 1998 a major initiative involving departmental strategic planning and performance measurement was launched to improve cabinet planning. By 2000 the two policy cabinet committees were charged with the responsibility of reviewing the strategic plans of individual departments and agencies along with the performance measures they suggested using to create a base line for future assessments concerning progress.

In the September 1999 election the Romanow government barely escaped defeat. To reduce the political uncertainty associated with a minority government, a coalition with three sitting Liberal members was created. Although two Liberal members entered cabinet, few if any formal changes were made to the cabinet planning structure. The Liberal members fully participated in both cabinet and cabinet committees as well as the annual cabinet planning retreat. Given the fragile political position of both caucuses within the coalition, however, more attention had to be devoted to shorter-term political positioning to avoid triggering an early election.

The Calvert Government, 2001 to the Present

In February of 2001 Roy Romanow was succeeded as premier by Lorne Calvert, a former minister in Romanow's cabinet. Calvert renegotiated a successor coalition agreement with the two remaining Liberal members and began government with the cabinet decision-making struc-

Figure 10.7. Calvert government, 2001–2004

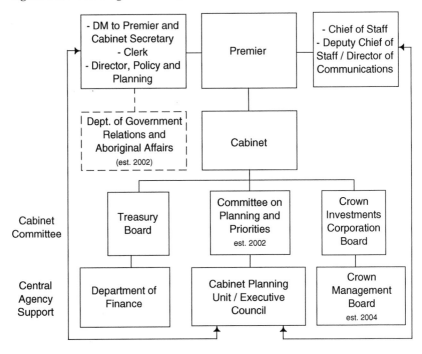

tures he inherited from Romanow.[33] Over time, some changes were made to the structure. In 2002 three formal changes were made but none marked a fundamental departure from the basic planning model that had been inherited from previous governments.

First, the previously single position of deputy minister to the premier and cabinet secretary was split into two, with Premier Romanow's former chief of staff appointed to the latter position. This change allowed the deputy minister to the premier, as head of the public service, to spend more time with the permanent heads of government departments and agencies. It also permitted the use of more informal coordination mechanisms, including creating subcommittees of the deputy ministers. This change was consistent with the increasing need for horizontal policy management. From the 1990s it had become clear that interdepartmental committees were essential to deal with the cross-cutting aspects of most policy initiatives of government and this, in turn, required small teams of civils servants from various areas to work together on time-limited projects whose goal was to produce actionable items for the cabinet committees and, ultimately, cabinet.

Second, the Department of Intergovernmental and Aboriginal Affairs was merged with the Department of Municipal Government to create a department called Government Relations and Aboriginal Affairs. Although given a more ambitious mandate to conduct intraprovincial municipal and Aboriginal government relations, this department continued its central agency role in terms of leading, and sometimes coordinating, the province's interprovincial, federal-provincial, and international relations.

Third, the Cabinet Committee on the Economy and the Cabinet Committee on Social Development were merged into a single Committee on Planning and Priorities, a reversion to the structure that existed in the first part of the Romanow administration. Again, this organizational change did not mark a fundamental shift in direction or management.

In 2004 the Crown Management Board was established to replace the Crown Investments Corporation Board. This organizational change reflects the desire of the Calvert government to inject a more explicit public policy agenda into the province's largest crown corporations. In particular, the holding company now has a mandate to ensure that Saskatchewan residents receive the lowest-cost utilities (as a package of services) in Canada. It is also responsible for a pro-active Aboriginal hiring and retention strategy. It is too early to evaluate whether this portends a major change in the GFO-CIC legacy of past administrations.[34]

Conclusions: Planning and Decision-Making in Saskatchewan

All provinces have a similar basic structure of cabinet decision-making given their similar constitutional requirements. Yet within the constraints of the common model of responsible government there has been a great deal of opportunity for variation. In the case of Saskatchewan there was the early establishment of a highly institutionalized cabinet decision-making structure in comparison with other provinces. This was based on a series of events and institutional changes that created the ideal conditions for this innovation. Most notably, of course, was the election of the CCF government which had a strong commitment to and need for a planning apparatus. This was coupled with the creation of an independent, career-based civil service which was freed from the influence of patronage and less susceptible to control by the governing party.[35] So successful were the CCF in the task of creating a modern, professional public service that one of the main criticisms that Seymour Martin Lipset levelled at the CCF government was its unwillingness to bring about the necessary personnel changes required to implement their ambitious policy agenda.[36]

Partly because of its conviction of the value of planning and partly because of a commitment to a career public service, the CCF pioneered the development of new cabinet decision-making structures. Rather than controlling government through the exercise of patronage, the CCF created a cabinet system of decision-making that would better reflect the preferences and priorities of the cabinet and premier. Indeed, one of the earliest rationales for moving from a disaggregated cabinet to the more institutionalized version is the belief that a better supported cabinet decision structure with key committees will bring greater overall coherence to the government's agenda. That is, in a system with both a disaggregated cabinet and a weak party system, coupled with an independent civil service, there is relatively little opportunity for political vision to animate the policy agenda. Seen in this light, the changing developments in the cabinet decision-making structures in Saskatchewan were designed to ensure that a strong political vision would be included in the decision-making process. Cabinet decision-making structures were not merely part of a technocratic exercise designed to improve the efficiency and coherence of the policy process at the bureaucratic level, but rather a step taken by political leaders in the province to ensure that their own agenda was forcefully articulated throughout the decision-making process of government.

The tripartite structure that developed in Saskatchewan has shown remarkable resilience, lasting through numerous decades and surviving two extended periods of non-NDP government. While both Ross Thatcher and Grant Devine showed some hostility to certain parts, particularly the GFO-CIC because of its close association with the CCF-NDP legacy, the structure endured. This endurance is based partly on the flexibility of the model, but more importantly it has endured because it developed into an institutionalized legacy that came to define the administrative style of the province. While the apparatus has not always been employed for planning purposes, it has worked best when planning has been at the centre of the system of executive decision-making in Saskatchewan.

If the institutionalized cabinet is defined as one in which cabinet committees along with their supporting central agencies coordinate decision-making, then Saskatchewan had such a system in fairly complete form by 1948. Today Saskatchewan looks little different from other systems of government in structural terms, even if its powerful emphasis on planning continues to set it apart.

Chapter 11

The Post-Institutionalized Cabinet: The Administrative Style of Alberta

KEITH BROWNSEY

Alberta political life has been shaped by a premier-centred politics. This style of governance and politics emerged in the first decade after Alberta became a province in 1905 and was reinforced by later events. While certain features have been adapted to meet the particular requirements of the current premier and government, this style of governance remains in place to the present day.

Alberta's premier-centred governance style can be divided into four periods. The first began with the ceding of the Hudson's Bay Company territory in the northwest to the Dominion of Canada in 1869. The governance of the territories and province was dominated by the dominion government and its appointed governor and later lieutenant-governor. The colonial phase did not end until control over natural resources was given to the three prairie provinces by the government of Canada in 1930. The second period, from the election of William Aberhart in 1935 and the succession of Ernest Manning in 1943, saw the establishment of a non-institutional type of decision-making centred on the premier. This system lasted until the defeat of the Social Credit government in 1971. The new Progressive Conservative premier, Peter Lougheed, set about to create a cabinet decision-making apparatus that could cope with the increasing array of governmental activity as Alberta moved from a rural, agricultural society to an industrialized, urban polity. The institutionalized decision-making process was dismantled by Premier Ralph Klein in December 1992. Klein replaced the cabinet committee system of the Lougheed (and Getty) era with a simplified structure that reinforced the position of the premier in the province's governance structure. The current period of Alberta governance can best be described as a post-institutionalized style with its mix of caucus committees, lack of ministerial control and focus on the premier and his few close advisers.

Over the course of its history as a territory and a province in Confederation, Alberta has been the home to a variety of new political movements. Of these the best known are Social Credit, the Progressives, the United Farmers of Alberta, and the Reform Party–Canadian Alliance. These new parties were created as a response to particular socioeconomic events such as the Great Depression of the 1930s or the collapse of oil and gas prices. Or to express anger at issues ranging from the collapse of the family farm to taxes to some perceived intrusion by the federal government into areas of provincial jurisdiction. Some have been enormously successful while others have vanished almost as quickly as they were formed. Collectively, they have given Alberta the image of a politics on the fringe of Canadian society.

There are two features to this phenomenon that have been generally overlooked. First, only four parties have ever governed the province: the Liberals from 1905 to 1921; the United Farmers of Alberta from 1921 to 1935; the Social Credit League from 1935 to 1971; and the Progressive Conservatives from 1971 to the present. The long tenure of these governments has led to a blurring of the distinction between party and state. Almost every aspect of social and economic and cultural life in Alberta has become a political act. This politicization is illustrated by the commonly held view that a seat on the Calgary Stampede Board is the first step into the provincial legislature and eventually cabinet. Within this highly politicized world individuals and groups who find themselves in conflict with the state or those who seek greater input into its decision-making processes are frustrated by the lack of points of access to the political system. This frustration tends to produce much of the discontent exhibited over the years by such political parties as the Confederation of Regions, the Western Canada Concept, Alberta First, Alberta Independence Party, and the Alberta Alliance, to name but a few.

The long tenure of provincial governments in Alberta also has led to a concentration of power in the hands of the premier and his advisers. While several lieutenant-governors exhibited a penchant for political control in the years immediately after provincial status was granted in 1905,[1] the premier has been the centre of political activity since the election of Social Credit and its first leader, William Aberhart, in 1935. As a former high school principal, Aberhart ran his cabinet the way he ran his high school. Legendary for both his organizational abilities and his work ethic, Aberhart controlled every aspect of his party, government, and bureaucracy.[2] This tradition continued under his successor, Ernest Manning. For twenty-five years Manning governed in a very personal fashion; no decision was ever taken without his knowledge and approval.[3]

The defeat of Social Credit in 1971 saw an increase in the scope and complexity of cabinet structure under the Progressive Conservative government of Peter Lougheed. With his activist provincial agenda, Lougheed found it necessary to mirror the decision-making capabilities of the federal government and, as importantly, have the ability to negotiate with the multinational oil and gas companies that operated in the province. When Lougheed left office in 1985, his successor, Don Getty, maintained most of the same ministers, the same cabinet size, staff assistance, cabinet committees, and central policy techniques as his predecessor. Although Getty was often inaccessible to his ministers and was thought to spend a great deal of time on various golf courses in Alberta and elsewhere, few discernable differences could be detected in the style of decision-making.

With the selection of Ralph Klein as premier in a Progressive Conservative leadership contest in late autumn 1992, an alternative style of administration quickly became apparent. While the Lougheed and Getty governments had created and maintained an institutionalized cabinet, Klein's administrative style can accurately be described as post-institutionalized. With his long-time assistant, Rod Love, Klein deconstructed the decision-making process in Alberta. Authority was concentrated in the office of the Premier, cabinet committees were abandoned, the central agencies of the bureaucracy were dismantled, executive assistants were hired on the basis of their political effectiveness rather than their administrative competence, and communications advisers were placed in every minister's office.[4] Moreover, the line between the caucus and the cabinet was blurred when caucus committees were established with non-cabinet members of the Legislative Assembly. This post-institutionalized style has allowed Klein to control all aspects of governance in the province. As a result, the premier frequently contradicts public statements of ministers and makes decisions with little or no formal consultation with cabinet. The post-institutionalized cabinet resembles an earlier premier-centred, informal style of decision-making. While this style of organization has many similarities to the styles of Aberhart and Manning, it is both more centralized and less structured in its approach.

Several important consequences flow from this administrative style. The first is that the premier has an unusual amount of power. Klein decides, with the advice of his political staff, what decisions will go forward. As a result, many decisions have been made without consultation with cabinet or caucus. Second, decisions are sometimes ill-conceived, with little or no planning of implementation or measurement of outcome or effectiveness. To understand the current administrative style in Alberta, it is necessary to review the development of the decision-making process of the executive council.

Institutions, Styles, and Governing

Much has been written about the concentration of power in the hands of the prime minister and a few key advisers at the federal level in Canada. Donald Savoie in *Governing from the Centre* and Jeffrey Simpson in *The Friendly Dictatorship* are only two better-known studies of the increasing power of the prime minister and his staff. The growth in the authority of the central executive has come as a surprise and is a concern to many observers of Canadian political life. Power has shifted, Savoie argues, from cabinet committees and cabinet to the prime minister and a few senior advisers. This style of management at the core of the Canadian state is unique. It is a mix of the Westminster parliamentary model and the efforts of the political executive since the late 1960s to rationalize and coordinate an increasingly complex state structure. The centralization of authority in the Prime Minister's Office and in the cabinet secretariat, the Privy Council Office, has been described as a reflection of the personal styles of the individuals who have held the office of prime minister.

Savoie makes the argument that power in the federal state has moved away from line ministers and their departments towards the centre, but little attention has been given to this phenomenon in the provinces. Although there are several interesting articles on the organization of provincial cabinets and the impact of the premier on the style of decision-making,[5] little effort has been made to understand the evolution of cabinet decision-making in the provinces. Nevertheless, the concentration of authority in Ottawa has its provincial counterpart in Alberta and other provinces. The circumstances are different but the outcomes are remarkably similar.

The factors promoting cabinet institutionalization and de-institutionalization in the provinces are a mix of history, ideology, and politics. Alberta, for example, has been guided by a history of right-wing populism and strong premiers who determined the policy agenda. While exogenous influences such as the expertise developed by other provinces and interest groups have played a part in the development of the particular style of Alberta cabinets, it is the province's history of near-autocratic leadership and populism that has played the key role in determining outcomes despite institutional arrangements.

While institutions do not determine outcomes, they do 'provide an enabling, restricting, or stimulating context for individual or corporate action.'[6] Although Alberta proceeded along a path similar to the other provinces and the federal government in institutionalizing cabinet committees and secretariats, certain features are unique to the province. In recent years the process of de-institutionalization of the cabinet has taken on features which are not found either at the provincial or federal level in Canada. The adaptation of the institutionalized cabinet to Alberta followed what March and Olsen describe as the 'logic of appropriateness.' The tradition of premier-centred decision-making structured the process of cabinet 'by affecting not only the strategies, but also the preferences of the relevant actors.'[7] While the Lougheed and Getty governments of the 1970s and 1980s may have adopted the features of the institutionalized cabinet, the new structures were deeply affected by the existing style of decision-making within the cabinet. The relative ease and success with which Klein dismantled the cabinet structure and replaced it with a hybrid model with the caucus and premier at the centre indicates a return to patterns that predate cabinet committees, the cabinet secretariat, central policy techniques, and staffing arrangements of the Lougheed and Getty era.

The development of the Alberta cabinet system has followed the logic of appropriateness: it has been change within the system rather than change of the system. Each re-organization of cabinet fell within the parameters of the existing style established years before under Aberhart and Manning. Their unaided premier-centred decision-making was replaced with a system of cabinet committees and a cabinet secretariat. These changes did not diminish the role of the premier in the process. It was only in the late 1980s and early 1990s, when Don Getty disengaged from the traditional role of premier, that the cabinet decision process was seen to be distant, over-bureaucratized, and ineffective. Klein's selection as party leader and premier signalled a return to an earlier model of cabinet style. The Getty government's forty-three-committee process was replaced by a fusion of caucus and cabinet committees with the Agenda and Priorities Committee at the centre of the system.

This new system blurred the lines between the cabinet and caucus but retained a central role for the premier. The premier, however, was not given the support that had existed under Getty and Lougheed. Instead, the formal distinction between the Executive Council Office and the Office of the Premier continued but only on paper. A new emphasis was place on a rapid response to emergent issues, bold initiatives, and control of the agenda. Love believed that the key to successful governance was to manage the media which, it was thought, had the power to sway an increasingly volatile electorate. Greater flexibility was needed in the cabinet process to cope with growing electoral instability. This highly politicized decision-making process, with its focus on the premier and his staff, defines the post-institutional cabinet in Alberta.

The Colonial Cabinet

The Alberta cabinet[8] dates from the first legislature of 1905. It was appointed by Lieutenant-Governor George Bulyea. A Liberal appointee charged with ensuring a Liberal government was put in place, Bulyea played a pivotal role in provincial politics until his retirement in 1915. The five members of the first Executive Council oversaw the creation of a variety of provincial institutions, from railways construction to a public health system to elementary schools. Although there was a statutory requirement for a Treasury Board, decisions were taken on all crucial issues by cabinet as a whole. Treasury Board made recommendations but did not have the place it would achieve under Ernest Manning thirty years later. No minutes were taken of cabinet proceedings and any decisions can only be surmised from the recorded votes in the legislature and the provincial budgets. Some archival records indicate a collective decision-making style where the lieutenant-governor had considerable political and policy influence. For example, when Bulyea replaced Premier Alexander Rutherford with Arthur Sifton in 1910, it was done in consultation with Prime Minister Wilfrid Laurier as a way to preserve Liberal political dominance.[9]

The election of the United Farmers of Alberta (UFA) government in 1921 saw a change in administrative style. The UFA had been very critical of traditional notions of cabinet government. Under Herbert Greenfield and John Brownlee the farmers' government sought to replace the traditional party system with a type of particpatory or dele-gate democracy.[10] Cabinet was to take direction from the UFA annual convention. But the concept of delegate democracy clashed with insti-tutionalized notions of responsible government, and the UFA was forced to modify its approach. Nevertheless, this style of cabinet deci-sion-making was in contrast to the traditional cabinet government of the Liberals.

No record exists of cabinet minutes or decisions, but the participa-tory style of the UFA indicates a willingness to reflect the wishes of the party meetings in legislation. The UFA had been elected to represent the interests of the agricultural community in Alberta, and the cabinet was quite willing to look to the party for direction. Although the exi-gencies of cabinet government forced a modification of some of the more participatory aspects of UFA philosophy, a compromise was reached between the desire for participation and the constraints of cabinet government.

Social Credit and the Pre-Institutionalized Cabinet

In the 1930s two events altered the administrative style of decision-making in Alberta. In 1930 the federal government passed control over natural resources to the prairie provinces. This provided Alberta with a new source of revenue and lessened the province's fiscal dependency on Ottawa. At the same time, the role of the lieutenant-governor was substantially reduced and the colonial period of administration was effectively at an end.

The second event that dramatically altered the course of Alberta politics and governance occurred in 1935. The charismatic, evangeli-cal, high school principal, William Aberhart, led his Social Credit party to an overwhelming victory in the provincial election. Aberhart was an autocrat who demanded loyalty from his party members and caucus. He appointed candidates in the constituencies, set party pol-icy, and reserved the right to expel members from the party. His view of democracy was very different from that espoused by the UFA. Aberhart believed that once the electorate had made its choice, the government was free to implement the will of the people. For exam-ple, when Attorney General John Hugill refused to guarantee that legislation did not violate the constitutional division of powers between the federal and provincial governments, Aberhart summarily dismissed him. Differing visions of what was meant by the will of the people led to a backbenchers' revolt in 1937. With promises of greater caucus participation, Aberhart quelled the revolt and was able to continue as premier. Increasingly disillusioned with government after 1937, Aberhart spent more and more time in Vancouver until his death in 1943.

Ernest Manning, Aberhart's former pupil and co-religionist, succeeded him as premier and party leader. Manning continued the same style of leadership as Aberhart, but abandoned Social Credit monetary theory and the worst aspects of its conspiracy theories. Cabinet continued in a non-institutionalized form. There was no agenda; ministers would approach the premier with proposals and ask that they be discussed. It was the premier's decision whether or not they were included. No minutes of meetings were taken; some notes were made by various cabinet ministers but no official record exists of decisions taken. Moreover, no officials attended cabinet meetings. The cabinet secretary was not in attendance.[11] It was a truly unaided cabinet.

The only standing cabinet committee was Treasury Board. While various ad hoc committees were formed over the years as issues arose, once a recommendation had been made or a decision taken they were disbanded. Chaired by the provincial treasurer and vice-chaired by the premier, Treasury Board served as a type of agenda and priorities committee for cabinet. A statutory committee, Treasury Board vetted all proposals for their financial implications. If a piece of legislation was too expensive, it was denied funding. The one outside member allowed to attend any meeting of cabinet or cabinet committee was the secretary to Treasury Board, who as a senior civil servant took minutes of the meetings and recorded the decisions taken.

This situation was even less complicated in that from 1944 to 1955 Manning served as provincial treasurer. Thus, for eleven years Manning was not only premier but provincial treasurer and chair of Treasury Board. Simply put, he controlled the three central political and administrative positions in his government.

This system of decision-making worked well as long as the agenda remained uncomplicated. Manning's legendary aversion to bureaucracy and to state programs left much space for a non-institutionalized system of cabinet decision-making. As well, Manning's dominant position over the rest of the government ensured that he would be the centre of authority in the cabinet process. Although there were several strong ministers, such as Alfred Hooke and Gordon Taylor, few others in cabinet could challenge the premier.

After twenty-five years in office Manning's style of leadership had become embedded in Alberta governance. When Harry Strom succeeded Manning in 1968, it was expected that he would continue in much the same style. But Strom was a controversial choice for premier. It had been expected that Gordon Taylor would take over, but Strom's victory was assured by the intervention of Social Credit campaign manager and party president Orvis Kennedy.[12] The divisions within the party caused by the leadership contest never healed. Instead, personal, urban-rural, and ideological resentments were left to fester. Cabinet meetings became more rancorous than they had been under Manning. While several innovative policies were introduced, the bickering in cabinet between rural and urban MLAs precluded any substantial change to administrative style or policies in a province that had moved well beyond the rural and agricultural predilections of Social Credit.

The unaided cabinet had been successful as long as the leader was able to control debate within cabinet and caucus. Ministers were left alone to administer their departments. No records were kept of cabinet meetings or decisions. The cabinet met on Tuesday mornings without the aid of a secretary. As his predecessors had done before him, Premier Strom set the agenda on the advice of his ministers. While cabinet meetings sometimes lasted all day if business required, many took just the morning. Caucus was consulted on a regular basis and the only cabinet committee was Treasury Board. When any question arose in the legislature or press about their conduct, Manning had been swift to act, either replacing the offending ministers or ensuring that they were protected from scrutiny. Strom did not have the authority to act in this type of decisive fashion.

Even though Manning had to deal with a resurgent Liberal party led by Harper Prowse in the 1950s, he had dominated provincial political life. Strom, however, stood across the legislative aisle from Peter Lougheed and his Progressive Conservative caucus. The provincial Conservatives did much to cast themselves as an acceptable alternative to the long-ruling Social Credit, and in the 1971 election they were able to portray Strom as the leader of an aging rural-based government that was out of touch with the new urban realities of Alberta.

The Institutionalized Cabinet: The Lougheed-Getty Years

The 1971 provincial election was a turning point in Alberta history. Not only did the Progressive Conservatives defeat the Social Credit government – one of the longest ruling governments in Canadian history – they set about a course of reform that updated and altered much of the traditional character of political life in Alberta. Not least were the innovations of cabinet. As one former Conservative member of the Legislative Assembly has stated, 'there was nothing there.'[13] When Peter Lougheed arrived at the legislature he knew that he would find no cabinet secretariat, staff assistance, or central policy coordination.

Along with the Treasury Board, Lougheed established four policy committees: Agenda and Priorities, Economic Planning, Social Planning, and Intergovernmental Relations. As well, the deputy minister of Executive Council attended meetings of the full cabinet, and there was help for all committees including the various ad hoc or special committees organized to meet specific, time-sensitive tasks. Minutes of all cabinet meeting were now kept and a record was made of all votes. In spring 1972 – for the first time in the history of the provincial legislature – Hansard was introduced.

Other changes occurred in the Executive Council Office. Using the model of the Prime Minister's Office and the Privy Council Office, the administrative and political functions were separated – a key feature of the process of institutionalization. Premier Lougheed gave responsibility for political duties to the staff of the Office of the Premier while allocating central agency functions to the Executive Council Office. The deputy minister of the Executive Council became the secretary to cabinet charged with all the functions that such a position entails, including hiring and firing staff, allocation of resources to various cabinet committees, and responding to the various policy initiatives of cabinet. Most importantly, agenda-setting priorities were assigned to the Executive Council Office. Cabinet agendas were now formalized. The deputy minister was assigned the task of preparing an agenda for cabinet meetings as well as the various standing and ad hoc committees. The two divisions under the direction of the deputy minister were the Cabinet Secretariat and the Administrative Services Centre. Lougheed also established the position of executive director – chief of staff – in the premier's office. This position is best described as a political deputy minister. The executive director was responsible for the Legislative

Affairs Branch, the Communications Office, the Correspondence Unit, and the Southern Alberta Office of the Premier.

The basic structure of this system remained in place through the Lougheed and Getty years. Minor modifications were made from time to time but the essential features were kept. In the last years of Lougheed's government, the Cabinet Secretariat became in fact, if not title, a cabinet planning secretariat. Cabinet design in this period reflected coordination between specialized political and policy functions, but also their separation. This style of administrative structure continued until the end of the Getty government in early December 1992.

The institutionalization of the cabinet process under Lougheed and Getty did not involve radical departures from traditional decision-making processes in Alberta. The institutionalization of cabinet procedures did add to the already considerable authority of the premier. With a long history of strong leadership, the formalization of cabinet procedures simply reinforced this dominant position. The authority of the centre was strengthened by the administrative reforms of the early 1970s. In fact, the Lougheed reforms fitted in with the tradition of a dominant premier in Alberta.

The Post-Institutionalized Cabinet

With the election of Ralph Klein as leader of the Progressive Conservatives, in December 1992, the process of de-institutionalization of cabinet began. Klein initiated several sweeping reforms that fundamentally altered the nature of decision-making in Alberta, but they nevertheless remained within the core of a premier-centred administrative style.

The first significant change came with the appointment of a communications officer in each minister's office. These communications officers were appointed by the executive director in the premier's office, and they reported to the director of communications in the Office of the Premier. As well, all ministerial executive assistants were interviewed as to their perception of their role. In the course of the interview, if it was determined that the executive assistants did not see their role as political they were terminated. While ministers were free to hire their own executive assistants, Klein's chief of staff, Rod Love, ensured that they viewed their role as political operatives and not as neutral members of the bureaucracy. This caused considerable problems for several ministers and their assistants. A number of ministerial aids had been seconded from the permanent bureaucracy, and the politicization of their role not only confused them but led to their dismissal.

Another major change in the cabinet process was the blending of cabinet and caucus committees into a hybrid American-style legislative committee system within the traditional parliamentary cabinet committee structure. Since copied by British Columbia, the goal of this new post-institutionalized cabinet structure was to simplify the decision-making process. It was not viewed as an effort to employ backbenchers, but as a means through which government caucus members could influence the policy process. The central unit in this new structure was the Agenda and Priorities Committee. Although the modifications were perceived as a necessary reform of an increasingly unwieldy structure, there was a blurring between the functions of the Executive Council and Office of the Premier. Klein and Love reduced the number of cabinet committees from fifteen to three: Agenda and Priorities, Treasury Board, and Legislative Review. Treasury Board and Agenda and Priorities each have ten members, three of them backbenchers.

In place of cabinet committees Love created what he described as Standing Policy Committees (SPCs). Comprised of both cabinet members and backbench MLAs, each standing policy committee is chaired by a private government member with the authority to hear public submissions. Ministers are appointed as vice-chairs of these committees. These chairpersons sit at the cabinet table to represent the views of their committee (see Figure 11.1).

The standing policy committees struck in 1992 were Agriculture and Rural Development, Community Services, Financial Planning, and Natural Resources and Sustainable Development. In October 1995 a standing policy committee on Health Restructuring was added. In March 1997, following the provincial election, the standing policy committees were restructured. The seven committees announced were: Agriculture and Rural Development, Community Services, Education and Training, Financial Planning and Human Resources, Health Planning, Jobs and Economy, and Sustainable Development and Environmental Protection.

In May 1999 the standing policy committees underwent a major restructuring. The seven existing committees were reduced to five:

Figure 11.1. Ministerial Report Decision Model

New government policy can be initiated from many sources (the general public, interest groups, industry, etc.) and it must be approved and sponsored by a Minister and researched and drafted by his/her department. The Minister will take the proposed policy to the Agenda and Priorities Committee which directs the item to one of five Standing Policy Committees. The Standing Policy Committee study the policy in detail, and their decision is sent to Cabinet and Caucus for final approval.

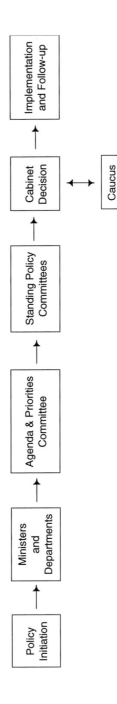

Source: Premier's Office.

Agriculture, Environment, and Rural Affairs; Economic Sustainability; Finance and Intergovernmental Relations; Health and Safe Communities; and Learning. After the March 2001 election there were six SPCs: Agriculture and Municipal Affairs, Economic Development and Finance, Energy and Sustainable Development, Health and Community Living, Justice and Government Services, and Learning and Employment. Each has between twelve and fourteen members. Not including the premier, who is an ex officio member, there are between three and five cabinet ministers on each committee, and they are dominated by backbenchers.

With ten members, three of whom are backbenchers, the Agenda and Priorities Committee coordinates the activities of the standing policy committees. Any subcommittee struck is to be task-oriented and have a maximum forty-five days of life. Each committee is given its own terms of reference and is able to review and make recommendations on policies, programs, and legislation and hear public submissions in its respective areas of competence.

The committees also monitor existing programs, services, and legislation. In addition, the committees consider the budgetary implications of each proposal as well as implementation and communications strategies, and they review the budgets of departments that impinge on their jurisdiction. For example, the standing policy committee on Agriculture and Municipal Affairs has jurisdiction over Municipal Affairs, Agriculture, Food and Rural Development, Infrastructure, Municipal Affairs, and Transportation. This oversight role was designed so that committee members would have the opportunity to provide comments and make recommendation for consideration by ministers in the preparation of the annual budget and the new three-year business plans for each department that were inaugurated by the Klein government. Each committee is assigned a cabinet policy coordinator (assistant deputy minister) who reports to the deputy minister of Executive Council. The cabinet policy coordinator oversees the administrative and policy requirements of each committee.

The creation of standing policy committees meant a transformation of the policy initiation process in the province. Policy initiatives must still be sponsored by a minister and drafted by his or her department. The minister then takes the proposed policy to the Agenda and Priorities Committee which will either reject it or send it to one of the seven standing policy committees. The committee then reviews the policy and its decision is sent to caucus and cabinet for final approval. If the policy initiative requires legislative changes, the proposal then goes to the Legislative Review Committee. This committee is comprised of ministers, MLAs, and legal counsel. It does a final review of legislation to ensure that the legal text contains the policies caucus intends. Once the Legislative Review Committee approves a draft, the legislation is printed and put on notice in the official papers of the Legislative Assembly.

Under this reformed cabinet system the deputy minister of Executive Council remains as secretary to cabinet. As with the Lougheed and Getty governments, the secretary to cabinet 'carries out functions associated with two distinct positions.' First, as clerk of the Executive Council, the position has overall responsibility for the administration of the Executive Council Office, cabinet, and its committees as well as the Office of the Lieutenant-Governor. There is a deputy clerk who acts as deputy secretary and is responsible for the day-to-day operations of the office. Second, as deputy minister of the Executive Council, the position is responsible for ensuring that government policies are communicated and coordinated on behalf of the Executive Council.

The Cabinet Secretariat organizes and coordinates the planning and policy meetings that take place within the government. It is also responsible for the administration and record-keeping of cabinet, standing policy committees, the Agenda and Priorities Committee, and the Legislative Review Committee. The secretariat also participates in the coordination of the Treasury Board fiscal and business planning process with the departments, the standing policy committees, and the Treasury Board. The policy coordination group provides administrative, policy, planning, and coordination support for the deputy minister of Executive Council.[14]

The position of the managing director of the Public Affairs Bureau is an anomaly within the cabinet structure. The managing director is a deputy minister who works out of the premier's office. The bureau is charged with helping 'the government in an ongoing dialogue with Albertans by providing quality, co-ordinated and cost-effective communication and consulting services.' This puts the bureau at odds with the Communications Office in the Office of the Premier. However, the Public Affairs Bureau is used as an information gathering arm of the Executive Council providing polling, media surveys, and other data to cabinet.

While much of the support structure was retained from the Lougheed and Getty years, the creation of standing policy committees created a very different type of administration than is found in the other provinces or at the federal level in Canada. Within the framework of political life in Alberta, Klein and Love designed a system of issue initiation and management that was described as participatory. Backbench MLAs are now included in cabinet deliberations, and they have an opportunity to put forward their own ideas. This system, however, has not been in keeping with the stated wish to give government back to the people. Replacing eleven committees of cabinet with standing policy committees that included a large number of backbench MLAs has served to focus decision-making authority within the ten-member Agenda and Priorities Committee chaired by the premier. The standing policy committees are not as powerful as the disbanded cabinet committees of the Getty and Lougheed administrations. Other than Treasury Board – which has a limited, fiscal mandate – there is no cabinet committee that is able to challenge the decision-making authority of Agenda and Priorities. This effort to streamline the policy process has led to a type of post-institutionalized cabinet. While coordinated, rational planning of the Lougheed-Getty years has not been entirely abandoned, the centralizing of authority in one cabinet committee, Agenda and Priorities, has re-established a style of governance not seen since the Social Credit era. This combination of different styles has created a hybrid system of decision-making and administration in Alberta, but one that continues the premier-dominated style of Alberta governance.

Conclusion

Executive decision-making in Alberta is a history of strong premier-led governments. Since the first Liberal government and continuing through the United Farmers, Social Credit, and the Progressive Conservatives, Alberta has been governed from the centre. Beginning with the Liberals in 1905 the executive has been the focus of institutional authority. With the election of William Aberhart in 1935, the authority of the premier was strengthened by his autocratic style. The pre-institutionalized cabinet of the Manning years gave the premier enormous authority over the provincial state. This premier-centred government was modified by the Progressive Conservative administration of Peter Lougheed. Lougheed established a system of coordinated planning that allowed the province to deal effectively with the federal government and the multinational oil and gas companies that had dominated

Alberta throughout the Social Credit years. The Lougheed-Getty governments saw the creation of an institutionalized cabinet in which cabinet decisions were taken in a coordinated fashion with the support of committees and administrative help.

The election of Ralph Klein as premier began an effort to dislodge the institutionalized cabinet. The decision-making process was seen as too cumbersome to take bold initiatives and control the political agenda. The cabinet committee system was replaced by a number of caucus committees that included both ministers and backbenchers. The one remaining cabinet committee of significance in this new process is the Agenda and Priorities Committee chaired by the premier. Authority for policy and legislative initiatives has, therefore, been placed almost entirely in this new inner cabinet. While the Legislative Review and Treasury Board committees of cabinet still exist, their mandates are limited to writing the appropriate legislation and examining the fiscal implications of any policy.

The centralization of power in an inner cabinet with a strong premier fits well with the administrative style found in Alberta. The province has a long history of centralized decision-making in the Office of the Premier. The administrative tradition of a strong leader and premier structured the process of adaptation to the new institutional arrangements by effecting not only the strategies but also the preferences of the relevant actors. Klein's post-institutional cabinet fits well with the existing rules and operating procedures.

The implementation effectiveness of the various types of cabinet organization depended on the institutional scope of the adaptations. Effective implementation was possible because of changes that followed the 'logic of appropriateness.' There are, however, problems with this new cabinet process. While Klein's post-institutional cabinet may be able to focus on one or two issues, such as the elimination of budget deficits, other programs are neglected. As the controversy surrounding the funding of public and separate school construction indicated in January 2003, there is a lack of coordination within the decision-making process in Alberta – reminiscent of an early pre-institutionalized structure.

The strong leader-centred administrative style set the parameters within which reforms would be considered, rather than what changes would be considered of provincial administrative institutions. Each of the four phases of cabinet development in Alberta fit in with the appropriate logic of existing administrative arrangements.

Chapter 12

The West Annex: Executive Structure and Administrative Style in British Columbia

NORMAN J. RUFF

A provincial bureaucracy is not a monolithic institution, and any attempt to define its administrative style must acknowledge the defining influences of both place and time. The public service of British Columbia is composed of a wide range of institutional structures, from traditional ministries headed by a cabinet minister to more autonomous Crown corporations and various boards and agencies. All these components have their own institutional histories, internal function-related demands, size-related managerial issues, and contextual influences of their own policy networks of organized interests that help shape their routine and administrative style. They are not static entities. Changing social, economic, and political environment shifts in policy programs and their priorities, and different generations of officials over time may produce a layering of different administrative styles as one succeeds another. The administrative style, for example, of a newly formed Revenue Ministry will differ from that of the Ministry of Health, which in turn may vary from the Ministry of Forests or Finance with their own particular professional outlooks. Yet all operate within a common institutional framework of a premier-led cabinet government that emanates its own all-penetrating cues as appropriate policy and behavioural dispositions. If there is an underlying British Columbia way of administering then it is perhaps found in the environmental cues emanating from the organization and practices found at the centre – that is, the Office of the Premier, which is located in the West Annex of the Parliament buildings in Victoria, and the Executive Council. This chapter considers the evolution of that institutional structure and its accompanying templates as they have defined British Columbia's administrative style.

As Richard Sigurdson has observed, there is greater executive dominance in provincial politics than in federal politics, although what provincial public policy is actually able to effect by way of economic and fiscal levers is more limited.[1] Certainly, the institutional power of political actors over bureaucratic executives has been more extensive in British Columbia because of the size and traditions of the centre located around the premier's office and the provincial cabinet. In most respects, the main characteristics of the British Columbia political system are very like those captured by Christoph Knill in his analysis of the administrative reform capabilities and administrative change in Great Britain. Strong executive leadership, malleable administrative structures, the politically contingent power of the bureaucracy with a separation of politics and administration in a model that demands 'not that civil servants be non-political but they be politically promiscuous'[2] all fit comfortably within the B.C. administrative style. British Columbia's post-2001 experience with administrative reform would also seem to confirm similar consequences for the provincial government's ability to implement a revolutionary policy paradigm shift in a Thatcherite fashion as seen in the case of Britain. Paradoxically, the British Columbia experience suggests that what were once constraints are now seen as institutional facilitators of administrative reform.

Values and Staffing the Centre

Historically, if a single administrative style had been attached to British Columbia it would have been one of laggardly insularity.[3] The stories that pre-1972 phone calls outside the province required approval from the premier and that officials' attendance at out-of-province conferences were discouraged are well worn, but not apocryphal. From the beginning of the twentieth century on, the B.C. provincial policy agenda was on the cutting edge of provincial state expansionism, for example, in workers compensation and public hospital insurance. The post-1952, twenty-year-old Social Credit regime of Premier W.A.C. Bennett nevertheless assiduously insisted on a traditional administration and politics that resemble Michael Harmon's description of low responsiveness and initiation predispositions as characteristic of a passive administrative style.[4] Administrative values in British Columbia lagged behind the changing scope and content of provincial public policy. Although not entirely unique to British Columbia, this held back the development of any institutionalized policy support at the centre outside of the person of the premier himself – with some assistance from his deputy minister of finance and the deputy provincial secretary. An un-institutionalized centre directly embodied the passive administrative style that the premier wished to convey throughout the provincial bureaucracy.

The election of a New Democratic government in 1972 brought an entirely new set of policy priorities, and these had a significant impact on ministry structures and policy outputs. The NDP also brought a shift in the administrative style of the senior bureaucracy because of the influx of 'parachutists' recruited for their compatability with the objectives and needs of the new government. Yet, despite the expected convergence with practices in the Saskatchewan home of the Canadian social democratic model, little changed at the centre because of a continuing concern for loss of political direction should the government become 'bureaucratized.'[5] Ministers pursued the particulars of their 1972 'New Deal' election platform, drawing on the resources of their own department and with little central coordination outside, or at times inside, the provincial cabinet room. Premier David Barrett later reflected, 'My policy from the start had been to delegate power to cabinet ministers. As a result, I was confronted in the House almost daily with issues I knew nothing about.'[6] Financial strains towards the end of that government's term, in 1975, and the availability of a trusted adviser[7] to go to Victoria, planted the first seed of institutionalized policy review with the creation of a small Office of the Planning Advisor to the Cabinet.

This political antipathy to a bureaucratized centre initially continued on the 1975 return of a Social Credit, under Premier Bill Bennett, who tentatively relied on a small central staff under the rubric of an Intergovernmental Relations Office. By 1982, however, Bennett had broken this insular mould and adopted of an Ottawa-style centre, with its Prime Minister's Office (PMO) to keep an eye on policy coordination. A principal secretary (later renamed chief of staff) was appointed, and as with the Privy Council Office (PCO) in Ottawa, created to maintain an administrative eye on governance in British Columbia, the Office of the Deputy Minister to the Premier and Secretary to Cabinet (first appointed in 1981) were established. This dual institutional structure provided direct support to both the premier and cabinet and has been retained by B.C.'s eight successive premiers over the past twenty years.

Such institutional continuity is particularly noteworthy given the post-1990 high turnover of premiers and their closest political advisers. A Cabinet Planning Secretariat provided comprehensive operational support and government-wide strategic planning assistance to provincial cabinet and its committees. A more active policy role for senior department executives was recognized in the institutionalization of a Deputy Ministers' Council, chaired by the deputy minister to the premier, with a mandate to review and make recommendations on common corporate issues – something that had been actively discouraged during the pre-1972 Bennett regime.[8] The council also gave support to cabinet committees and carried out ad hoc policy reviews.

The continuity in the division of labour at British Columbia's institutionalized centre was not immune to the impact of the different leadership styles of the various premiers.[9] The dangers of the populist style of Premier Bill Vander Zalm, for example, resulted in such controversies as those surrounding the sale of Expo lands and the sale of his private Fantasy Gardens property and ultimately forced his resignation. Such dangers were readily apparent from the outset in Vander Zalm's 1986 attempt to abandon the stable dualism of the deputy minister–chief of staff model. The post-1991 chairman-of-the-board style attributed to Premier Mike Harcourt appeared to lean in an irresolute direction that informed a centre described as a 'the premier in a plexiglass bubble' with a detached splendid isolationism. In due course this would cost Harcourt the premiership as the 'Bingogate' (Nanaimo Commonwealth Holding Society) charity money scandal unfolded in 1995.[10] The more colleague-intimidating, proactive, get-things-done policy style of his successor Glen Clark may be similarly tagged as responsible for the controversies regarding the 1996–7 estimates for a balanced budget, and the fast-tracked approval for construction of the ill-fated aluminium-hulled fast ferries. This style may have also fed the accusations of breach of trust and the charge of accepting a favour in connection with the Burnaby casino licensing application that led to Clark's resignation in 1999. The Clark style and its consequences were pointedly referred to in the 29 February 2000 cabinet swearing-in speech of the last NDP premier Ujjal Dosanjh, who promised, 'to replace executive government run out of the Premier's office with Cabinet government.' He may not have been entirely successful in this. Within a year, Dosanjh's minister of highways resigned, complaining that decisions were being made in the premier's office with little or no input from caucus and cabinet.[11]

Save for briefly under Premier Vander Zalm, when there was only a chief of staff, staffing of the centre has throughout retained much the same dual-function division. The Office of the Deputy to the Premier has generally adopted a non-party, although policy partisan, orientation to policy review and government operations. The status and functioning of the more partisan chief of staff position has been prone to high turnover while shifting in importance with the administrative style of each premier and the personal political crises confronting him.[12] During the Clark administration, for example, its policy significance was partially eclipsed by the close relationship to the premier enjoyed by a powerful head of the Cabinet Policy and Communications Secretariat (CPCS – or as it was soon tagged 'cupcakes'). Located in the Ministry of Finance, CPCS was an attempt to provide a more coordinated approach to policy formation and assistance to cabinet, and it had reported through the deputy to the premier, Doug McArthur, during the Harcourt administration. Under Premier Clark it took on a more prominent status on the appointment of Tom Gunton as the secretariat's own deputy minister.

Post-2001 West Annex

The 2001 Campbell government greatly expanded the capabilities and range of the centre. Two deputy ministers share the Office of the Deputy Minister to the Premier, one as the traditional cabinet secretary and the other for Corporate Planning Restructuring to oversee the post-2001 core service review of all provincial government activities (see Figure 12.1). The responsibilities of the chief of staff were extended to provide not only strategic advice and issues management support to the premier but also liaison with the government caucus and management of external relationships with communities and organizations outside government.[13] The twin deputy ministers to the premier continue to be the primary agents for cross-ministry policy development and policy coordination, with added leverage over the ministries in the review and restructuring of government services. In November 2003 the Office of the Premier added a third deputy minister for strategic policy, the economy, and the environment.

As of 2001, the premier's office also absorbed the Crown Agencies Secretariat, the Chief Information Office, the Public Affairs Bureau, and the Intergovernmental Relations Secretariat. Each has its own deputy minister. New policy priorities resulted in the transfer of the

Figure 12.1. Staffing the centre – Office of the Premier, 2002

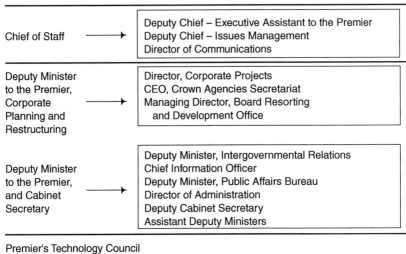

Chief of Staff	Deputy Chief – Executive Assistant to the Premier Deputy Chief – Issues Management Director of Communications
Deputy Minister to the Premier, Corporate Planning and Restructuring	Director, Corporate Projects CEO, Crown Agencies Secretariat Managing Director, Board Resorting and Development Office
Deputy Minister to the Premier, and Cabinet Secretary	Deputy Minister, Intergovernmental Relations Chief Information Officer Deputy Minister, Public Affairs Bureau Director of Administration Deputy Cabinet Secretary Assistant Deputy Ministers

Premier's Technology Council

B.C. Progress Board

Crown Corporations Secretariat from the Ministry of Finance and Corporate Relations. The secretariat provided support to various ministers, the Treasury Board, and to the cabinet on the operational management and strategic policy issues of Crown corporations and drafted related policy directives. Renamed the Crown Agencies Secretariat (CAS) and relocated in the premier's office,[14] this secretariat now has extended responsibilities in the strategic oversight of all 730 provincial Crown agencies (Crown corporations plus agencies and boards and commissions) in an effort to reduce policy fragmentation and improve accountability. As the government moves towards an implementation of a 'strong minister / strong board' approach to agency governance, CAS shifted its focus from detailed operational and financial management issues to a more strategically oriented oversight role. The twin scissors of government restructuring under the core services review and the expenditure reductions needed to balance the 2004–5 provincial budget gave the CAS a significant role in the wind-down of Crown agencies as well as the down-sizing of the secretariat itself.[15]

The growth in size of the cabinet and in staff support for the premier's office out of Bill Bennett's fledgling Office for Intergovernmental Relations is an indication of the centre's vigilance over external as well as more immediate domestic provincial public policy. The continuation of a small Intergovernmental Relations Secretariat, reporting to the deputy to the premier, with its own minister or a junior minister of state, institutionalized the goal of external policy coherence in British Columbia's relations with the federal and other governments. Such concerns as the constitutional preoccupations of the 1980s and of today's social union framework stem from external agendas and naturally fall to the centre. The secretariat also has a critical role as the cabinet's custodian of a shared interministerial style and policy positioning in all areas of intergovernmental relations.[16] British Columbia has not typically been seen as a major player in federal-provincial relations and the Office of the Premier has attempted to define the objectives and strategies required to improve effectiveness of B.C.'s federal, interprovincial, and international relations.

Similarly, the Office of the Premier's director of communications and the post-2001 formation of the Public Affairs Bureau institutionalize another concern – that of seeking coherence and overall control over the government's policy messages. A review of the government's entire communications process was prepared by David Brown in 1976, and it had rejected the Alberta centralized model. It recommended, instead, that departmental informational officers be retained but it also proposed that a communications planning adviser be attached to the Executive Council and that all government programs should include a communications plan. As elsewhere, drawing the line between government information and party-serving, image-building propaganda raises some delicate distinctions, which can be exacerbated by the centralization of the provision or the contracting out of government communications with the general public. Premier Harcourt, for example, was the subject of a conflict-of-interest review and party to an investigation by the B.C. auditor general in the awarding of communications contracts. No favouritism was found and the premier was cleared of the charge. But although the overseeing of contracts by the Government Communications Office and the coordination of public opinion research through the Public Issues and Consultation Office may be appropriate for effective management, their reporting links to the premier's office and cabinet can feed political innuendo.

Concern for coordination from the centre and a heightened concern for 'new era' policy consistency by individual ministers and their ministries have recently brought British Columbia back to the Alberta model. All information officers were brought under the rubric of the Office of the Premier's Public Affairs Bureau, and in June 2002, all 270 of them were terminated as public service employees. Some 160 were subsequently rehired by order-in-council. This new centralizing communications model has been said to 'demand a new work ethic and political culture that ensures all Public Affairs Bureau employees work together as one team with all ministers and their staff to meet the government's communications needs and objectives.' A 'silos' approach to ministry communications was replaced by a 'far greater interministry coordination.' The new Public Affairs Bureau Communications Division is staffed by order-in-council appointees. The latter report to the premier's chief of staff while a Support Services and Operations Division is staffed by a mix of excluded public service employees, order-in-council appointments, and contractors who report through an assistant deputy minister to both of the premier's chief advisers, the deputy minister to cabinet and the chief of staff. The increased politicization as well as centralization of the communications function was directly acknowledged in an admission that 'this change reflects the unique and demanding nature of communications work required by ministers to properly communicate within the broad political context in which they operate. It acknowledges that communications is inescapably a function aimed at giving expression to the vision and priorities for which the government is politically accountable.'[17] Or, as it was still more candidly put by the premier, 'this is not just a straight union job. This is a job that is going to require commitment to the government's goals and objectives.'[18]

A central media relations unit, said to operate on a '24/7' basis, supplements media relations within the provincial ministries, and continuous monitoring of the media attempts to help ministries provide instant responses to developing public issues and 'respond quickly to public statements that are misleading or factually incorrect.' Nine large ministries and the treaty negotiations office have been allocated their own communications staff while the smaller ministries share with two or three others. All communications directors are accountable to the premier as well as to the minister of their assigned ministry. Within this fine-tuning of central supervision over communications, it should be noted, communications officers were removed from involvement in ministry staff preparation of such cabinet documents as ministry submissions or cabinet briefing notes and such tasks as ministry intranet services and community liaison.[19]

Two new advisory bodies add to the policy intelligence and advice coming directly to the premier. The Premier's Technology Council provides advice on economic issues in the technology industry and a Progress Board, made up of business representatives, now monitors the province's economic performance. Somewhat similar to the Progress Board pioneered by Oregon State in 1989, the latter is an independent performance measurement and policy advisory body to the premier setting benchmarks for the growth of the provincial economy and identifying specific economic goals for tax, regulatory, and fiscal reform in its biannual reports.[20]

In the first year of the new B.C. Liberal government, the Office of the Premier had grown from forty full-time positions and annual operating expenditures of $3 million to 470 staff and a $56 million revised 2001–2 budget. As discussed above, this was due in large part to the absorption of the Crown Agencies Secretariat, the Public Affairs Bureau, and all government communications staff into the Office of the Premier. The 2004–5 service plan subsequently envisaged 298 positions and a $44.1 million operating budget with 209 of the positions and 75 per cent of that expenditure allocated to the Public Affairs Bureau. Today's centre has become as much preoccupied with getting its message out as it is with directing policy.

Defining the Style of a New Administration

The administrative style and cues of Premier Gordon Campbell are still evolving but, despite the maintenance of the basic B.C. institutional forms at the centre, it is already clear that there is little administrative continuity with his predecessors. The premier's second deputy minister was charged with the core services review, which was seen as a 2001 electoral mandate for its 'new era' party platform. This fundamental direction to all policy matters may be largely attributable to a populist impulse to live up to the party's 'covenant with the people,' but the ubiquitous mandate also provided a policy coherence that flowed from the centre to permeate throughout the provincial government. Many of the commonly regarded key tasks of the centre regarding policy coordination, inter-minister and inter-ministry conflict resolution, and legitimation were not entirely eliminated. However, they were significantly reduced in importance by an unyielding adherence to the two-hundred-item mix of general and specific new era policy blueprints. If there is a newly emergent British Columbia administrative style it is that of a corporate collegiality facilitated by the shared political mandate, which must be referred to by every cabinet member, and which in turn has informed the sweeping core services review and the rolling three-year strategic plans that began in 2002.

Experimentation with more transparent government resulted in twenty-nine open cabinet meetings in the first thirty-four months of the Campbell administration. Such meetings are called on twenty-four hours public notice, with the proceedings televised and web cast and with subsequent online postings of the cabinet submissions, executive summaries, and transcripts of their proceedings. They have become occasions for policy information updates and policy announcements on such issues as the deregulation of liquor sales, the elimination of business subsidies, and restructuring of health authorities, as well as such presentations as the Gary Filmon Report on the Firestorm 2003 Provincial Review. The open cabinets focus on detailed minister-by-minister staged presentations and too often give the appearance of a 'power point' driven policy process, and the exchange of mutual compliments that accompany the open cabinet discussions at times sound like a contrived congratulatory chorus. Nevertheless, they also convey an image of a shared corporate vision. The new device of enforcing ministerial responsibility by withholding a portion of each minister's salary for an individual and collective cabinet failure to meet budgetary limits, itself a new era commitment, no doubt also reinforces the sense of a common enterprise behind the cabinet chorus.

Centre-defined cues as to the administrative styles deemed appropriate for the new provincial government were set forth in some detail in a remarkable letter of instructions sent each new minister on 25 June 2001. It informed all twenty-eight cabinet members on the appropriate organization of their offices and also on their relationships with their executive staff, with the premier's officials, and with the new cabinet structures, plus specific references to their own particular sets of policy responsibility. The carefully defined parameters began with a reminder that this was to be a lean and efficient government and that the structuring and staffing of each minister's office (confined to a single ministerial and single executive assistant) would be arranged by the premier's chief of staff. Coordination of the implementation of the political agenda was to be through the Office of the Premier's communications director working with the caucus communications director. The Public Affairs Bureau provided communications planning services such as media monitoring and advertising in each ministry.[21] For the ministers' executive staff, the instructions stressed that 'all Deputy Ministers, Assistant Deputy Ministers and equivalents are appointments of the Premier' and these had a 'dual reporting relationship' to their minister and to the deputy to the premier.[22] The respective roles of the minister and deputy were given careful definition to match the new provincial administrative style of both elected and unelected provincial officials: 'These appointees are civil servants in the fullest sense of the term. They obviously must maintain your confidence and respect, but their role is to give you good policy advice and professional execution of government directions and programs; they are not your political advisors. Similarly your role is to ensure that policy issues are identified, properly analyzed and either resolved through your discretion as Minister or brought to Cabinet on those matters requiring a broader perspective. I would caution that your role is not to become the chief executive officer of your Ministry. That is the purview of your deputy.'[23]

Recent British Columbia political history no doubt informed the letter's reminder of another set of administrative values implicit in the province's conflict-of-interest legislation and the premier's own statement of standards. It stressed that 'the hallmark of this administration is one founded upon the high ethical conduct of every member of our government, but first and foremost among all members of the Executive Council.'

The Office of the Premier's three-year strategic service plans also give out an integrated corporate leadership–central command set of administrative values. A statement of strategic shifts to achieve the New Era vision envisages movement from 'coordination, micro-management and confidentiality [to] leadership, innovation, transparency and accountability' and a shift from a 'lack of clarity and responsibility for overall priorities and core services' to a focus on key priorities and ministerial responsibility along with integrated service delivery, consistent cross-government intergovernmental relations, and an integrated communications network.[24] This redefinition of some of the administrative features of B.C. provincial cabinet government and a de-emphasis of policy co-ordination rests on an assumed team spirit derived from the notion of an electorally mandated policy framework and its specific party policy commitments. Diminished possibilities of conflict are hopefully assumed to obviate the institution-building, policy coordination obsession of its predecessors.

Cabinet Committee Structures

Over time, the development of staff support within British Columbia's centre has run parallel to the growth of cabinet (from seventeen ministers, fourteen of them salaried, in 1967 to twenty-three, nineteen salaried, in 1973, up to the 2001 record of twenty-eight members)[25] and a cabinet committee system served by a Cabinet Secretariat under the deputy minister to the premier. From a fledgling two statutory committees in 1972, the Harcourt administration redesigned the 1980s cabinet committee structure to four major elements: the Planning Board, chaired by the premier as the central policy and planning committee on all major policy issues and government legislative and strategic policy priorities with its own working groups in specific policy areas; Treasury Board, chaired by the minister of finance, with statutory authority under the Financial Administration Act over all financial management and budgetary policy, with primary responsibility in the development and review of economic, fiscal, and taxation policy, as well as preparation of the budget and estimates of expenditures; the Cabinet Committee on Regulations and Orders in Council, chaired by the attorney general; and the Public Issues Committee supported by the Public Issues and Consultation Office within the Ministry of Government services. By the end of the NDP's ten-year term in office, backbenchers were also brought into cabinet committees and working groups.

The much enlarged Campbell cabinet of 2001, with twenty-one full ministers and seven ministers of state, has addressed the danger of policy fragmentation (and the concerns of an over-wieldy seventy-seven member government caucus in a seventy-nine seat legislature) through an elaborate network of cabinet and legislative committees. Based on the Alberta model, working legislative committees operate in tandem with an integrated two-way flow between five government caucus committees (GCCs) vice-chaired by a minister, and five cabinet committees (CCs) which themselves include backbench members. (For the 2004 structure see table 12.1.) At the outset, the overriding preoccupation of the new government, with the implementation of its 2001 policy platform, alongside the commitment to balance the budget, made the Core Review and Deregulation Committee of Cabinet the most influential ministerial group that became chaired by the premier.[26] This was complemented by the pressing perspectives emanating from Treasury Board, which in 2002 struggled with a record $4.4 billion deficit, and the

Table 12.1. British Columbia Legislative and Cabinet Committee Systems, 2004

Legislative Assembly	Cabinet	
Select Standing Committees (SSCs)	Government Caucus Committees (GCCs)	Cabinet Committees (CCs)
Aboriginal Affairs	Communities and Safety	Agenda and Priorities
Crown Corporations		
Education	Economy and Government	
Operations		
Finance and Government Services	Education	Environment and Resource
Development		
Health		Legislative
Review		
Parliamentary Reform, Ethical Conduct, Standing Orders, & Private Bills	Cross Government Initiatives	Treasury Board
Public Accounts		
Legislative Initiatives		

Other caucus committees have included task forces on leaky condominiums, pine beetle infestation, offshore oil and gas, and the Northern and the Kootenay regional caucuses. The original 2001 GCCs included separate committees for the economy and government operations and also a committee on natural resources. Education and cross government initiatives are 2004 additions.

There is no readily identifiable inner cabinet, and the potential candidate in the form of the Agenda and Priorities Committee is primarily concerned with policy review flows and routings through the committees and cabinet.

necessities of the government's strategic plan and ministry plans for services if the 2004–5 budget is to be balanced.

The GCCs occupy a unique position. They are composed of governing party caucus members (unlike the Legislative Assembly's SSCs, which contain an opposition presence, insofar as since 2001 there is one with only two NDP members), and as cabinet committees, they are staffed by cabinet operations staff and bound by cabinet confidentiality vis-à-vis their caucus colleagues. GCCs have become more than make-work arenas for a bulging caucus; they provide policy advice and budgetary review input. Originally they also received public submissions but any propensity for them to act as an additional access point for organized policy interests was short-lived. GCCs significantly extend the fusion of the province's executive and legislative functions in British Columbia, and funding for GCCs is through the Legislative Assembly budget. The importance of the cabinet and full caucus relationships was highlighted in the premier's June 2001 instructions to ministers requiring their attendance at all government caucus meetings and meetings of government caucus committees. Committee organizational charts too often provide an aura of planning and policy activity that does not extend very far beyond their 'power point' presentation. Even so, in the opening years of the Campbell government, the new committee networks helped maintain a cohesive administrative style and policy uniformity through this fusion of executive and legislative functions and the quasi-co-optation of the governing party caucus into the centre.

The Post-Institutionalized Cabinet and Executive-Driven Fusion

The past thirty years of organizational change surrounding British Columbia's political executive, as described above, parallel development patterns in other provinces and the transitions to an institutionalized cabinet identified by Christopher Dunn. In many instances, the British Columbia bureaucracy has tended to be a straggler relative to other jurisdictions. Its institutional reforms have replicated developments in other provinces or reflected negative as well as positive lessons in drawing from their experiences. But although not an administrative innovator, there remains a 'made-in-B.C.' quality to the province's performance both in the timing of change and in some underlying continuities that differentiate it from the experience elsewhere.

At the outset, the institutionalized cabinet came relatively late to British Columbia because of a fundamental concern for the dangers of bureaucratic control that institutionalization might bring. The 1972 NDP victory was seen as a grand window of opportunity for British Columbia to emulate the Saskatchewan model of a well-served cabinet. But a continuing preoccupation with direct cabinet ministerial control prevailed. The subsequent government turnover in 1975 was more propitious in opening the policy window on administrative reform. Cautiously drawn lessons from Alberta and Ottawa helped shape the fledgling premier's and cabinet operations offices and the introduction of a Treasury Board staff and Employee Relations Bureau. What John Kingdon has identified as the three elements shaping policy agenda – the problem, policy, and political streams – had finally merged.[27] A 1986 atavistic attempt to return to pre-1972 practices under Premier Vander Zalm provided a brief reminder that populist influences could still haunt the centre. By the 1990s the main tendency in British Columbia's governance appeared to be an increasingly fragmented centre (despite the efforts of a cabinet committee coordinating group) with the proliferation of central agencies and staff in the Cabinet Planning Secretariat and Intergovernmental Relations Branch in the Cabinet Office, as well as Treasury Board staff in Finance, the Public Issues and Consultation Office, and Government Communications within the Ministry of Government Services, and later, the Cabinet Policy and Communications Secretariat within Finance.

Beneath its organizational jigsaw, British Columbia had many of the characteristics of what Dunn has described as a post-institutionalized cabinet, with an increase in the already considerable concentration of power within the Office of the Premier at the expense of cabinet. The 1996–9 Clark administration had many post-institutionalized features, including a shrunken cabinet and heightened control through his main advisers, his chief of staff, his deputy minister for communications and operations, and his deputy minister in the Policy Secretariat. With the exception of an enlarged Liberal cabinet, more recent developments have increased B.C.'s premier-driven post-institutionalization characteristics. These include several additional emulations of other jurisdictions such as the adoption of the Alberta-style three-year service plans, core services review, the B.C. Progress Board, and the government caucus committee structure.

It would be a mistake, however, to assume that British Columbia has simply acquired a taste for synchronicity with other provinces. As Tom Christensen et al. have argued, the leeway for administrative reform is influenced by the instrumental-structural features of the polity and a leadership attentive to an active administrative policy. They interact with such environmental factors as economic crises or exposure to global prescriptions and their own historical–institutional cultural contexts to constrain or create opportunities to launch reform.[28] In the case of

British Columbia's initial post-1975 reform phase, the transformation of the centre began with an element of catch-up with practices elsewhere alongside a critical loosening of the cultural constraints against a proactive bureaucracy. In its post-2001 reform phase the centre has been shaped by the immediate B.C. imperatives of an unprecedented government majority plus the accompanying self-perception of a binding mandate to rethink the entire nature of provincial government.

Taking a long view, the evolution of the centre within the institutions of British Columbia governance has matched the changing scope of provincial government and its associated administrative values over the past thirty years. From the early 1970s open acceptance of a greater role policy-making for senior B.C. executives and increasing levels of policy partisanship, from the initial NDP 1972–5 agenda shift through the Bill Bennett 1983 program of restraint down to the present-day corporate model of the goal-defined 'chief executive officer,' there has been a significant shift in the underlying administrative culture of British Columbia. The expectations of elected and unelected officials are far different to those of a generation ago. As of 2004, the governance of British Columbia and its administrative styles embodies a remarkable paradox. The new policy agenda has accelerated a sweeping redefinition of the role of provincial government, its services, regulatory activities, and policy instruments. Reprofiling, restructuring, results-based administration, deregulation, policy flexibility and responsiveness, transparency, increased accountability, contracting-out, and affordability are the language of a new agenda that brings many of the components of performance management more explicitly into provincial administrative and managerial practice. Alongside this is an offloading regionalization of social services, increased agency and local autonomy, privatization, and public-private partnerships. All of these potentially feed fragmentation of the B.C. government in fulfilment of the 'hollow crown'[29] projection of a governmental centre with a weakened capacity to provide coherent coordination or direction and policy response. As the provincial government downsizes the public service over the three years from 2002 to 2005, each year's surviving cohort of executives, managers, and support staff are engaged in a restructuring that will eventually eliminate a good number of their own functions and positions.

In the meantime, British Columbia's institutional framework and practices of the political executive have moved in an opposite direction to any 'hollowing out' by actively conserving power at the centre.

Such devices as the notion of a policy mandate and the integration of cabinet and caucus committees in shaping policy direction enhance the centre by enlarging its compass and implicating senior ministry officials as committee policy advisers. The defining characteristic of any Westminster-style parliamentary framework has always been the fusion of the executive and legislative functions. British Columbia's reforms dramatically extend such fusion and the underlying reality of executive dominance from the West Annex. With the core service and strategic policy reviews there has been an unprecedented degree of policy integration and command. Indeed, these two phenomena have a joint impact through their constraints and incentives that project powerful and mutually reinforcing cues in administrative style and policy control not approached since the zenith of the W.A.C. Bennett regime. Where British Columbia's current course may eventually lead remains uncertain. As March and Olsen observe, 'the transformation of institutions is neither dictated completely by exogenous conditions nor controlled precisely by intentional actions.'[30] For the moment, the intentions of the Campbell administration have only just begun to be tested.

Part IV

CONCLUSION

Chapter 13

Conclusion: Executive Institutional Development in Canada's Provinces

LUC BERNIER, KEITH BROWNSEY,
AND MICHAEL HOWLETT

This book has investigated a particular aspect of the Canadian political-administrative style, that is, the relatively long-term relationship existing between the institutions and behaviour of government at the provincial level. While chapters in the book provided a general overview of the development of executive agencies and governments in each of Canada's eleven major jurisdictions, and addressed the ten major questions set out in Chapter 1, each author has focused upon the nature of the style of executive government of one jurisdiction in this country and how it has changed over time.

The authors discovered that the dominant role of the premier or prime minister is not assured in Canadian government. As the analysis of important jurisdictions such as Quebec showed, first ministerial dominance is conditional upon a relatively long-term stay in office, the continued success of the governing party at the polls, and the ability of premiers to retain the support of their party machinery and caucus. Without such support, a first minister can often rule only very uneasily, without being able to ensure that his or her initiatives will be successfully translated into policy or law.

On the relationship between the first minister and other cabinet ministers, the authors revealed the importance of extra-cabinet staff and support agencies in allowing a premier to control powerful rivals. Although the exact mechanism of control has evolved considerably over time, the development of central agencies, and especially control over activities such as communications and legislative agendas coming to rest in the Premier's Office, has greatly extended the ability of even weak premiers to control their cabinets.

Cabinet committees and committee structures were seen to have varied tremendously between governments and, over time, within them as well. While ostensibly created in an effort to make the institutionalized cabinet operate more efficiently and effectively through the delegation of time and the coordination of policy-making, cabinet committee systems also fragment the decision-making process and provide additional levers through which central agencies and premiers have been able to exercise a controlling influence on overall cabinet deliberations and direction.

Part and parcel of cabinet 'committee-ization' has been the creation of de facto or, in some cases, de jure inner cabinets within the institutional model. Although most provinces have not gone as far down this road as has the federal government, the expansion of cabinet size has been a major characteristic of executive development across Canada over the past several decades and has contributed to the development of specialized committees whose main role is to oversee or coordinate lesser ones. Like the well-known early Trudeau-era federal cabinet, many provinces have created priorities and planning committees, which amount to defacto inner cabinets of key ministers who are able to help the premier steer cabinet initiatives in a desirable direction or, at least, delay or shelve initiatives that they do not favour. Staffing these key committees, of course, is one of the central techniques by which first ministers retain control over the executive branch of the state.

Each of the chapters has provided a great deal of information on the structure, evolution, and role played by central agencies in the executive branch. Although many of these agencies, such as Treasury Board and the Privy Council Office, pre-date the modern executive machinery of government, their size and role have evolved dramatically, and this has aided the development of the independent policy capacity of Canadian cabinets. While the exact nature and evolution of central agencies is unique in each jurisdiction, there is no doubt that the development of such agencies is a key characteristic of the transition from the traditional to the departmental or institutionalized cabinet in all Canadian jurisdictions.

The pattern of evolution of central agencies has also affected the nature of the first minister's and cabinet's relations with departmental deputy ministers. That is, in the traditional and departmental cabinets, deputy ministers played a significant role as purveyors of information, knowledge, expertise, and advice as required by the cabinet in making well-informed policy choices and decisions. However, as central agencies expanded and grew, a separate layer of administration appeared between the administrative and political arms of the executive, filtering and impeding direct links between senior departmental officials and executive members.

Directly related to the above point, the decline of the deputy minister has been accompanied by the simultaneous rise of the cabinet secretary as 'deputy-minister' to cabinet, standing at the apex of power, serving as the lynch-pin linking central agencies and departments to the institutional cabinet. Of course, as some jurisdictions have developed a post-institutionalized cabinet, the role of the cabinet secretary has suffered at the expense of the growth of the role and significance of the premier's secretary.

Although in contemporary Canadian cabinets few independent sources of power exist outside the central agencies, inner cabinets, and premier's offices, several authors have discerned the continued ability of specialized financial ministries and ministers to monopolize information and expertise on government expenditures and revenues upon which the other major players of Canadian executive government rely in making their decisions. Although the ability of a Ministry of Finance to do more than set the general tone of fiscal restraint or largesse of government depends in many jurisdictions upon its ability to encompass the traditional budgeting and auditing role of Treasury Board, in some jurisdictions ministers of finance continue to exist as independent challengers to the monopolization of information and expertise in the other parts of Canadian executive agencies.

Finally, this volume provides ample evidence of one of the key mechanisms used by premiers' offices in jurisdictions such as British Columbia, Ontario, and the federal government to overtake central agencies in the domination of cabinet activities: the control over the communications function of government. This usurps one of the last tools of influence left in the hands of departments, as well as the cabinet as a whole and the central agencies that support it. Now they must bow down to the ability of the Premier's Office to generate a picture of harmony and solidarity in the portrayal of the smooth sailing of the ship of state so important to voters, media relations, and party members.

This book has thus revealed a pattern of evolution of cabinet government in the provinces which is quite different from the better-known
features of the federal government in Ottawa. By illuminating these
differences, the authors provide a more detailed portrait of Canadian
executive governance than has previously been available.

The contributions of these chapters, however, are more than just
descriptive and empirical in nature. As was suggested in Chapter 1,
the authors have also collectively addressed theory in this area. The
principle contribution made has been to systematically apply to the
Canadian context the insights of previous studies of the evolution of
federal and provincial cabinets, notably the Dupré-Dunn-Savoie model
of a four-stage process of executive office development in Canada. As
this book reveals, while the government in Ottawa has moved through
four stages since Confederation – from the traditional unaided cabinet,
to the departmental cabinet of strong ministers and departments, to
the institutional cabinet with central agency support, and finally to the
prime-minister centred post-institutional model – not all the provinces
have moved to the fourth stage. In addition, the timing of developments in the provinces has not been the same as that of the federal government. In some, it has taken much longer to emerge from the
traditional model, and they have generally compressed the transition
between stages into a shorter period of time than did their federal
counterpart.

Only three jurisdictions (Alberta, British Columbia, and Ontario)
developed along post-institutional lines. Examining the reasons for the
evolution, or lack of it, towards a premier-centred model in different
jurisdictions, it appears that the main criterion for assessing this development is not the personality of the premier, since strong and weak, or
active and passive, premiers can be found in all eras of cabinet government in Canada. Rather the key dimension has to do with the increasing autonomy of the Premier's Office, first from the legislature, then
from ministers and deputy-ministers, then from cabinets and cabinet
committees, and finally from central agencies and cabinet secretaries.
That is, a key institutional element of the Westminster model of government – the fusion of legislative and executive powers – has gradually been altered as, first, the executive developed an ever-greater
capacity to control the legislature and evade or override traditional
controls and limits placed on executive behaviour, and, second, the
Premier's Office attained considerable independent capacity and
autonomy from the rest of the executive branch.

This process of the accretion of control in the Premier's Office has been accomplished in several stages as (1) full cabinets take over control of the legislative agenda in the transition from the traditional to the departmental cabinet; (2) the capacity of central agencies to deal with complex policy issues is enhanced in the transition from the departmental to the institutionalized cabinet, and (3) the machinery of cabinet government developed in the institutionalized phase is 'seized' by the Premier's Office in the transition to (4) the post-institutionalized phase – including the centralization of communications activity and the establishment of caucus committees that allow the Premier's Office to extend its control back into the legislature.

Notes

Chapter 1

1 See Paul G. Thomas, 'Ministerial Responsibility and Administrative Accountability,' in M. Charih and A. Daniels, eds., *New Public Management and Public Administration in Canada* (Toronto: IPAC, 1997), 143–63.

2 See R.A.W. Rhodes, and P. Weller, eds., *The Changing World of Top Officials* (Buckingham: Open University Press, 2001).

3 Donald J. Savoie, *Governing from the Centre: The Concentration of Power in Canadian Politics* (Toronto: University of Toronto Press, 1999), and Donald J. Savoie, 'The Rise of Court Government in Canada,' *Canadian Journal of Political Science* 32, no. 4 (1999): 635–64.

4 Herman Bakvis, 'Prime Minister and Cabinet in Canada: An Autocracy in Need of Reform?' *Journal of Canadian Studies* 35, no. 4 (2001): 60–79.

5 On this question, see Graham White, 'Mother Teresa's Biker Gang or Cabinet Democracy in Canada' in *Canada Today: A Democratic Audit* (Canadian Study of Parliament Group / Canadian Studies Programme, Mount Allison University, 30 November 2001).

6 Christopher Dunn, *The Institutionalized Cabinet: Governing the Western Provinces* (Montreal: McGill-Queen's University Press, 1995); 'Premiers and Cabinets,' in C. Dunn, ed., *Provinces: Canadian Provincial Politics* (Peterborough: Broadview, 1996), 165–204; 'The Central Executive in Canadian Government: Searching for the Holy Grail,' in C. Dunn, ed., *The Handbook of Canadian Public Administration* (Don Mills: Oxford University Press, 2002), 305–40.

7 Michael Howlett, 'Administrative Styles and the Limits of Administrative

Reform: A Neo-Institutional Analysis of Administrative Culture,' *Canadian Public Administration* 46, no. 4 (2004): 471–94.

8 Michael Howlett, 'Understanding National Administrative Cultures and Their Impact upon Administrative Reform: A Neo-Institutional Model and Analysis,' *Policy, Organization and Society* 21, no. 1 (2002): 1–24.

9 See Max Weber, *Economy and Society: An Outline of Interpretive Sociology* (Berkeley: University of California Press, 1978), and S.E. Eisenstadt, *The Political Systems of Empires* (London: Collier, 1963).

10 See, for example, Dwight Waldo, *The Administrative State: A Study of the Political Theory of American Public Administration* (New York: Ronald Press, 1948), and Ernest Barker, *The Development of Public Services in Western Europe 1660–1930* (Oxford: Oxford University Press, 1944).

11 See Christoph Knill, 'European Policies: The Impact of National Administrative Traditions,' *Journal of Public Policy* 18, no. 1 (1998): 1–28; Christoph Knill, 'Explaining Cross-National Variance in Administrative Reform: Autonomous versus Instrumental Bureaucracies,' *Journal of Public Policy* 19, no. 2 (1999): 113–39; and Adrienne Heritier, Christoph Knill, and Susanne Mingers, *Ringing the Changes in Europe: Regulatory Competition and the Transformation of the State. Britain, France, Germany* (Berlin: Walter de Gruyter, 1996).

12 See Hans Bekke, James L. Perry, and Theo Toonen, 'Comparing Civil Service Systems,' *Research in Public Administration* 2 (1993): 191–212; Hans Bekke, James L. Perry, and Theo A.J. Toonen, eds., *Civil Service Systems in Comparative Perspective* (Bloomington: Indiana University Press, 1996); Hans Bekke, James L. Perry, and Theo A.J. Toonen, 'Introduction: Conceptualizing Civil Service Systems,' ibid., 1–12; Hans Bekke and Frits M. van der Meer, eds., *Civil Service Systems in Western Europe* (Cheltenham: Edward Elgar, 2000); and Hans Bekke, 'Studying the Development and Transformation of Civil Service Systems: Processes of De-Institutionalization,' *Research in Public Administration* 5 (1999): 1–18.

13 Elisabeth S. Clemens and James M. Cook, 'Politics and Institutionalism: Explaining Durability and Change,' *Annual Review of Sociology* 25 (1999): 441–66.

14 See Junko Kato, 'Review Article: Institutions and Rationality in Politics – Three Varieties of Neo-Institutionalists,' *British Journal of Political Science* 26 (1996): 553–82; and Peter A. Hall and Rosemary C.R. Taylor, 'Political Science and the Three New Institutionalisms,' *Political Studies* 44 (1996): 936–57.

15 A useful definition of institutions used in this approach was put forward by Robert Keohane who described them as 'persistent and connected sets of

rules (formal or informal) that prescribe behavioural roles, constrain activity, and shape expectations.' Robert O. Keohane, *International Institutions and State Power: Essays in International Relations Theory* (Boulder: Westview Press, 1989), 163.

16 Elinor Ostrom, 'Institutional Rational Choice: As Assessment of the Institutional Analysis and Development Framework,' in P.A. Sabatier, ed., *Theories of the Policy Process* (Boulder: Westview Press, 1999), 35–71.

17 James G. March, and Johan P. Olsen, 'Institutional Perspectives on Political Institutions,' *International Political Science Association* (1994): 5.

18 Morten Egeberg, 'The Impact of Bureaucratic Structure on Policy Making,' *Public Administration 77*, no. 1 (1999): 159.

19 Graham T. Allison and Morton H. Halperin, 'Bureaucratic Politics: A Paradigm and Some Policy Implications,' *World Politics 24*, no. (Supplement) (1972): 40–79; Alexander L. George, 'The "Operational Code": A Neglected Approach to the Study of Political Leaders and Decision-Making,' *International Studies Quarterly 13* (1969): 190–222.

20 Thomas H. Hammond, and Jack H. Knott, 'Political Institutions, Public Management, and Policy Choice,' *Journal of Public Administration Research and Theory 9*, no. 1 (1999): 33–85. See also Thomas H. Hammond, 'Agenda Control, Organizational Structure, and Bureaucratic Politics,' *American Journal of Political Science 30*, no. 2 (1986): 379–420. More generally, see Fritz W. Scharpf, 'Games Real Actors Could Play: The Problem of Mutual Predictability,' *Rationality and Society 2* (1990): 471–94, and Fritz W. Scharpf, 'Political Institutions, Decision Styles, and Policy Choices,' in R.M. Czada and A. Windhoff-Heritier, eds., *Political Choice: Institutions, Rules and the Limits of Rationality* (Frankfurt: Campus Verlag, 1991), 53–86.

21 On ideas and their impact, see John L. Campbell, 'Institutional Analysis and the Role of Ideas in Political Economy,' *Theory and Society 27*, no. 5 (1998): 377–409; and Peter A. Hall, 'Policy Paradigms, Experts, and the State: The Case of Macroeconomic Policy-Making in Britain,' in S. Brooks and A.G. Gagnon, eds., *Social Scientists, Policy, and the State* (New York: Praeger, 1990), 53–78. On calculations of feasibility, see Ralph K. Huitt, 'Political Feasibility,' in A. Ranney, ed., *Political Science and Public Policy* (Chicago: Markham Publishing Co., 1968), 263–76; Giandomenico Majone, 'On the Notion of Political Feasibility,' *European Journal of Political Research 3* (1975): 259–74; and Arnold J. Meltsner, 'Political Feasibility and Policy Analysis,' *Public Administration Review 32* (1972): 859–67.

22 John Zysman, 'How Institutions Create Historically Rooted Trajectories of Growth,' *Industrial and Corporate Change 3*, no. 1 (1994): 243–83.

23 Graham White, 'Adapting the Westminster Model: Provincial and Territo-

rial Cabinets in Canada,' *Public Money and Management* 21, no. 2 (2001): 17–24.

24 Bekke, Perry, and Toonen, 'Introduction: Conceptualizing Civil Service Systems,' in Bekke, Perry and Toonen, eds., *Civil Service Systems*, 4.

25 For example, see Stefan Dupré, 'Reflections on the Workability of Executive Federalism,' in R. Simeon, ed., *Intergovernmental Relations* (Toronto: University of Toronto Press, 1985); and Dunn, *The Institutionalized Cabinet*.

26 Savoie, *Governing from the Centre*, 325.

27 Dunn, *Handbook of Canadian Public Administration*, 312–13.

Chapter 2

1 See, among others, Andrew Coyne, 'Stop me if you've heard this,' *National Post* (Toronto), 29 July 2002, A4.

2 Gordon Robertson, 'The Changing Role of the Privy Council Office,' *Canadian Public Administration* 14, no. 4 (Winter 1971): 497.

3 Canada, *Responsibility in the Constitution* (Ottawa: Privy Council Office, 1993).

4 See Stefan Dupré, 'The Workability of Executive Federalism in Canada,' in H. Bakvis and W. Chandler, eds. *Federalism and the Role of the State* (Toronto: University of Toronto, 1987), 238–39.

5 Based on material provided to me by a former senior official with the Federal-Provincial Relations Office, Ottawa, January 1993.

6 Donald J. Savoie, *Governing from the Centre: The Concentration of Power in Canada* (Toronto: University of Toronto Press, 1999), 153.

7 Andrew F. Cooper, *In Between Countries: Australia, Canada and the Search for Order in Agricultural Trade* (Montreal and Kingston: McGill-Queen's University Press, 1997), 217.

8 See David Cameron and Richard Simeon, 'Intergovernmental Relations and Democratic Citizenship,' in B. Guy Peters and Donald J. Savoie, eds., *Revitalizing the Public Service: A Governance Vision for the Twenty-First Century* (Montreal: McGill-Queen's University Press, 2000), 58–118.

9 See, among others, Donald J. Savoie, *The Politics of Public Spending in Canada* (Toronto: University of Toronto Press, 1990).

10 See, among many others, Donald Johnston, *Up the Hill* (Toronto: Optimum Publishers International, 1986); John C. Crosbie, *No Holds Barred: My Life in Politics* (Toronto: McClelland and Stewart, 1997); and Erik Nielsen, *The House Is Not a Home* (Toronto: Macmillan of Canada, 1989).

11 Richard Johnston et al., *Letting the People Decide: Dynamics of a Canadian Election* (Montreal: McGill-Queen's University Press, 1992), 244.

12 Quoted in Sharon L. Sutherland, 'Does Westminster Government Have a

Future?' (Ottawa: Institute of Governance, Occasional Paper Series, 11 June 1996), 5.

13 Ibid., 11.

14 See Crosbie, *No Holds Barred*, 301.

15 Public Opinion, *This Morning*, 3 December 1997.

16 Edward Greenspon and Anthony Wilson-Smith, *Double Vision: The Inside Story of the Liberals in Power* (Toronto: Doubleday, 1996), 7.

17 Quoted in Savoie, *Governing from the Centre*, 330.

18 Thomas S. Axworthy, 'Of Secretaries to Princes,' *Canadian Public Administration* 31, no. 2 (Summer 1988): 245.

19 Al Johnson, *What Is Public Management in Government?* (Ottawa: Canadian Centre for Management Development, May 1993).

20 See Canada, *Budget des dépenses pour l'année financière se terminant le 31 mars 1969* (Ottawa: Imprimerie de la Reine, 1969), 106, 109, 349, 365, 436, 438; and *Part III Estimates, 1996–97*. Consultations with an official with the Privy Council Office, Ottawa, 1 March 1999.

21 See Marc Lalonde, 'The Changing Role of the Prime Minister's Office,' *Canadian Public Administration* 14, no. 4 (Winter 1971): 532.

22 Ibid., 520.

23 A.D.P. Heeney, 'Mackenzie King and the Cabinet Secretariat,' *Canadian Public Administration* 10 (September 1967): 367.

24 See the mandate discussion in Canada, *Privy Council Office 1997–98 Estimates*.

25 Quoted in Savoie, *Governing from the Centre*, 122.

26 'Chrétien set to remake top court,' *Ottawa Citizen*, 14 December 1997, A7.

27 Quoted in Savoie, *Governing from the Centre*, 283.

28 Donald J. Savoie, 'Globalization, Nation States, and the Civil Service,' in B. Guy Peters and Donald J. Savoie, eds., *Governance in a Changing Environment* (Montreal and Kingston: McGill-Queen's University Press, 1995), 82–110.

29 Harland Cleveland, 'The Twilight of Hierarchy: Speculations on the Global Information Society,' *Public Administration Review* 45, no. 1 (January/February 1985): 195.

30 Quoted in Greenspon and Wilson-Smith, *Double Vision*, 48.

31 Jeffrey Simpson, *Spoils of Power: The Politics of Patronage* (Toronto: Collins, 1988), 367. See also John Sawatsky, *The Insiders: Government, Business, and the Lobbyists* (Toronto: McClelland and Stewart, 1987).

32 Jean Chrétien, *Straight from the Heart* (Toronto: Key Porter Books, 1985), 85.

33 Sharon Sutherland, 'Responsible Government and Ministerial Responsibil-

ity: Every Reform Is Its Own Problem,' *Canadian Journal of Political Science* 24, no. 1 (March 1991): 101.

34 'Spending limits irk cabinet,' *Globe and Mail*, 3 December 1997, A1, A28.

35 Canada, *The Functioning of the Privy Council Office* (Ottawa: Privy Council Office, December 1978), 4–8.

36 Mitchell Sharp, 'Relations Between Politicians and Public Administrators,' in *Bulletin* (Toronto: Institute of Public Administration, 1985), 1.

37 Jacques Bourgault and Stephane Dion, 'The Changing Profile of Federal Deputy Minister, 1867 to 1988,' Research Paper no. 2 (Ottawa: Canadian Centre for Management Development, March 1991), 28, 39.

38 Frank Swift, 'Strategic Management in the Public Service: The Changing Role of the Deputy Minister' (Ottawa: Canadian Centre for Management Development, November 1993), 63.

39 Canada, 'Discussion Paper on Values and Ethics in the Public Service' (Ottawa: Privy Council Office, December 1996), 45.

40 Swift, 'Strategic Management in the Public Service,' 23.

41 Consultation with Mitchell Sharp, Ottawa, March 1998.

42 Consultation with a former deputy minister, Ottawa, March 1998.

43 Jacques Bourgault, 'De Kafka au Net: la lutte incessante du sous-ministre pour contrôler son agenda,' *Gestion* 22, no. 2 (Summer 1997): 21–2.

44 Quoted in Greenspon and Wilson-Smith, *Double Vision*, 212.

45 Axworthy, 'Of Secretaries to Princes,' 247, 262.

46 'Penalty killer PM plays rough,' *Globe and Mail*, 1 December 2000, A4.

Chapter 3

1 See also Christopher Dunn, 'The Newfoundland Public Service: The Past as Prologue?' in Evert Lindquist, ed., *Government Restructuring and Career Public Service in Canada*, Monographs on Canadian Public Administration No. 23 (Toronto: Institute of Public Administration of Canada, 2000), 173–207.

2 Ross A. Johnson, 'Cabinet Decision-Making Structures: Taking Issues out of Politics?: The Newfoundland Case,' paper presented at the annual meeting of the Canadian Political Science Association, Quebec, 30 May–2 June 1976.

3 John C. Crosbie, *No Holds Barred: My Life in Politics* (Toronto: McClelland and Stewart, 1997), 57.

4 Interview with John Crosbie, St John's, 10 September 2002.

5 Interview with Ed Roberts, St John's, 14 August 2002.

6 John C. Crosbie, *No Holds Barred*, 66–8.

7 Interview with John Crosbie, St John's, 10 September 2002.

8 Throne Speech debate, 3 March 1970, quoted in Richard Gwyn, *Smallwood:*

The Unlikely Revolutionary (Toronto: McClelland and Stewart, rev. ed. 1999), 357.

9   Much of what follows is based on two informative articles by Randy Joyce, a staff writer at the *Evening Telegram* in St John's: 'Moores' rise and entrenchment,' 14 May 1977, and 'Restructuring: Old Wine in Recycled Bottles,' 21 May 1977.

10 Government of Newfoundland, *Excepts from the Report of the Committee on Government Administration and Productivity,* St John's, December 1972, 2.

11 Calculated from figures provided in ibid., 20

12 Ibid., 19.

13 Government of Newfoundland, *Government White Paper on The Organization of the Public Service of Newfoundland and Labrador* (St John's, November 1972).

14 The COGAP report said, for example, that 'The Treasury Board has been in operation in this Province for comparatively few years and, when it was first activated, there was an understandable tendency to extend its control over a wide field of expenditures. For these reasons, many departments feel that the effective carrying out of their programs and operations is being handicapped by the constant necessity to submit contemplated expenditures to the Board for expenditures.' *Excerpts,* 13.

15 Joyce, 'Restructuring: Old Wine in Recycled Bottles.'

16 The duties of the commission were to manage and supervise public service recruitment, selection, appointment, promotion, transfers, personnel planning, staff evaluation and staff procedure manuals.

17 Channing's career spanned a large part of Newfoundland history. He had spent forty-four years in the public service, half of it in the position of senior public servant, in fact if not always in name. In later years he was deputy minister of provincial affairs from 1956 to 1968, then deputy minister to Premier Smallwood, and from 1972 to 1978, when he retired, headed the Cabinet Secretariat, as clerk.

18 David Vardy received training in commerce, economics and political science at Memorial University, and went to receive an MA in economics from both the University of Toronto and Princeton. In December of 1972, fresh from a teaching stint at Queen's University, he became director of economic and resource policy in the Planning and Priorities Secretariat and secretary to the Resource Policy Committee of Cabinet. He was deputy minister in the P&P Secretariat from 1975 to 1978, and then clerk of the Executive Council and secretary to cabinet from September 1978 to February of 1985. His analytical abilities continued to manifest themselves long after his time in the secretariat, having been called upon for a host of major arm's-length policy studies and public offices.

19 *Building on Our Strengths*, Report of the Royal Commission on Employment and Unemployment (St John's, Newfoundland: Queen's Printer, 1986), 420.
20 Ibid. See recommendations 235, 237, 238.
21 J.D. House, *Against the Tide: Battling for Economic Renewal in Newfoundland and Labrador* (Toronto: University of Toronto Press 1999), 11.
22 *Canadian Public Administration* 69 (Spring 1991), entire edition.
23 Newfoundland and Labrador, *Budget 1992*, appendix A, A-3; *Budget 1993*, Appendix, 1; *Budget 1994* and *Budget 1995*, Appendix in each; and *Budget 1995*, Appendix, 1.
24 The same act solidified the control of the premier as the gatekeeper for intergovernmental agreements: section 1 said that 'Notwithstanding another Act or law, every intergovernmental agreement shall, before it is executed be submitted to the Premier, and except an agreement in respect of which the Lieutenant-Governor in Council by order directs otherwise, *every intergovernmental agreement shall be signed by the Premier* as well as the minister of the government of the province administering the department to which it relates, *and an intergovernmental agreement which is not executed in accordance with this section is not binding on the province or an agency or official of the province'* (emphasis added). Premier Tobin would change this back to the former, non-specific designation in 1997. Statutes of Newfoundland 1997, ch. 25, An Act to amend the Intergovernmental Affairs Act (Assented to 19 December 1997).
25 Government of Newfoundland and Labrador, *Public Consultation Process on the Strategic Economic Plan: Report to the Public* (St John's: Advisory Council on the Economy, April 1992). The Report contained 134 recommendations.
26 Government of Newfoundland and Labrador, *Challenge and Change: A Strategic Economic Plan for Newfoundland and Labrador* (St John's: Queen's Printer, June 1992).
27 As of writing, only one has been released: Government of Newfoundland and Labrador, *Meeting the Challenge: Status Report on the Implementation of the Strategic Economic Plan* (St John's: n.p., January 1994).
28 A 1978 graduate of Osgoode Hall Law School, Rowe had been assistant clerk of the Newfoundland House of Assembly and then joined the Department of External Affairs. From 1984 to 1996 he practised law in Ottawa. Tobin liked his intellect, which he first discovered in a Rowe paper when he assumed the Fisheries and Oceans portfolio in 1993. Tobin entrusted the clerkship/secretary position to him in March 1996, where he served until June 1999, when he was appointed a justice of the Trial Division of the Supreme Court of Newfoundland. Since December of 2001 he has been a Justice of the Court of Appeal in St. John's. (See Brian Tobin, with John Lawrence Williams, *All in Good Time* [Toronto: Penguin Canada, 2002], 164.)

29 There were many changes in 1999–2000 in central agency officials, reflecting the change in regimes. Malcolm Rowe was replaced on 9 June 1999 by John R. Cummings, Q.C., as clerk of Executive Council and secretary to the cabinet, and on that date Gary Norris became the new deputy clerk of Executive Council and associate secretary to the cabinet. Veteran provincial Liberal politician Beaton Tulk replaced Tobin as premier from October 2000 to February 2001, a comfort to the party because of his experience and because he did not intend to run himself. On 14 November 2000 Premier Tulk announced that Cummings had been appointed deputy minister of justice and that Gary Norris had moved from deputy clerk to clerk of the Executive Council and secretary to cabinet. Andrew Noseworthy replaced Norris as deputy clerk of the Executive Council and associate secretary to cabinet, rising from his previous position of deputy minister, Intergovernmental Affairs Secretariat. On 12 February 2001, Tulk, operating on behalf of premier-designate Roger Grimes, announced that Deborah Fry had been appointed clerk of the Executive Council and secretary to cabinet, replacing Gary Norris, who became deputy minister of intergovernmental affairs.

30 Brian Tobin, *All in Good Time* (Toronto: Penguin Canada, 2002), 158–9.

31 Deborah Fry had previously been deputy minister of health and community services, deputy minister of human resources and employment, deputy minister of education, and deputy minister of employment and labour relations. A person with a wide experience – she held both a B.Sc.N. and an LLB. – she had practised law with the Department of Justice of Newfoundland and Labrador, and has worked in public health and nursing education in Saskatchewan and Australia. Fry, originally from Saskatchewan, was also the first non-native Newfoundlander/Labradorian to serve as clerk. Fry was dismissed in September of 2004 by Williams, in connection with the resignation of Elizabeth Marshall, the health minister, for reasons that were not made clear to the public.

32 David R. Cameron and Graham White, *Cycling into Saigon: The Conservative Transition in Ontario* (Vancouver: UBC Press, 2000), 6.

Chapter 4

1 See, for example, Colin Campbell and George Szablowski, *The Superbureaucrats: Structure and Behaviour in Central Agencies* (Toronto: Macmillan of Canada, 1979); W.A. Matheson, *The Prime Minister and the Cabinet* (Toronto: Methuen Publications, 1976); R.M. Punnett, *The Prime Minister in Canadian Government and Politics* (Toronto: Macmillan of Canada, 1977); Walter Stewart, *Shrug: Trudeau in Power* (Toronto: New Press, 1971); and Thomas A.

Hockin, ed., *Apex of Power: The Prime Minister and Political Leadership in Canada* (Scarborough: Prentice-Hall of Canada, 1971).

2 Donald J. Savoie, *Governing from the Centre: The Concentration of Power in Canadian Politics* (Toronto: University of Toronto Press, 1999); Christopher Dunn, *The Institutionalized Cabinet: Governing the Western Provinces* (Montreal and Kingston: McGill-Queen's University Press, 1995).

3 Jeffrey Simpson, *The Friendly Dictatorship* (Toronto, Ontario: McClelland and Stewart, 2001).

4 R.A. Young, 'Teaching and Research in Maritime Politics: Old Stereotypes and New Directions,' *Journal of Canadian Studies* 21, no. 2 (Summer 1986): 133–56.

5 For instance, McKenna's name reportedly appeared in the headline or first paragraph of more than three hundred stories in the *Globe and Mail* during his ten years as premier. Philip Lee, *Frank: The Life and Politics of Frank McKenna* (Fredericton: Goose Lane Editions, 2001), 15.

6 Richard Starr, *Richard Hatfield: The Seventeen Year Saga* (Halifax: Formac Publishing Company, 1987); Michel Cormier and Achille Michaud, *Richard Hatfield: Power and Disobedience*, translated by Daphne Ponder (Fredericton: Goose Lane Editions, 1992); Lee, *Frank.*

7 Rand Dyck, *Provincial Politics in Canada: Towards the Turn of the Century,* 3rd ed. (Scarborough: Prentice Hall Canada, 1996), 167–209; Hugh Mellon, 'New Brunswick – The Challenge of New Brunswick Politics,' in Keith Brownsey and Michael Howlett, eds., *The Provincial State in Canada: Politics in the Provinces and Territories* (Peterborough: Broadview Press, 2001), 75–109; Della M.M. Stanley, *Louis Robichaud: A Decade of Power* (Halifax: Nimbus Publishing, 1984), 137–62; R.A. Young, 'Remembering Equal Opportunity: Clearing the Undergrowth in New Brunswick,' *Canadian Public Administration* 30, no. 1 (Spring 1987): 88–102; and *The Robichaud Era, 1960–70: Colloquium Proceedings* (Moncton: Canadian Institute for Research on Regional Development, University of Moncton, 2001).

8 Dyck, *Provincial Politics in Canada,* 185–87; Mellon, 'New Brunswick,' 81–2; and J.D. Love, 'The Merit Principle in the Provincial Governments of Atlantic Canada,' *Canadian Public Administration* 31 no. 3 (Fall 1988): 342–45.

9 Mark Pedersen, 'The Transition from Patronage to Media Politics and Its Impact on New Brunswick Political Parties' (MA thesis, Queen's University, 1982).

10 Stanley, *Robichaud,* 179–89 and 222; Lee, *Frank,* 139–64.

11 Arthur T. Doyle, *The Premiers of New Brunswick* (Fredericton: Brunswick Press, 1983), vii, viii.

12 Donald J. Savoie, 'Governing a "Have-Less" Province: Unravelling the New Brunswick Budget Process in the Hatfield Era,' in Allan M. Maslove,

ed., *Budgeting in the Provinces: Leadership and the Provinces*, Monographs on Canadian Public Administration, no. 11 (Toronto: Institute of Public Administration of Canada, 1989), 34.

13 Ralph R. Krueger, 'Changes in the Political Geography of New Brunswick,' *Canadian Geographer* 19, no. 2 (Summer 1975): 121–34.

14 R.V. Stewart Hyson, 'New Brunswick's Electoral Redistribution of 1990–94: A Structural Approach to Redistribution Policy' (PhD dissertation, Ottawa, Carleton University, 1998), 82–126.

15 Young, 'Teaching and Research in Maritime Politics,' 137–42; and Robert E. Garland, *Promises, Promises ... An Almanac of New Brunswick Elections, 1870–1980*, Social Science Monograph Series, Special Issue No. 1 (Saint John: University of New Brunswick, 1979), 48–56.

16 John Garner, 'The Ballot in the British North American Colonies,' in J.H. Aitchison, ed., *The Political Process in Canada: Essays in Honour of R. MacGregor Dawson* (Toronto: University of Toronto Press, 1963), 17–35.

17 Hugh G. Thorburn, *Politics in New Brunswick* (Toronto: University of Toronto Press, 1961), 135–43; Dalton Camp, *Gentlemen, Players and Politicians* (Toronto: McClelland and Stewart, 1970), especially 1–94; Hyson, *New Brunswick's Electoral Redistribution of 1990–94*, 113–23; and Mellon, 'New Brunswick,' 85–7.

18 The reference to MLAs here in the masculine is appropriate because there were no female MLAs until the modern period. The first woman (Brenda Robertson) was elected in 1967. See Elspeth Tulloch, *We, the Undersigned: A Historical Overview of New Brunswick Women's Political and Legal Status, 1784–1984* (Moncton: New Brunswick Advisory Council on the Status of Women, 1985), 73.

19 H.J. Whalen, *The Development of Local Government in New Brunswick* (Fredericton: Queen's Printer, 1963); and Ralph R. Krueger, 'The Provincial-Municipal Government Revolution in New Brunswick,' *Canadian Public Administration* 13, no. 1 (Spring 1970): 51–99.

20 R.A. Young, Philippe Faucher, and André Blais, 'The Concept of Province-Building: A Critique,' *Canadian Journal of Political Science* 17, no. 4 (December 1984): 783–818.

21 Dunn, 'The Central Executive in Canadian Government: Searching for the Holy Grail,' 307.

22 Ibid.

23 Stanley, *Robichaud*, 1–14.

24 Depending on the criteria used, the French-speaking population (mostly Acadians) now constitutes about one-third of the province's population. For much of the province's history, English-French disputes had occurred within the Roman Catholic Church and the two communities had lived

separately; French was seldom used in the legislature – simultaneous translation in the legislature was introduced in 1967 – or in the senior ranks of government. Further elaboration on biculturalism and bilingualism in New Brunswick may be found in the following sources: Edmund A. Aunger, *In Search of Political Stability: A Comparative Study of New Brunswick and Northern Ireland* (Montreal: McGill-Queen's University Press, 1981); Pierre A. Coulombe, *Language Rights in French Canada*, Francophone Cultures and Literatures, Vol. 2 (New York: Peter Lang Publishing, 1995); Dyck, *Provincial Politics in Canada*, 172–5 and 185–202; David L.E. Peterson, 'New Brunswick: A Bilingual Assembly for a Bilingual Province,' in Gary Levy and Graham White, eds., *Provincial and Territorial Legislatures in Canada* (Toronto: University of Toronto Press, 1989), 156–65; Catherine Steele, *Can Bilingualism Work? – Attitudes Toward Language Policy in New Brunswick: The 1985 Public Hearings on the Poirier-Bastarache Report* (Fredericton: New Ireland Press, 1990); and Richard Wilbur, *The Rise of French New Brunswick* (Halifax: Formac Publishing Company, 1989).

25 Mellon, 'New Brunswick,' 90–2.
26 Aldéa Landry's spouse, Fernand, was also McKenna's first deputy minister of the Premier's Office. Lee, *Frank*, 26.
27 Stanley, *Robichaud*, 150–1.
28 Ibid., 123–62.
29 Pedersen, *The Transition from Patronage to Media Politics*, 16–94.
30 For a more in-depth account of Hatfield's government, see Hugh P. Mellon, 'Political Communications and Government Reform: New Brunswick under Richard Hatfield' (Kingston: PhD dissertation, Queen's University, 1990).
31 For a fascinating political biography of Hatfield, see Cormier and Michaud, *Richard Hatfield*.
32 Henry J. Llambias, 'The New Brunswick Ombudsman' (Ottawa: PhD dissertation, Carleton University, 1979), 48–67.
33 For greater elaboration, see Savoie, 'Governing a "Have-Less" Province,' 31–54; and Paul C. Leger, 'The Cabinet Committee System of Policy-making and Resource Allocation in the Government of New Brunswick,' *Canadian Public Administration* 26, no. 1 (Spring 1983): 16–35.
34 Cormier and Michaud, *Richard Hatfield*, 63. Later on in their careers, both Massé and Murray were to move to federal politics, although the latter continued occasionally to serve Hatfield as an adviser and speechwriter.
35 Lee, *Frank*, 139–64.
36 Donald J. Savoie, *Pulling against Gravity: Economic Development in New Brunswick during the McKenna Years* (Montreal: Institute for Research on Public

Policy, 2001), 85. Also on McKenna's record, see William J. Milne, *The McKenna Miracle: Myth or Reality?* (Centre for Public Management, Faculty of Management, University of Toronto, 1996).

37 Stewart Hyson, 'Electoral Boundary Redistribution by Independent Commission in New Brunswick, 1990–94,' *Canadian Public Administration* 43, no. 2 (Summer 2000): 174–97.

38 Stewart Hyson, 'Where's "Her Majesty's Loyal Opposition" in the Loyalist Province?' *Canadian Parliamentary Review* 11, no. 2 (Summer 1988): 22–5.

39 Philip Lee's biography of McKenna, *Frank*, provides a most thorough account of these close advisers to the premier.

40 Interview with a former McKenna cabinet minister, 23 October 2002.

41 The official party standings resulting from the general election of 9 June 2003 were: twenty-eight Progressive Conservative, twenty-six Liberal, and one NDP. See New Brunswick, Office of the Chief Electoral Officer, '2003 Election Results.' Online. http://www.gnb.ca/elections/03prov/03recapsheet-e.asp, accessed 20 March 2004.

42 Stewart Hyson, 'New Brunswick's Gamble on VLTs – Was This the Way to Conduct a Referendum?' *Canadian Parliamentary Review* 24, no. 4 (Winter 2001–2): 19–26.

43 Interviews, 23 October 2002 and 6 November 2002.

44 The Lord government's ineffective handling of the high increases in car insurance rates by the private insurers was seen by most observers as the key factor in the government's loss of support, with the Progressive Conservative party escaping with only the narrowest of victory in 2003. Weir's committee report is expected to be delivered later in 2004.

Chapter 5

1 Donald J. Savoie, *Governing from the Centre: The Concentration of Power in Canadian Politics* (Toronto: University of Toronto Press, 1999).

2 Christopher Knill, 'European Policies: The Impact of National Administrative Traditions,' *Journal of Public Policy* 18, no. 1 (1998): 1–28; Hans Bekke, James L. Perry, and Theo Toonen, 'Comparing Civil Service Systems,' in *Research in Public Administration* 2 (1993): 191–212; and James G. March and Johan P. Olsen, 'The New Institutionalism: Organizational Factors in Political Life,' *American Political Science Review* 78, no. 3 (1984): 734–49.

3 Christopher Dunn, 'Premiers and Cabinets,' in Christopher Dunn, ed., *Provinces: Canadian Provincial Politics* (Peterborough: Broadview Press, 1996), 195.

4 Rand Dyck, *Provincial Politics in Canada: Towards the Turn of the Century,* 3rd ed. (Scarborough: Prentice Hall, 1996), 139.

5 J. Murray Beck, *Politics in Nova Scotia, Volume Two, 1896–1988* (Tantallon, Four East Publications, 1988).

6 With a legislature averaging forty seats between 1867 and 1978, this would mean that provincial cabinets would typically encompass a clear majority of the governing caucus. This reality would ostensibly give the government caucus much greater weight in governmental priority-setting and policy and program decision-making than would be the case of other caucuses in other provinces with larger legislative assemblies.

7 Christopher Dunn, *The Institutionalized Cabinet: Governing the Western Provinces* (Toronto: University of Toronto Press, 1995), and Agar Adamson and Ian Stewart, 'Party Politics in the Not So Mysterious East,' in Hugh G. Thorburn, ed., *Party Politics in Canada*, 7th ed. (Scarborough: Prentice Hall, 1996), 121.

8 David J. Elkins and Richard Simeon, *Small Worlds: Provinces and Parties in Canadian Political Life* (Toronto: Methuen, 1980).

9 Kenneth Bryden, 'Cabinets,' in David J. Bellamy, Jon H. Pammett, and Donald C. Rowat, eds., *The Provincial Political Systems: Comparative Essays* (Toronto: Methuen, 1976). 317.

10 Peter Kavanagh, *John Buchanan: The Art of Political Survival* (Halifax: Formac Publishing, 1988), 81.

11 Kavanagh, *Buchanan*, 81–2.

12 Peter Aucoin, 'Nova Scotia: Government Restructuring and the Career Public Service,' in Evert Lindquist, ed., *Government Restructuring and Career Public Services* (Toronto: The Institute of Public Administration of Canada, 2000), 236.

13 Ibid., 236–9.

14 Ibid., 239.

15 Dunn, 'Premiers and Cabinets,' 196; Peter Clancy, James Bickerton, Rodney Haddow, and Ian Stewart, *The Savage Years: The Perils of Reinventing Government in Nova Scotia* (Halifax: Formac Publishing, 2000), 72.

20 Aucoin, 'Nova Scotia,' 251–5.

Chapter 6

The author would like to thank Douglas Boylan, former clerk of Prince Edward Island's Executive Council, for his helpful comments on this chapter, and Cynthia Anne McKenna of the University of Prince Edward Island's Robertson Library for research assistance.

1 See David A. Milne, 'Prince Edward Island: Politics in a Beleaguered Garden,' in Keith Brownsey and Michael Howlett, eds., *The Provincial State in*

Canada: Politics in the Provinces and Territories (Broadview: Peterborough, 2001), especially 125–7.

2 Kenneth Bryden, 'Cabinets,' in David J. Bellamy, Jon H. Pammett, and Donald C. Rowat, eds., *The Provincial Political Systems: Comparative Essays* (Toronto: Methuen, 1976), 311.

3 See Leopold Kohr, *The Overdeveloped Nations: The Diseconomies of Scale* (New York: Schoken Books, 1978).

4 See Blair Weeks, ed., *Minding the House: A Biographical Guide to Prince Edward Island MLAs, 1873–1993* (Charlottetown: Acorn Press, 2002).

5 Calculated from Statistics Canada, *Employment and Average Weekly Earnings (including overtime), Public Administration, Canada, the Provinces and Territories* (Ottawa: Department of Supply and Services, 2000).

6 This statement is based on combined provincial and federal employment, but, because many functions that would otherwise be municipal are provincial in PEI, that may not be the case if municipalities in other provinces were included.

7 See J.T. Croteau's *Cradled in the Waves: The Story of a People's Cooperative Achievement in Economic Betterment on Prince Edward Island, Canada* (Toronto: Ryerson Press, 1951).

8 See Harry Baglole and David Weale, eds., *Cornelius Howatt: Superstar!* (Belfast, PEI: privately published, 1974).

9 See David Milne, 'Politics in a Beleaguered Garden,' in Keith Brownsey and Michael Howlett, eds., *The Provincial State in Canada* (Peterborough: Broadview Press, 2001), 111–38.

10 John Crossley, 'A United Elite and a Compliant Public: A Preliminary Look at Government Reform in Prince Edward Island,' presented at the annual conference of the Atlantic Provinces Political Studies Association, St Francis Xavier University, 15–17 October 1993, 11.

11 Rand Dyck, *Provincial Politics in Canada: Towards the Turn of the Century,* 3rd ed. (Scarborough: Prentice Hall, 1996), 92.

12 Neil Nevitte, *The Decline of Deference : Canadian Value Change in Cross-National Perspective* (Peterborough: Broadview Press, 1996).

13 Donald J. Savoie, *Governing from the Centre: The Concentration of Power in Canadian Politics* (Toronto: University of Toronto Press, 1999); Mancur Olson, *The Logic of Collective Action: Public Goods and the Theory of Groups* (Cambridge, Mass.: Harvard University Press, 1971); Gunnar Myrdal, 'The Principle of Circular and Cumulative Causation,' chap. 2, in *Economic Theory and Under-Developed Regions* (London: Gerald Duckworth & Co., 1957).

14 S.J.R. Noel, 'Leadership and Clientism' in David J. Bellamy et al., eds., *The*

Provincial Political Systems: Comparative Essays (Toronto: Methuen, 1976), 197.

Chapter 7

1 See Luc Bernier and Evan Potter, *Business Planning in Canadian Public Administration*, New Directions, No. 7 (Toronto: Institute of Public Administration of Canada, 2001).

2 See Luc Bernier, 'The Beleaguered State: Québec at the End of the 1990s', in Keith Brownsey and Michael Howlett, eds., *The Provincial State in Canada* (Peterborough: Broadview, 2001).

3 Hubert Guindon, 'The Modernization of Quebec and the Legitimacy of the Canadian State,' in Daniel Glenday, Hubert Guindon, and Allan Torowetz, *Modernization and the Canadian State* (Toronto: Macmillan, 1978), 212–46; Kenneth McRoberts, *Quebec: Social Change and Political Crisis*, 3rd ed. (Toronto: McClelland and Stewart, 1993).

4 Daniel Salée, 'Reposer la question du Québec? Notes critiques sur l'imagination sociologique,' *Revue québécoise de science politique* 18 (1990): 83–106.

5 Gérard Pelletier, *Les années d'impatience, 1950–1960* (Montréal: Stanké, 1983), 6.

6 R.A. Young, Philippe Faucher, and André Blais, 'The Concept of Province-Building: A Critique,' *Canadian Journal of Political Science* 17 (1984): 783–818.

7 Kenneth McRoberts, *Quebec: Social Change and Political Crisis*, 3rd ed. (Toronto: McClelland and Stewart, 1993).

8 Claude Morin, *Mes premiers ministres* (Montréal: Boréal, 1991).

9 Among other accounts, see Peter Debarats, *René, a Canadian in Search of a Country* (Toronto: Seal Books, 1977). See also Pierre O'Neill and Jacques Benjamin, *Les mandarins du pouvoir* (Montréal: Québec/Amérique, 1978).

10 Graham Fraser, *PQ, René Lévesque and the Parti québécois in power*, 2nd ed. (Montreal: McGill-Queen's University Press, 2001).

11 See Jean Crète, ed., *Générations et politiques* (Boucherville: Gaëtan Morin Éditeur, 1989).

12 Kenneth Kernaghan, Bryan Marson, and Sandford Borins, *The New Public Organization* (Toronto: Institute of Public Administration of Canada, 2000); Mohamed Charih and Art Daniels, eds., *Nouveau management public et administration publique au Canada* (Toronto: Institute of Public Administration of Canada, 1997); Robin Ford and David Zussman, eds., *La prestation de rechange de services: pour une gouvernance partagée au Canada* (Toronto: Institute of Public Administration of Canada, 1997).

13 P.R. Bélanger, 'Les nouveaux mouvements sociaux à l'aube des années 90,'

Nouvelles Pratiques Sociales 1, No. 1 (1988): 101–14; P.R. Bélanger and B. Lévesque, *Le modèle québécois: corporatisme ou démocratie sociale?* (Montréal: Cahiers du Crises No. 0111, 2001); Yves Bélanger, *Québec Inc.: L'entreprise québécoise à la croisée des chemins* (LaSalle: Éditions Hurtubise HMH, 1998).

14 Marie Bouchard, Gilles Bourque, and Benoît Lévesque, 'L'évaluation de l'économie sociale dans la perspective des nouvelles formes de régulation socio-économique de l'intérêt général,' *Cahiers de recherche sociologique* (March 2001): 31–53; Gilles L. Bourque, *Le modèle québécois de développement: de l'émergence au renouvellement* (Sainte-Foy: Presses de l'Université du Québec, 2000).

15 Guy Lachapelle, 'Identity, Integration and the Rise of Identity Economy: The Québec Case in Comparison with Scotland, Wales and Catalonia,' 211–31 in Guy Lachapelle and John Trent, *Globalization, Governance and Identity: The Emergence of New Partnerships* (Montréal: Presses de l'Université de Montréal, 2000).

16 B. Lévesque, 'Le partenariat: Une tendance lourde de la nouvelle gouvernance à l'ère de la mondialisation. Enjeux et défis pour entreprises publiques et d'économie sociale,' *Annales de l'économie publique, sociale et coopérative* 72, no. 3 (September 2001): 323–38; B. Lévesque, *Le modèle québécois: Un horizon théorique pour la recherche, une porte d'entrée pour un projet de société?* (Montréal: Cahiers du Crises, No. 0105, 2001).

17 B. Lévesque, P.R. Bélanger, M. Bouchard, and M. Mendell, *Le Fonds de solidarité FTQ, un cas exemplaire de nouvelle gouvernance* (Montréal: Fonds de solidarité, 2001).

18 See David Waldner, *State Building and Late Development* (Ithaca: Cornell University Press, 1999) and D. Michael Shafer, *Winners and Losers* (Ithaca: Cornell University Press, 1994). On Quebec, see Jean-Pierre Dupuis, ed., *Le modèle québécois de développement économique* (Cap-Rouge: Presses Inter universitaires, 1995).

19 Graham Fraser, *P.Q.: René Lévesque and the Parti Québécois in Power* (Toronto: Macmillan, 1984).

20 Employees in the Quebec public and parapublic sectors are remunerated through appropriations voted by the National Assembly and include the public service, the health and social services network, and the elementary and high schools in the education system

21 See Gilbert Leduc, 'L'État, ce monstre insaisissable,' *Le Soleil*, 5 April 2003, D-1.

22 Jeanne Laux and Maureen Appel Molot, *State Capitalism in Canada* (Ithaca: Cornell University Press, 1988).

23 Peter Aucoin, *The New Public Management: Canada in Comparative Perspective* (Montreal: Institute for Research on Public Policy, 1995); David Osborne and Ted Gaebler, *Reinventing Government: How the Entrepreneurial Spirit is Transforming the Public Sector* (Reading, Mass: Addison-Wesley, 1992).

24 See Louis Côté, 'La modernisation de l'administration publique québécoise à la lumière de l'expérience étrangère,' *Coup d'oeil* (ENAP) 8, no 1 (April 2002): 9–12.

25 L.E. Lynn, Jr., C.J. Heindrich, and C.J. Hill, 'Studying Governance and Public Management: Challenges and Prospects,' *Journal of Public Administration Research and Theory* 10, no. 2 (2000): 233–61; Vincent Lemieux, *Les rôles du gouvernement dans la gouvernance* (Canadian Centre for Management Development, 2000).

Chapter 8

At the time this article was researched and written, the author worked in Ontario's Cabinet Office and Management Board Secretariat. The views expressed in this paper are exclusively those of the author and do not necessarily reflect those of the Government of Ontario. An earlier version of this chapter was published in *Canadian Public Administration* (vol. 44, no. 2) as 'Politics, Leadership and Experience in Designing Ontario's Cabinet.'

1 Christoph Knill, 'European Policies: The Impact of National Administrative Traditions,' *Journal of Public Policy* 18, no. 1 (1998): 1–28; and Christoph Knill, 'Explaining Cross-National Variance in Administrative Reform: Autonomous versus Instrumental Bureaucracies,' *Journal of Public Policy* 19, no. 2 (1999): 113–39.

2 See, for example, Colin Campbell, 'Cabinet Committees in Canada: Pressures and Dysfunctions Stemming from Representational Imperative,' in Thomas Mackie and Brian Hogwood, eds., *Unlocking the Cabinet: Cabinet Structures in Comparative Perspective* (London: Sage Publications, 1995); Peter Aucoin, 'Prime Minister and Cabinet,' in James Bickerton and Alain-G. Gagnon, eds., *Canadian Politics*, 2nd ed. (Peterborough: Broadview Press, 1994); and Christopher Dunn, *The Institutionalized Cabinet: Governing the Western Provinces* (Montreal and Kingston: McGill-Queen's University Press, 1995).

3 Christopher Dunn has written extensively on the evolution of institutional cabinets. See his 'Premiers and Cabinets,' in Christopher Dunn, ed., *Provinces: Canadian Provincial Politics* (Peterborough: Broadview Press, 1996); and his *The Institutionalized Cabinet: Governing the Western Provinces* (Montreal and Kingston: McGill-Queen's University Press, 1995). See also Leslie

Pal and David Taras, eds., *Prime Ministers and Premiers: Political Leadership and Public Policy in Canada* (Scarborough: Prentice-Hall, 1988).

4 In 1948 one of the first moves toward institutionalization occurred with the appointment of a cabinet secretary who was not a member of cabinet. In the 1950s cabinet minutes and submission formats became standardized, and in the 1960s the Executive Council Office was expanded under the direction of the cabinet secretary to coordinate the work of largely ad hoc cabinet sub-committees and serve as a liaison between cabinet and the growing number and size of operating departments. See Dunn's discussion of Ontario in his 'Premiers and Cabinets.'

5 J. Stefan Dupré, 'Reflections on the workability of executive federalism,' in Richard Simeon, ed., *Intergovernmental Relations* (Toronto: University of Toronto, 1985), 3.

6 For an insider's account of the implementation of the COGP, see James Fleck, 'Restructuring the Ontario Government,' *Canadian Public Administration* 16, no. 1 (Spring 1973). On the long-term impact of the COGP reforms, see Evert Lindquist and Graham White, 'Streams, Springs and Stones: Ontario Public Service Reform in the 1980s and 1990s,' *Canadian Public Administration* 37, no. 2 (Summer 1994).

7 The committees were Resources Development, Social Policy, and Justice.

8 The committees were Emergency Planning; Native Affairs; Northern Development; Race Relations; Housing and Community Development; Education, Training and Adjustment; and Drug Abuse. The chairs of these committees were members of P&P. See Ontario, Cabinet Office, *New Cabinet System: September 1989* (Toronto: Cabinet Office, 1989).

9 These committees were Economic and Labour, Social, Environment, and Justice.

10 See, in general, Mark McElwain, 'Ontario's Budget Process,' in Graham White, ed., *Government and Politics of Ontario*, 4th ed. (Toronto: Nelson, 1990).

11 Over the past thirty years, various expenditure management and reduction programs have been grafted onto this basic decision-making process. Under the NDP, for example, the Multi-Year Expenditure Control Plan (MYERP) was introduced to require ministries to meet base expenditure reduction targets set by cabinet and to ensure that new initiatives be considered and ranked by policy committees within funding envelopes established by cabinet. Similar, more informal 'envelope' exercises were conducted in almost every year after 1995.

12 See, for example, David Wolfe, 'Queen's Park Policy-making Systems,' in Sid Noel, ed., *Revolution at Queen's Park* (Toronto: James Lorimer, 1997), 156.

13 See Richard Loreto, 'Changes in the Ontario Cabinet System under Premier Rae,' *Public Sector Management* (Spring 1991).

14 While the Premier's Office and Cabinet Office were initially separate structures headed by a deputy minister to the premier and a secretary to cabinet respectively, Premier Davis appointed Dr Edward Stewart to both senior positions in January 1976. This fusion had the effect of politicizing Cabinet Office, an effect enhanced by the employment of such high-profile Conservative party activists as Hugh Segal and John Tory. See Graham White, 'Governing from Queen's Park: The Ontario Premiership,' in Pal and Taras, eds., *Prime Ministers and Premiers*, 162.

15 Between 1972 and 1993, the Ministry of Government Services supported cabinet's physical asset and technology decisions. In 1993, it was merged with Management Board.

16 Intergovernmental Affairs was separated as a distinct ministry in 1978.

17 Treasury Board Secretariat's planning and estimates function as well as staff support returned to Management Board. The Office of the Budget moved to the new Ministry of Finance created in 1993. This move returned Management Board to its pre-1991 status as the key agency responsible for expenditure management and the Ministry of Finance as the government's chief economist and forecaster.

18 David Cameron and Graham White, 'Cycling into Saigon: The Tories Take Power in Ontario,' paper presented at the annual meeting of the Canadian Political Science Association, June 1996, 21. On this point, see also Richard Loreto, 'Making and Implementing the Decisions: Issues of Public Administration in the Ontario Government,' in Graham White, ed., *The Government and Politics of Ontario*, 5th ed. (Toronto: University of Toronto Press, 1997), 103.

19 Business planning was introduced upon the recommendation of the Ontario Financial Review Commission (OFRC), which was appointed in 1995 to review and comment on the financial practices of the Ontario Public Service and its agencies. As part of a proposed 'integrated framework for ministries' activities that better links planning, monitoring, reporting and evaluation to improve the management and accountability processes,' the OFRC recommended that 'each ministry prepare a three-year business plan, updated annually, that reflects the Government's priorities.' For more detailed information, see David Fulford, 'Business Planning in Ontario,' in Luc Bernier and Evan Potter, eds., *Business Planning in Canadian Public Administration* (Toronto: Institute of Public Administration of Canada, 2001).

21 By 1999–2000, Management Board began fine-tuning the business planning

process by focusing on such things as linking operating and capital allocations with non-tax revenues and training on business planning for OPS
managers. This fine-tuning continued in 2000–01 with the identification of
corporate management principles, improved performance measurement
reporting, development of a business planning directive, and electronic
submission of plans.

22 John Ibbitson provides a detailed account of the Premier Harris's first two
years in office in *Promised Land: Inside the Mike Harris Revolution* (Scarborough: Prentice-Hall Canada, 1997).

23 These committees were Policy and Priorities, Jobs and the Economy, Federal-Provincial Relations, Restructuring and Local Services, and Cabinet
Committee on Privatization.

24 Disentanglement also involved devolution of some social assistance, public
transit, water and sewers, highways, public health, and subsidized housing
responsibilities to municipalities in return for provincial assumption of
education funding.

25 Ibbitson, *Promised Land*, 261.

26 When the Conservatives came to power, an ADM was in charge of both
communications and corporate services in Cabinet Office. A director of
communications was in charge of a ten-person branch and reported to this
ADM.

27 In September 2001 minor changes were introduced to this model as well.
First, the position of deputy minister, communications, was abolished and
replaced with an associate deputy minister to whom individual ministries'
communications directors report. Second, one of the three ADM communications positions was eliminated, and a new executive coordinator position
responsible for communications were added to each of the two policy
divisions an effort to streamline communications and policy decision-
making.

28 Ibbitson, *Promised Land*, 152–53.

29 Donald Savoie explains in great detail why Prime Minister Chrétien
retained the preinstitutionalized St Laurent cabinet decision-making model
in his *Governing from the Centre: The Concentration of Power in Canadian Politics* (Toronto: University of Toronto Press, 1999).

30 For example, the Common Sense Revolution committed to reducing the
public service by fifteen thousand. The Blueprint, by contrast, committed to
making the Ontario public service 'the best in the world – smaller, quicker,
less bureaucratic, less expensive and more responsive.'

31 These decisions include the allocation of annual capital expenditures,
opportunities to leverage private sector and non-provincial government

contributions, and the sale or commercialization of government assets and services with significant capital requirements.

32 SuperBuild is a crown agency established by regulation under the Ontario Development Corporations Act, with an advisory board of directors, which has representation from the private and public sectors. The chief executive officer and the chair of the board of directors of SuperBuild, David Lindsay, reports to the minister of finance.

33 Strategic Resources Group, *Managing the Environment: A Review of Best Practices* (Toronto: Strategic Resources Group, 2001).

34 See Hugh Segal, 'The Evolving Ontario Cabinet: Shaping the Structure to Suit the Times,' in Donald MacDonald, ed., *The Government and Politics of Ontario*, 3rd ed. (Scarborough: Nelson Canada, 1985).

35 Premier Eves created two associate ministers of municipal affairs and housing (one for rural affairs and one for urban affairs), one associate minister of health and long-term care, one for francophone affairs, and one for enterprise, opportunity and innovation.

36 It is interesting to note how the nomenclature of the new Liberal committee structure marks a return to the pre-1999 conventions originally recommended by the COGP. For example, PPCB has returned to being the Planning and Priorities Board and the Statutory Business Committee has become the Legislation and Regulations Committee once again.

37 Non-ministers involved in cabinet deliberations are required to swear an oath of secrecy in order to be privy to the Executive Council documents, just like their ministerial colleagues.

38 In recent years, Ontario's premier has not been a member of any committee other than P&P/PPCB.

Chapter 9

1 The NDP captured thirty-two (44 per cent of the popular vote) of the fifty-seven seats in the legislature. The Progressive Conservative party won twenty-four seats and the Liberal party won one seat. The NDP secured thirty-five seats as a result of the June 2003 election (49 per cent of the popular vote). The PC won twenty seats; the Liberal party captured two.

2 Legislative Assembly of Manitoba, Speech from the Throne, 25 November 1999.

3 Herman Bakvis and David MacDonald, 'The Canadian Cabinet: Organization, Decision-Rules, and Policy Impact,' in Michael M. Atkinson, ed., *Governing Canada: Institutions and Public Policy* (Toronto: Harcourt Brace, 1993), 54–5.

4 Errol Black and Jim Silver, *A Flawed Economic Experiment: The New Political Economy of Manitoba* (Winnipeg: Canadian Centre for Policy Alternatives, June 1999), 4.

5 Alex Netherton, 'Paradigm and Shift: A Sketch of Manitoba Politics,' in Keith Brownsey and Michael Howlett, eds., *The Provincial State in Canada: Politics in the Provinces and Territories* (Peterborough: Broadview Press, 2001), 225.

6 Black and Silver, *A Flawed Economic Experiment*, 18.

7 The Conference Board of Canada, 'Manitoba: Steady as She Goes,' *Provincial Outlook: Economic Forecast* (Ottawa: Author, 1999), 27.

8 Black and Silver, *A Flawed Economic Experiment*, 23.

9 Social Planning Council of Winnipeg, *Promises Not Kept: 2001 Report on Child Poverty in Manitoba*, mimeo.

10 Currently, there are sixty-two First Nations communities in the provinces. Manitoba also has a significant Métis community. According to the 1996 census, 12.8 per cent of Manitoba's population was Aboriginal.

11 Darren Lezuski, Jim Silver, and Errol Black, 'High and Rising: The Growth of Poverty in Winnipeg,' in Jim Silver, ed., *Solutions That Work: Fighting Poverty in Winnipeg* (Winnipeg and Halifax: Canadian Centre for Policy Alternatives – Manitoba and Fernwood Publishing, 2000), table 10, p. 36. Furthermore, the unemployment rate of Aboriginal peoples on reserves, especially northern communities, would be even higher.

12 Manitoba Government, 'Preliminary Response Outlined to Deloitte and Touche Report,' *News Release*, 19 November 1999.

13 For a complete listing and substantive explanation, see Christopher Dunn, *The Institutionalized Cabinet: Governing the Provinces* (Kingston and Montreal: Institute of Public Administration of Canada and McGill-Queen's University Press, 1995), 279–85.

14 Ibid., 134–6.

15 Ibid., 17 and 198.

16 Helen Fallding and Paul Samyn, 'Doer offers up recipe for NDP success,' *Winnipeg Free Press*, 24 November 2001, A4.

17 Personal interview with Paul Vogt, secretary, Policy Management Secretariat, Manitoba Government, 26 April 2002. After assuming office, the NDP government did not commission a firm or person to undertake a review of cabinet structure and effectiveness as had been done by many previous governments in Manitoba. See Dunn, *The Institutionalized Cabinet*, 189.

18 Interview with clerk of the Executive Council, 2 May 2002. It was related to the author that months past 11 September the Homeland Security committee no longer holds regular meetings. It is likely that this committee will be

phased out as security initiatives are taken on and implemented at the departmental level.

19 Ken Rasmussen, 'The Manitoba Civil Services: A Quiet Tradition in Transition,' in Evert Lindquist, ed., *Government Restructuring and Career Public Services* (Toronto: Institute of Public Administration of Canada, 2000), 351.

20 Manitoba Government, 'Community and Economic Development Committee of Cabinet Launched,' *News Release*, 28 March 2000.

21 Interview with Eugene Kostyra, secretary to Community and Economic Development Committee, Manitoba government, 24 July 2002.

22 Manitoba Government, 'Inner-City Youth Leadership Program to Receive Provincial Funding,' *News Release*, 21 August 2002.

23 Dunn, *The Institutionalized Cabinet*, 186.

24 Christopher Dunn, 'Premiers and Cabinets,' in Christopher Dunn, ed., *Provinces: Canadian Provincial Politics* (Peterborough: Broadview Press, 1996), 191.

25 B. Schwartz and D. Rettie, 'Interview: Rick Mantey: Exposing the Invisible,' *Manitoba Law Journal, Underneath the Golden Boy: A Review of Recent Manitoba Laws and How They Came to Be*, 28, no. 2 (2001): 187–8.

26 Dunn, 'Premiers and Cabinets,' 175.

27 Graham White, 'The Interpersonal Dynamics of Decision Making in Canadian Provincial Cabinets,' in Michael Laver and Kenneth A. Shepsle, eds., *Cabinet Ministers and Parliamentary Government* (Cambridge: Cambridge University Press, 1994), 261.

28 Ibid., 263.

29 Howard Pawley and Lloyd Brown-John, 'Transitions: The New Democrats in Manitoba,' in Donald J. Savoie, ed., *Taking Power: Managing Government Transitions* (Toronto: Institute of Public Administration of Canada, 1993), 164.

30 Bakvis and MacDonald, 'The Canadian Cabinet,' 57.

31 Dunn, 'Premiers and Cabinets,' 165.

Chapter 10

1 Christopher Dunn, *The Institutionalized Cabinet: Governing the Western Provinces* (Kingston and Montreal: McGill-Queen's University Press, 1995).

2 J.L. Granatstein, *The Ottawa Men:The Civil Service Mandarins, 1935–57*, 2nd ed. (Toronto: University of Toronto Press, 1998); Ken Rasmussen, 'The Canadian Civil Service at War: From Patronage to Planning,' in Fabio Rugge, ed., *Administration and Crisis Management: The Case of Wartime* (Brussels: International Institute of Administrative Sciences, 2000), 69–89.

3 Della M.M. Stanley, *Louis Robichaud: A Decade of Power* (Halifax: Nimbus, 1984), 93–4.

4 Robert I. McLaren, *The Saskatchewan Practice of Public Administration in Historical Perspective* (Lewiston, NY: Edwin Mellon Press, 1998), 95, where he refers to the 'forty or so people' who formed the original nucleus of more senior administrators and central agency analysts upon which the stellar reputation of the Saskatchewan civil service rested.

5 Ibid., 82.

6 George Cadbury, 'Planning in Saskatchewan,' in Laurier LaPierre et al., eds. *Essays on the Left: Essays in Honour of T.C. Douglas* (Toronto: McClelland and Stewart, 1972).

7 Dale Eisler, *Rumours of Glory: Saskatchewan and the Thatcher Years* (Edmonton: Hurtig, 1987); James Pitsula and Ken Rasmussen, *Privatizing a Province: The New Right in Saskatchewan* (Vancouver: New Star Books, 1990).

8 This was true of Ottawa at this time as well. See Gordon Robertson, 'The Changing Role of the Privy Council Office,' *Canadian Public Administration* 14 (Winter 1971): 487–508.

9 Thomas H. McLeod and Ian McLeod, *Tommy Douglas: The Road to Jerusalem* (Edmonton: Hurtig, 1987), 128.

10 Meyer Brownstone, 'The Douglas-Lloyd Governments: Innovation and Bureaucratic Adaptation,' in LaPierre, ed., *Essays on the Left*, 65–70.

11 Cadbury, 'Planning in Saskatchewa,' 52.

12 A.W. Johnson, *Dream No Little Dreams: A Biography of the Douglas Government of Saskatchewan, 1944–1961* (Toronto: University of Toronto Press, 2004).

13 On the career of George Cadbury, see Robert I. McLaren, 'George Woodall Cadbury: The Fabian Catalyst in Saskatchewan's "good public administration"' *Canadian Public Administration* 38, no. 3 (Fall 1993).

14 See A.W. Johnson's articles: 'The Treasury Board in Saskatchewan,' in *Proceedings of the 7th Annual Conference* (Toronto: Institute of Public Administration of Canada, 1955); and 'Government Organization and Methods Units,' *Proceedings of the 4th Annual Conference* (Toronto: Institute of Public Administration of Canada, 1952).

15 Colin Campbell and George Szablowski, *The Super-Bureaucrats: Structure and Behaviour in Central Agencies* (Toronto: Macmillan of Canada, 1979).

16 Cadbury, 'Planning in Saskatchewan,' 64.

17 Dunn, *The Institutionalized Cabinet*, 43–56.

18 D. Stephens, 'The Saskatchewan Public Administration Foundation, 1963–1966,' *Canadian Public Administration* 24, no. 2 (Summer 1981): 295–300; Evelyn Eager, *Saskatchewan Government: Political and Pragmatism* (Saskatoon: Prairie Books, 1980), 144.

19 Dunn, *The Institutionalized Cabinet*, 53, 55.

20 Douglas F. Stevens, *Corporate Autonomy and Institutional Control: The Crown Corporation as a Problem in Organizational Design* (Montreal and Kingston: McGill-Queen's University Press, 1993), 117.

21 Kenneth Bryden, 'Cabinets,' in David Bellamy, Jon Pammet, and Donald Rowat, eds., *The Provincial Political Systems: Comparative Essays* (Toronto: Methuen, 1979).

22 Eager, *Saskatchewan Government*, 54.

23 John Richards and Larry Pratt, *Prairie Capitalism Power and Influence in the New West* (Toronto: McClelland and Stewart, 1979), 257–75.

24 Interview, Allan Blakeney, 7 November 2002.

25 Tom Waller, 'Framework for Economic Development: The Role of Crown Corporations and the Crown Investments Corporation of Saskatchewan,' in Eleanor D. Glor, ed., *Policy Innovation in the Saskatchewan Public Sector, 1971–82* (Toronto: Captus Press, 1997). Stevens, *Corporate Autonomy and Institutional Control*, chapter 5.

26 Howard Leeson, 'The Intergovernmental Affairs Function in Saskatchewan, 1960–1983,' *Canadian Public Administration* 30, no. 3 (Fall 1987): 399–420.

27 Crown Investments Review Commission, *Report to the Government of Saskatchewan* (Regina, December 1982).

28 Stevens, *Corporate Autonomy*, 123.

29 Dunn, *The Institutionalized Cabinet*, 103.

30 The interesting fact to keep in mind is that Premier Romanow did not chair (or attend) Treasury Board or CIC board meetings. And although he was formally chair of the Priorities and Planning Committee, he rarely attended meetings, preferring to receive his minister's recommendations without his influence and instead make a final judgment on the matter in cabinet. This was certainly an additional reason why cabinet committee recommendations were not simply ratified at cabinet meetings.

31 Privy Council Office, Government of Canada, *Decision-Making Processes and Central Agencies in Canada: Federal, Provincial and Territorial Practices* (Ottawa: Privy Council Office, 1998), 2.

32 Gregory P. Marchildon and Brent Cotter, 'Saskatchewan and the Social Union,' in Howard Leeson, ed., *Saskatchewan Politics: Into the Twenty-First Century* (Regina: CPRC Press, 2001), 367–80.

33 One Liberal member left the coalition cabinet to sit as an independent Liberal while the other two Liberal members of the coalition eventually lost their status as Liberal members but continued to sit in cabinet as independent members. Both ran in the 2003 election as NDP candidates.

34 It should be noted, however, that the individual hired to become the new

president of the Crown Management Board was the vice-president of CIC during the Blakeney era.

35 Howard A. Scarrow, 'Civil Service Commissions in the Canadian Provinces,' *The Journal of Politics* 19, no. 2 (May 1857): 240–61.

36 Seymour Martin Lipset, *Agrarian Socialism* (Berkeley: University of California Press, 1971), 307–32.

Chapter 11

1 Lewis Thomas, *The Liberal Party in Alberta. A History of Politics in the Province of Alberta* (Toronto: University of Toronto Press, 1959), and Douglas R. Babcock, *A Gentleman of Strathcona. Alexander Cameron Ruthford* (Edmonton: Alberta Culture, Historical Resources Division, 1980).

2 See John A. Irving, *The Social Credit Movement in Alberta* (Toronto: University of Toronto Press, 1959), C.B. Macpherson, *Democracy in Alberta. Social Credit and the Party System*, 2d ed. (Toronto: University of Toronto Press, 1963), and J.R. Mallory, *Social Credit and the Federal Power in Canada* (Toronto: University of Toronto Press, 1954), for descriptions of Aberhart's autocratic style of governance.

3 Interview with Albert Ludwig, Calgary, 16 May 2002.

4 Rod Love, lecture given at Mount Royal College, Calgary, Alberta, 1 March 1999.

5 Christopher Dunn, *The Institutionalized Cabinet. Governing the Western Provinces* (Toronto: University of Toronto Press, 1996), Terence Morley, 'The Government of the Day: The Premier and Cabinet in British Columbia,' in R.K. Carty, ed., *Politics, Policy, and Government in British Columbia* (Vancouver: University of British Columbia Press, 1996), pp. 143–63, and Mark Crawford, 'Coordination of Communications and Policy Functions in the B.C. NDP Government,' paper presented to the British Columbia Political Science Association meeting, Victoria, May 2000.

6 Christoph Knill, 'European Policies: The Impact of National Administrative Traditions,' *Journal of Public Policy* 18, no. 1 (1998): 1–28.

7 Ibid., 3.

8 Alberta does not have a cabinet; the formal title given to the political executive in the province is Executive Council.

9 Thomas, *The Liberal Party in Alberta*, chapter 1.

10 David Laycock, *Democratic Thought on the Prairies 1910–1944* (Toronto: University of Toronto Press, 1990); William Irvine, *The Farmers in Politics* (Ottawa: Carleton University Press, 1978); and Macpherson, *Democracy in Alberta*, 217 ff.

11 Interview with Arthur W. Dixon, Calgary, Alberta, 14 May 2002.

12 Interview with Albert Ludwig, Calgary, Alberta, 16 May 2002.
13 Interview with Ron Ghitter, Calgary, 6 June 2002.
14 Premier's Office, *Office of the Premier and Executive Council* (Edmonton: Office of the Premier, n.d.)

Chapter 12

1 Richard Sigurdson, 'The British Columbia New Democratic Party: Does It Make a Difference?' in R.K. Carty, ed., *Politics, Policy and Government in British Columbia* (Vancouver: University of British Columbia Press, 1996), 311.
2 Christoph Knill, 'Explaining Cross-National Variance in Administrative Reform: Autonomous versus Instrumental Bureaucracies,' *Journal of Public Policy* 19, no. 2 (1999): 127–36.
3 On main characteristics of B.C. provincial bureaucracy, see Norman Ruff, 'Provincial Governance and the Public Service: Bureaucratic Transitions and Change,' in Carty, ed., *Politics, Policy and Government in British Columbia*, chapter 10, and Norman Ruff, 'Managing the Public Service.' in J.T. Morley, et al., *The Reins of Power* (Vancouver: Douglas & McIntyre, 1983).
4 Michael M. Harmon, *Action Theory for Public Administration* (New York: Longmans, 1981).
5 Paul Tennant, 'The NDP Government of British Columbia: Unaided Politicians in an Unaided Cabinet,' *Canadian Public Policy* 3 (Autumn 1977): 489–503, and Christopher Dunn, *The Institutionalized Cabinet: Governing the Western Provinces* (Montreal: McGill-Queen's University Press, 1995), Part Four.
6 See Dave Barrett and William Miller, *Barrett: A Passionate Political Life* (Vancouver: Douglas & McIntyre, 1995), 97.
7 Mark Eliesen, a former federal government economist, research director for the federal NDP, and latterly a Manitoba senior provincial deputy minister.
8 This group left a tangible record of some of its later work in British Columbia, Auditor General and Deputy Ministers' Council, *Special Reports: Enhancing Accountability for Performance in the British Columbia Public Sector* (June 1995 and January 1998) and *Framework and Implementation Plan* (April 1996). *Towards a More Accountable Government: Putting Ideas into Practice* (March 2000).
9 For discussions of pre-1996 premier-cabinet relationships see Terence Morley, 'The Government of the Day: Premier and Cabinet in British Columbia,' in Carty, ed., *Politics, Policy and Government in British Columbia*, chapter 9, and Walter Young and J.T. Morley, 'The Premier and Cabinet,' in *The Reins of Power*.

10 For discussions of leadership style under Premier Harcourt, see Dan Gawthrop Dan, *High Wire Act: Power, Pragmatism and the Harcourt Legacy* (Vancouver: New Star, 1996), and Mike Harcourt with Wayne Skene, *Mike Harcourt: A Measure of Defiance* (Vancouver: Douglas & McIntyre, 1996). For a critical look at the Clark administration, see Mark Milke, *Barbarians in the Garden City: The BC NDP in Power* (Victoria: Thomas & Black, 2001). Keith Baldrey also provides some insights in chief of staff–premier relations in 'Adrian Who?' *BC Business Magazine* (February 1997), 23.

11 'Lali quits the cabinet, criticizes leadership,' *The Province*, 9 February 2001.

12 The departure of Premiers Vander Zalm and Clark's closest personal advisers from this position (David Poole in August 1988 and Adrian Dix in March 1999) foreshadowed their own ultimate resignations as premier.

13 As was the case with previous premierships, these positions comprise an inner circle of established confidants. The cabinet secretary, Ken Dobell, was formerly Vancouver City manager during Gordon Campbell's term as mayor, and Lara Dauphinee, deputy chief of staff, was Mr Campbell's executive and, before that from 1993, his constituency assistant. Martyn Brown as chief of staff followed a typical career path to that position as the senior political and electoral strategy adviser to Gordon Campbell, 1998–2001. The corporate planning deputy minister, Brenda Eaton, is a career public servant.

14 The CAS reports through the deputy minister to the Premier for Corporate Planning and Restructuring together with Board Resourcing and Development that is responsible for the appointment of crown agency boards.

15 Crown Agencies Secretariat, *Service Plan 2002/03 – 2004/05*. It projected a 61 per cent reduction in the CAS budget to $1.8 million and a drop in full-time positions from twenty-two to nine. By 2004 the later had grown back to fourteen.

16 The appointment of the former president of the B.C. Liberal party as the secretariat's deputy minister in 2001 may have added a further consideration to its role and links to the Premier's Office.

17 Office of Premier, 'Explanatory Note: Government communications restructuring' (26 June 2002).

18 As quoted by Jim Beatty, 'Staff must support our goals: premier,' *Vancouver Sun*, 28 June 2002.

19 Ministry staff assigned these responsibilities by the minister and deputy minister, in consultation with the deputy minister to cabinet.

20 British Columbia Progress Board, *BC Progress Board 2001 Report* (15 February 2002). The B.C. Board tracks twenty-six measures of performance on the economy, innovation, education, environment, health, and social condition

and compares British Columbia's performance with other Canadian provinces and three U.S. states: Washington State, Oregon, and California.

21 When the new government met heavy weather and declining popular confidence in its policy management one year into its term, it adopted a new communications strategy to try to ensure its message got out.

22 Any adjustments at the executive level of the public service in deputies and assistant deputies following the initial 5 June deputy minister appointments were to be arranged by the deputy minister to the premier, Executive Council.

23 This admonition ended by stating that 'any clarification of these points should be discussed by my Deputy Minister, Executive Council, Ken Dobell.'

24 British Columbia, Office of the Premier, *2002/3 to 2004/05 Service Plan Summary.*

25 The first Harcourt cabinet in 1991 had a membership of twenty. Clark's first cabinet in 1996 was trimmed down to just fifteen.

26 The role of the Crown Agencies Secretariat in the core services review similarly brought this office back to an earlier level of importance at the centre. It encompasses the Board Resourcing and Development Office responsible for directorship appointments to crown corporations, agencies, boards and commissions.

27 John W. Kingdon, *Agendas, Alternatives and Public Policies* (Boston: Little, Brown, 1984), 174.

28 Tom Christensen, Per Laegreid, and Lois R. Wise, 'Transforming Administrative Policy,' *Public Administration* 80, no. 1 (2002): 158–60.

29 See Patrick Weller, Herman Bakvis, and R.A.W. Rhodes, eds., *The Hollow Crown: Countervailing Trends in Core Executives* (New York: St Martin's Press, 1997) for explorations of this concept.

30 James G. March and Johan P. Olsen, *Rediscovering Institutions: The Organizational Basis of Politics* (Glencoe: Free Press, 1989), 170.

Contributors

Luc Bernier, Ecole Nationale d'Administration Publique, Quebec

Keith Brownsey, Public Policy, Mount Royal College, Alberta

Peter Buker, Corran Ban, Prince Edward Island

Christopher Dunn, Department of Political Science, Memorial University, Newfoundland

Ted Glenn, The Business School, Humber College Institute of Technology & Advanced Learning, Ontario

Joan Grace, Department of Politics, University of Winnipeg, Manitoba

Michael Howlett, Department of Political Science, Simon Fraser University, British Columbia

Stewart Hyson, Department of Political Science, University of New Brunswick – Saint John, New Brunswick

David Johnson, Department of Political Science, University College of Cape Breton, Nova Scotia

Gregory P. Marchildon, Canada Research Chair in Public Policy and Economic History, Faculty of Administration, University of Regina, Saskatchewan

Ken Rasmussen, Faculty of Administration, University of Regina, Saskatchewan

Norman Ruff, Department of Political Science, University of Victoria, British Columbia

Donald J. Savoie, Senior Canada Research Chair in Public Administration and Governance, Université de Moncton, New Brunswick

The Institute of Public Administration of Canada Series
in Public Management and Governance

Networks of Knowledge: Collaborative Innovation in International Learning, Janice
  Stein, Richard Stren, Joy Fitzgibbon, and Melissa Maclean
*The National Research Council in the Innovative Policy Era: Changing Hierarchies,
  Networks, and Markets,* G. Bruce Doern and Richard Levesque
*Beyond Service: State Workers, Public Policy, and the Prospects for Democratic
  Administration,* Greg McElligott
*A Law unto Itself: How the Ontario Municipal Board Has Developed and Applied
  Land Use Planning Policy,* John G. Chipman
Health Care, Entitlement, and Citizenship, Candace Redden
*Between Colliding Worlds: The Ambiguous Existence of Government Agencies for
  Aboriginal and Women's Policy,* Jonathan Malloy
The Politics of Public Management: The HRDC Audit of Grants and Contributions,
  David A. Good
*Dream No Little Dreams: A Biography of the Douglas Government of Saskatchewan,
  1944–1961,* Albert W. Johnson
Governing Education, Ben Levin
*Executive Styles in Canada: Cabinet Structures and Leadership Practices in Canadian
  Government,* edited by Luc Bernier, Keith Brownsey, and Michael Howlett
The Roles of Public Opinion Research in Canadian Government, Christopher Page
The Politics of CANDU Exports, Duane Bratt
Policy Analysis in Canada: The State of the Art, edited by Laurent Dobuzinskis,
  Michael Howlett, and David Laycock
Digital State at the Leading Edge: Lessons from Canada, Sanford Borins, Kenneth
  Kernaghan, David Brown, Nick Bontis, Perri 6, and Fred Thompson
*The Politics of Public Money: Spenders, Guardians, Priority Setters, and Financial
  Watchdogs inside the Canadian Government,* David A. Good
Court Government and the Collapse of Accountability in Canada and the U.K.,
  Donald Savoie
Professionalism and Public Service: Essays in Honour of Kenneth Kernaghan, edited
  by David Siegel and Ken Rasmussen
Searching for Leadership: Secretaries to Cabinet in Canada, edited by Patrice Dutil
Foundations of Governance: Municipal Government in Canada's Provinces, edited
  by Andrew Sancton and Robert Young
Provincial and Territorial Ombudsman Offices in Canada, edited by Stewart Hyson
*Local Government in a Global World: Australia and Canada in Comparative
  Perspective,* edited by Emmanuel Brunet-Jailly and John F. Martin
Behind the Scenes: The Life and Work of William Clifford Clark, Robert A.Wardhaugh

The Guardian: Perspectives on the Ministry of Finance of Ontario, edited by Patrice Dutil

Making Medicare: New Perspectives on the History of Medicare in Canada, edited by Gregory P. Marchildon

Overpromising and Underperforming? Understanding and Evaluating New Intergovernmental Accountability Regimes, edited by Peter Graefe, Julie M. Simmons, and Linda A. White